op cloth

PB 22⁰⁰

D0741859

5c
½

Several scholars have written about how authoritarian or democratic political systems affect industrialization in the developing countries. There is no literature, however, on whether democracy makes a difference to the power and well-being of the countryside. Through the example of India, which enjoys the longest-surviving democracy of the developing world, this book investigates how the countryside uses the political system to advance its interests.

It is first argued that India's countryside has become quite powerful in the political system, exerting considerable pressure on economic policy. The countryside is typically weak in the early stages of development, growing more powerful as the size of the rural sector becomes as proportionately small as in the developed world. India's rural sector defies this historical trend and already exerts remarkable influence. Nevertheless, constraints on rural power exist. The most important constraint stems from the inability of economic interests to override abiding, ascriptive identities; and until an economic construction of politics subdues identities and noneconomic interests, farmers' power, though greater than ever before, will remain self-limited. Political economy addresses interests, but this book shows that it must also engage identities in seeking to explain several key phenomena, such as the evolution of economic policy.

Democracy, development, and the countryside

CAMBRIDGE STUDIES IN COMPARATIVE POLITICS

General editor
PETER LANGE   Duke University

Associate Editors
ELLEN COMISSO   University of California, San Diego
PETER HALL   Harvard University
JOEL MIGDAL   University of Washington
HELEN MILNER   Columbia University
RONALD ROGOWSKI   University of California, Los Angeles
SIDNEY TARROW   Cornell University

This series publishes comparative research that seeks to explain important, cross-national domestic political phenomena. Based on a broad conception of comparative politics, it hopes to promote critical dialogue among different approaches. While encouraging contributions from diverse theoretical perspectives, the series will particularly emphasize work on domestic institutions and work that examines the relative roles of historical structures and constraints, of individual or organizational choice, and of strategic interaction in explaining political actions and outcomes. This focus includes an interest in the mechanisms through which historical factors impinge on contemporary political choices and outcomes.

Works on all parts of the world are welcomed, and priority will be given to studies that cross traditional area boundaries and that treat the United States in comparative perspective. Many of the books in the series are expected to be comparative, drawing on material from more than one national case, but studies devoted to single countries will also be considered, especially those which pose their problem and analysis in such a way that they make a direct contribution to comparative analysis and theory.

OTHER BOOKS IN THE SERIES

Allan Kornberg and Harold D. Clarke   *Citizens and Community: Political Support in a Representative Democracy*
David D. Laitin   *Language Repertoires and State Construction in Africa*
Catherine Boone   *Merchant Capital and the Roots of State Power in Senegal, 1930–1985*
Ellen Immergut   *Health Politics: Interests and Institutions in Western Europe*
Sven Steinmo, Kathleen Thelan, and Frank Longstreth, eds.   *Structuring Politics: Historical Institutionalism in Comparative Analysis*
Thomas Janoski and Alexander M. Hicks, eds.   *The Comparative Political Economy of the Welfare State*

Continued on page following the Index

Democracy, development, and the countryside

Urban–rural struggles in India

ASHUTOSH VARSHNEY
Harvard University

CAMBRIDGE
UNIVERSITY PRESS

Published by the Press Syndicate of the University of Cambridge
The Pitt Building, Trumpington Street, Cambridge CB2 1RP
40 West 20th Street, New York, NY 10011-4211, USA
10 Stamford Road, Oakleigh, Melbourne 3166, Australia

First published 1995

Printed in the United States of America

Library of Congress Cataloging-in-Publication Data
Varshney, Ashutosh, 1957–

Democracy, development, and the countryside : urban–rural
struggles in India / Ashutosh Varshney.

p.   cm. – (Cambridge studies in comparative politics)

Includes bibliographical references and index.

ISBN 0-521-44153-6

1. Rural development – India.   2. Urbanization – India.   3. India –
Politics and government – 1947–   I. Title.   II. Series.
HN690.Z9C6846   1995
338.954 – dc20   94-27665
CIP

A catalog record for this book is available from the British Library.

ISBN 0-521-44153-6 hardback

To my parents

Contents

Preface

This book has been long in the making. I began working on it when political economy as an area of inquiry *within political science* was still new. In the mid-1980s, the leading political science departments in the United States were investing a good deal of their professional energy in developing the field. The book was completed when, several years later, political economy had stabilized itself as a field of specialization. Confronted with a rising ethnic explosion in the world, the heady enthusiasm of the early years had dissipated; and rationality as a governing principle of human behavior, though relevant, seemed more limited than was generally assumed in the 1980s. An unarticulated awareness that a field at the intersection of politics and economics must also pay attention to identities, and not simply to interests, has finally crept in. As a result, a certain mellowness is in evidence, showing signs of the emerging intellectual maturity of the field.

This book follows what has come to be called the rational-choice method without, however, accepting all the substantive assumptions of those who work in the field. The method is used first to explain why rural India has become so powerful, a development that is theoretically and historically counterintuitive. The same method is then used to show the limits on rural power. The argument in the end is that religious, caste, and ethnic identities – or at any rate noneconomic interests defined in ethnic, caste, and religious ways – are now blocking the economic construction of rural interests. These identities, moreover, are unlikely to be subdued by the economic thrust of the farmers' movement and politics.

Two institutions – Harvard University, where I teach, and MIT, where I studied – have in various ways left their stamp on this book. The book was born as a doctoral dissertation at MIT. The political science department at MIT encouraged graduate students specializing in political economy to take classes in economics as well. Between 1983 and 1989, I spent roughly half of my time taking courses and interacting with economists at Harvard and MIT. It was invaluable training. I had earlier done political economy of the Marxian kind. Exposure to micro, macro, development, and international economics made me better appreciate economic arguments. It also sensitized me to the limits of economic argumentation.

My dissertation was supervised by two political scientists – Myron Weiner (chair) and Suzanne Berger – and two economists – Lance Taylor and Peter Timmer. Because two different kinds of disciplines were involved, the dissertation took longer than expected. I was, however, the beneficiary of the time spent on it. Without the well-rounded and close scrutiny it received from all four committee members, the book would have been quite different. I am indebted to all four of them. They were not simply rigorous supervisors, but at various points sensitive friends as well. Ph.D. students need both! MIT also gave my thesis the Daniel Lerner Prize for the best dissertation in 1989–90, a prize I shared with my friend Gary Herrigel.

Since the completion of the dissertation in 1989, I have incurred many more debts. Robert Bates, Peter Hall, Ronald Herring, Robert Keohane, Mick Moore, the late D. S. Tyagi, Samuel Popkin, and four anonymous referees at Cambridge University Press and the University of California Press read the manuscript in its entirety, or large parts of it, offering excellent advice and comments. On individual chapters, useful suggestions were made by Jorge Dominguez, Jonathan Fox, Sanjiv Goel, Stephan Haggard, David Laitin, John Mellor, Kalypso Nicolaidis, Ashwini Saith, and James Scott. The Comparative Politics Group at Harvard, chaired by Jorge Dominguez, commented on the last two chapters. Baldev Raj Nayar, Ajit Jha, John Echeveri-Gent and Ashwini Saith arranged presentations at McGill, UCLA, the University of Virginia, and the Institute of Social Studies at The Hague. In India, the two people who gave much of their time and expertise are no more. Raj Krishna and D. S. Tyagi would have loved to see this book in print. The Ministry of Agriculture of the Government of India, especially its Commission for Agricultural Costs and Prices, was very supportive. This was the first time I realized what more experienced social scientists already know – that the writing of a book is a collective enterprise!

The various stages of research and writing were funded by The Ford Foundation, The American Institute of Indian Studies, The Institute for the Study of World Politics, and the Department of Government at Harvard. My grateful thanks to all of these institutions.

Finally, some personal debts. Because of the time it takes and the demands it makes, a Ph.D. from the United States can be very trying – not simply for students but also for their families. My parents, in their old age, and my siblings watched the entire process with remarkable patience. Their love sustained me in moments of fatigue, of which there were many. A year after my dissertation was done, my wife, Vibha, arrived in my life. The book was still not in press and the second project had already commenced when we got married. There wasn't enough time left to be together. Vibha, I know, is very pleased by the publication of the book.

Cambridge, Massachusetts
October 1994

A note on primary sources

With isolated exceptions, political economy work on India's economic policy has tended to "read off" the *reasons* underlying state behavior either from the *results* of state action, or from the interests of powerful interest groups, such as the rich farmers and industrialists. The former is a case of methodologically inadmissible functionalism; and the latter, if unproved, is primarily an analytic imputation of power or influence, not its demonstration. Very few researchers have gone "inside" the state institutions to examine what forces, considerations, and interests actually shape the economic behavior of the state. Aiming to do the latter, this book is based on three new kinds of empirical materials: 27 years of published but unused government reports, 26 years of parliamentary debates, and about 70 interviews with the past and present policy makers. Published documents include: reports of the Commission for Agricultural Costs and Prices between 1965–92; *Lok Sabha* (Lower House of Indian Parliament) Debates on agricultural policy and town–country struggles between 1965–91; statistical reports of the Finance, Planning, and Agriculture ministries; and the reports of the various special government committees set up to look into agricultural policy since 1965. These documents shed considerable light on the struggles within the state institutions. However, a fuller picture emerged only after interviews with policy makers were conducted. Those interviewed included: most ministers and secretaries of Finance, Food and Agriculture since 1965; selected chairmen and members of Planning Commission; chairmen of the Commission of Agricultural Costs and Prices between 1965 and 1991; and several state chief ministers. Finally, to understand the peasant mobilization, many peasant leaders and activists were also interviewed. Wherever necessary, these materials were supplemented with newspaper reports.

Introduction

Just what does modernization mean for the peasantry beyond the simple but brutal truth that sooner or later they are its victims?
—Barrington Moore, Jr., *Social Origins of Democracy and Dictatorship*, 1967

A new specter of peasant power is likely to haunt India in coming years.
—*The Times of India*, February 3, 1988

In the autumn of 1989, thousands of farmers arrived in Delhi around the time Prime Minister Rajiv Gandhi wished to hold a massive rally of the Congress party. The farmers were agitating for higher agricultural prices and subsidies, and for a better allocation of resources for the countryside. India's cities, they argued, were pampered, whereas the villages, where most Indians still lived, were badly served. The farmers were led by M. S. Tikait, a man who had rarely traveled beyond his region, a man most metropolitan journalists had found difficult to interview, for he could not even speak Hindi properly. He spoke a dialect of Hindi incomprehensible to the powerful, English-language media. In the end, Tikait's farmers held their demonstration in the heart of Delhi; Rajiv Gandhi moved his rally to the outskirts. The Prime Minister thought it wise not to confront the farmers.

Before religious issues overwhelmed India's politics in the early 1990s, Tikait's march into Delhi was among the more striking political images of the 1980s. Rajiv Gandhi was discovering firsthand what a score of district administrators and several state governments had experienced in a more overpowering way throughout the 1980s. Sit-ins lasting for weeks had already sensitized them to the arrival of rural power in local and state politics. As for Delhi, most politicians were urban in the 1950s, and quite a number Oxbridge-trained. The arena of rural politicians was in the districts and state capitals. By the late 1970s, however, Delhi had become a prime object of rural attention. "Agriculturists," as they are called in official discourse, were the largest single group in India's parliament. Moreover, most parties had become ruralized.

The Tikait–Rajiv image raises the principal question underlying this book.

What happens to the countryside – its power and welfare – when development takes place in a democratic framework? Surprising as it may seem, there is no literature on this subject. Scholars have thought about the relationship between democracy and industrialization, but not about democracy on the one hand and rural power and well-being on the other.[1]

The rural sector is typically weak in the early stages of development. In the literature on the role played by the countryside in the process of industrialization, rural power is conspicuous by its absence. Although powerful in the villages, the landlords either give in to the new industrial forces or, as happened in England, become the industrial entrepreneurs themselves. As for the peasants, a powerless and dwindling peasantry is either held to be a condition for the rise of a modern society or is shown to be its consequence.[2]

One qualification needs to be made, however. Once the process of industrialization reaches a point matching that of the currently developed world, an empowerment of the rural sector takes place.[3] The historical trajectory of rural power, therefore, has been paradoxical in nature. In the early phases of development, when rural dwellers constitute a majority of a country's population, they have historically been the weakest. As the process of industrialization makes a society overwhelmingly or predominantly urban, the power of the rural sector increases.

It is widely recognized that the power of farm groups in advanced industrial countries is reflected in the high protection granted to agriculture.[4] The explana-

---

1 A partial exception is Amartya Sen, 1989, "Food and Freedom," *World Development*, August. Sen argues that famines have not occurred and are unlikely to have taken place in a democracy. His focus is not on the rural sector, but on poverty and extreme forms of hunger.

2 As argued in Barrington Moore, Jr., 1966, *Social Origins of Dictatorship and Democracy: Lord and Peasant in the Making of Modern World*, Boston: Beacon Press.

3 The terms "rural sector," "peasantry," and "farmers" are used interchangeably in this book, despite a tradition of controversy on this point. It has often been argued that a distinction needs to be drawn between "peasants" and "farmers": the former being defined as those producing for home consumption, the latter, for the market. While this duality may be perfectly legitimate for historical cases drawn from Europe, advances in agricultural technology are making this distinction increasingly anachronistic. In terms of economic motivations and participation in market exchange, the upper and middle peasantry, and even the lower peasantry, no longer appear to be fundamentally different from the class of farmers. Social distinctions within the rural sector exist, but they have to be construed differently, not in terms of "peasants" and "farmers." With the scientific advances of the last three decades, the so-called peasantry in many parts of the third world has used the new technology in a rational manner, thereby aiding the process of modernization rather than impeding it. One major objection to using the term "rural sector" remains, however. In the third world, increases or decreases in rural power and welfare may not affect the class of landless agricultural laborers. Therefore, the term "rural sector," whenever used in this book, makes no assumptions about the directionality in the welfare or power of agricultural laborers. The awkward position of landless agricultural laborers in the rural sector is discussed in detail in Chapter 5.

4 The best account of the extent of protection accorded to agriculture in industrial societies is Kym Anderson and Yujiro Hayami, 1986, *The Political Economy of Agricultural Protection*, Sydney: Allen and Unwin.

tions for why this is so are both political and economic. Mancur Olson's argument about the organizational advantage of small groups is normally used to account for the high level of rural organization.[5] Compared to the developing world, the size of the farming community in the developed world is smaller, making it easier for the rural sector to organize for political action. The economic argument, on the other hand, is that, being small relative to other sectors in the economy, the farm sector can be subsidized by the government with less fiscal strain than if it were large. Moreover, as specified in Engels's law, an increasingly smaller proportion of rising per capita incomes is spent on food, making it possible for governments in the developed world to raise farm prices without hurting consumers much. In a typical household budget of the developed world food does not constitute a large expense.

The historical paradox of rural power can thus be stated as follows: although in the process of economic development the populous countryside loses power, the combination of a democratic polity and an industrialized economy later seems to empower it.[6] India defies this historically derived paradox. It is a low-income country, with over 65 percent of the population still dependent on agriculture; yet the rural sector has acquired substantial power in the polity. By now, over 40 percent of India's parliament has a rural background, as opposed to about 20 percent in the 1950s. Rural mobilization on prices, subsidies, and loans flourished in the 1980s. *All* political parties support the rural demand for more "remunerative" agricultural prices and for higher investment of public resources in the countryside. A considerable fraction of outstanding agricultural loans was waived in 1989–90. Finally, some of the key bureaucratic bodies involved in policy making in Delhi are by now substantially rural in social origins (though for rural politicians that may still not be adequate).

What explains the progressive empowerment of India's rural sector? Has the introduction of universal franchise in an early stage of development led to such an exceptional outcome? Universal franchise in the currently advanced countries was introduced after the industrial revolution; not so in India. Independent India was born agrarian as well as democratic. Democracy *preceding* an industrial revolution, this book argues, has led to the empowerment of the rural sector in the polity.

If democracy has indeed empowered the peasantry, does not the fact that India remains a poor economy impose some constraints on rural power? The demand for higher crop prices, lower farm input prices, waiver of agricultural loans, and higher rural investment is routed through the state (which makes the decisions on input and crop prices, loans, and public investment). If the state, to satisfy

5 Mancur Olson, 1965, *The Logic of Collective Action*, Cambridge, MA: Harvard University Press.
6 It is important to stress the combination of democracy and an industrialized society for this observation. In the alternative combination – communism and industrialism – the rural sector did not, it seems, make comparable gains. The rural population was not an active political actor in these centralized political systems, though the passive resistance of the rural folk to state-legislated activities, particularly to collectivization, frustrated many objectives of the state.

farmers, responds by increasing crop prices, lowering input prices, and waiving loans from India's nationalized banking system, it must raise resources to finance these transfers, or bear a burden of subsidy. Both ways are fraught with difficulty. While a whole range of measures aimed at raising resources for the transfer can be envisaged and are discussed in Chapter 7, let us consider an example of the difficulty involved. Suppose the state wishes to increase consumer prices to finance the rise in farm prices. With incomes as low as they are in India, increasing food prices for consumers has a limit. Higher prices will only lead to a lower food intake (by the poor in particular), which in turn will lead to accumulating food surpluses. Indeed, in contrast to the bleak production scenario of the mid-1960s, India since the late 1970s has witnessed the anomaly of a food surplus coexisting with widespread hunger.

For the state, one way to deal with this situation is to increase producer prices (to appease the farmers), not raise consumer prices, and subsidize the difference. How plausible is this scenario? Agriculture being the largest sector in a poor economy, the scale of subsidy required is potentially very large. Unlike in advanced industrial economies, where agriculture constitutes a small proportion of the GDP, subsidization of the large agricultural sectors in the third world is inherently fiscally problematic – as indeed it has become in India. The second argument of this book is that these two tendencies – the political deriving from a parliamentary democracy and the economic arising from the aggregate poverty of the country – are increasingly at odds. India's poverty and the demands of economic development are stemming the political rural tide.

The economic constraint on rural power, however, is not the only constraint. The third argument of the book is that, in the ultimate analysis, rural power is *self-limiting*. For the farmers to push the state and economic policy more in their favor, they must present themselves as a cohesive force united on economic interests (expressed as higher producer prices, larger subsidies, and greater investment). The farmers, however, have elected not to construct their interests in entirely economic terms. Although politics based on economic demands is stronger than before, politics based on other cleavages – caste, ethnicity, religion – also continues to be vibrant. Politics based on economic issues has the potential to unite much of the countryside against urban India: politics based on identities divides them, for caste, ethnicity, and religion cut across the urban and the rural. There are Hindu villagers and Hindu urbanites, Muslim peasants and Muslim urban professionals; and "backward castes" are found both in cities and villages. Until an economic construction of politics completely overrides identities and noneconomic interests, farmers' power, though greater than ever before, will remain self-limited. The ultimate constraint on rural power thus may not be the "urban bias" of the power structure, as the influential urban-bias theorists (Lipton, Bates, Schultz) have argued.[7] It may well stem from how human beings perceive themselves – as

7 Michael Lipton, *Why Poor People Stay Poor: Urban Bias in World Development*, Cambridge, MA: Harvard University Press, 1977; Robert Bates, *Markets and States in Tropical Africa*, Berkeley,

people having multiple selves. An abiding preponderance of the economic over the noneconomic is not how this multiplicity is necessarily resolved.

Interests and identities can be constructed in several ways. Farmers are members of a farming community as well as of caste, linguistic, and religious groups. Democratic freedoms permit political parties and organizations to mobilize and draw support on the basis of their preferred espousal of these interests and identities. Some farmers respond to the economic interests; others, to a different construction of who they are. In short, while democracy tends to empower the countryside in a largely rural society, it also places an inherent check on the evolution of rural power. If rural India were more united, the fiscal constraints would be attacked more centrally and to appease farmers, more nonrural corners would be cut in the budget.

Let me sum up the argument so far. A democratic system introduced *before* an industrial revolution has empowered India's countryside. Rural power, however, is subject to some serious constraints: the first emerges from the poverty of the country. A second, running deeper than the economic constraint, stems from cross-cutting cleavages, or multiple rural selves. Can the rural self be politically constructed in purely economic terms? The answer is no – in all probability. Rural empowerment is thus self-limited.

These constraints notwithstanding, an empowered rural sector at an early stage of development is a relatively exceptional occurrence.[8] To those familiar with the

---

CA: University of California Press, 1981; Theodore Schultz, *Distortion of Agricultural Incentives*, Bloomington: Indiana University Press, 1980. Also see Ashutosh Varshney, ed., 1993, "Beyond Urban Bias," a special issue of *The Journal of Development Studies*, Vol. 29, no. 4 July.

8 To the extent that rural empowerment is attributed to a democratic polity in this study, one should expect that in other democracies in the third world a similar tendency would obtain. Stable third world democracies have been few and far between. The link has been briefly noticed, though not yet systematically developed. For some first thoughts, see the studies in Varshney, ed., "Beyond Urban Bias," *The Journal of Development Studies*. Also see Michael Bratton, 1987, "The Comrades and the Countryside: The Politics of Agricultural Policy in Zimbabwe," *World Politics*, vol. 36, no. 2 (January); and Jeffrey Herbst, 1988, "Societal Demands and Government Choices: Agricultural Producer Price Policy in Zimbabwe," *Comparative Politics*, vol. 20, no. 1, (April). For Sri Lanka, Mick Moore notes that ethnic identities overwhelmed farm identities in Sri Lankan democracy, as a result of which Sri Lanka's rural sector did not acquire the same power as India's did. Cf. Moore, 1985, *The State and the Peasant in Sri Lanka*, Cambridge: Cambridge University Press. Ronald Herring points out that the rural folk in Sri Lanka had no special reason to organize as economic (as opposed to ethnic) political groups, as the economic policy of the Sri Lankan government was already substantially pro-rural (Review of Mick Moore, *Economic Development and Cultural Change*, vol. 36, no. 3 [April 1988]). While arguing a case for Kenya's rural exceptionalism in Africa, Bates notes how the pursuit of power got interlinked with a nurturing of the rural constituency in Kenyan politics, and how electoral competition, though more limited than in Asian democracies but keener than in most African polities, produced a tendency toward pro-rural economic policies in Kenya. See Robert Bates, 1989, *Beyond the Miracle of the Market: The Political Economy of Agrarian Development in Kenya*, Cambridge: Cambridge University Press. It would be interesting to see whether other democracies in the third world – Botswana, Trinidad, Tobago, Jamaica, Venezuela since 1959, and Chile between 1932 and 1972 – support the proposed link between democracy and rural power in the developing world.

rural landscape of India, still dotted with backwardness despite gains, the claim about an empowered rural sector may sound like a paradox, a statement that contradicts their visual impressions. The nature of this claim therefore needs to be clarified.

Whether or not an empowerment of the rural sector has taken place is basically a comparative issue. Comparative judgments about India's rural sector can be of three kinds: (1) comparisons with *other countries* at a similar level of development (or what would be functionally equivalent, comparisons with Europe in the early stages of industrialization); (2) comparisons with an *earlier time* in India's history; and (3) comparisons with respect to the *potential* power of the countryside. Considerations (1) and (2) make India's rural sector appear powerful. Consideration (3) is normally invoked by rural politicians on the ground that rural India, still the home of 65 percent of Indians, must be invested with greater power and economic resources. This, however, is a statement about how rural partisans would like the political and economic world to be, not how it has historically been. My claim about rural power in India is primarily based on the more empirically and historically grounded considerations (1) and (2).

It should be emphasized that, despite the sectoral nature of political mobilization, the class of landless agricultural laborers has been left out of it. Given that between one-fourth to one-third of rural India belongs to this category, one might say that a claim about sectoral rural power cannot be made. This would be an implausible objection, however. When one talks of urban bias or of the power of urban groups, the implication is not that *all* urban groups are powerful. Living in slums, the urban poor may well be below the poverty line, and may comprise as large a proportion of the city as the rural poor do of the countryside. (Like the rural poor, India's urban poor are one-fourth to one-third of India's total urban population.) Yet the claim about an urban bias is made because most other urban groups are politically significant. Arguments about sectoral power are partly about where the major benefits flow, and partly about *how power is ideologically and politically structured.* Much of India's politics has in the last decade and a half been conducted along the urban–rural (India-Bharat) lines. A large number of its politicians come from rural backgrounds. Rural benefits from economic policy have continued to grow, including a waiver of loans in 1990. The middle and small peasants participate in political mobilization, not simply the upper peasantry. The plight of the landless is particularly awkward, but that does not detract from arguments about sectoral rural power – just as the presence of unorganized urban poor, in itself, does not destroy the urban-bias view.

RURAL POWER AND ECONOMIC POLICY

These arguments emerge from a study of India's economic policy, with a focus on town–country issues. Unlike the mid-1960s, when India's capacity to feed its people was very much in doubt, the country over the last twenty years has solved the problem of production. The problem of distribution, however, remains. More

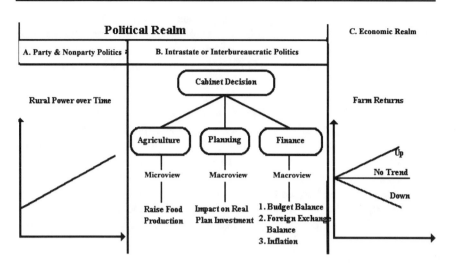

Figure 1.1. The policy process.

people than ever before have been fed, but many remain hungry. In India today, food surpluses coexist with hunger.

A new agricultural policy in the mid-1960s brought about the change. Under Nehru (1947–64), agricultural policy was based on land reforms and cooperatives, and no significant progress was made on either front. Rural India did not respond as expected. The population grew, but agricultural production stagnated, especially in the first half of the 1960s. Post-Nehru political elites gave farmers price incentives and invested in technology. A green revolution occurred. The current surpluses are a direct result of the green revolution on the supply side.

In the process, however, a serious politicization of economic policy has taken place. Concessions to farmers' demands have led to considerable interbureaucratic struggles *within* the government, as also *between* the government and the rural politicians and parties. Politicians representing rural India have also formed the government as part of ruling coalitions. In such situations, the state–countryside struggle has been intensely waged, not simply on the streets and in the halls of Parliament, but also in the relatively cloistered top levels of government bureaucracies.

Because higher prices and subsidies, greater public investment, and waiver of loans have been the demands of rural politicians, virtually all economic ministries are involved in the decisions. Three ministries are, however, critical: Food and Agriculture, Planning, and Finance. The power of the rural sector, and its limits, are ultimately played out in the state organs, so a brief overview of the process is necessary here.

The policy process is analytically represented in Figure I.1. It is divided in two realms, political and economic. The pressure outside the state (executive) organs comes from two sources: party politics and nonparty politics, the latter representing political mobilization undertaken by organizations that are political but do not generally contest elections. Party politicians pressure the government in Parliament; and when they become ministers, they bring their views right into the heart of the decision-making process.

Inside the state, the three critical bureaucracies – Agriculture, Planning, and Finance – are driven partly by their institutional concerns. The Agriculture Ministry's task is to increase agricultural production. If price incentives and input subsidies are deemed necessary to achieve that goal, as is likely to be true in the short run, a case for higher prices and subsidies will be made. Investments in research, extension, and technology may also increase production, but they typically do so in the medium and long run. Bureaucrats in the Agriculture Ministry are taken to task if production falls or levels off in the absence of weather calamities. Short-run concerns are constantly played out against the long-run concern.

The first pressure on the Agriculture Ministry may arise from within the Ministry if the Food Department is placed within it, which is often the case. The functioning of the Food Department/Ministry is aimed at food distribution, not production. To encourage higher take-off from the public distribution network, it may wish to lower the consumer price. Further pressure against higher food prices typically emanates from the Planning Ministry. Because food prices have a large weight in the various price indices (typically, 25–30 percent of the wholesale price index and 65–70 percent of the consumer price index), they affect the general price level – that is, inflation – in the economy and, by extension, the real value of plan investments. The Planning Ministry would like greater agricultural production, but the economywide macroimplications of food prices are normally its greater concern. It prefers non-price measures.

The most powerful representative of the intersectoral view, however, is the Finance Ministry. The Planning Ministry deals mostly with the design of economic policy; the Finance Ministry is involved both with the design and the actual, day-to-day functioning of economic policy. Finance is powerful because it holds the governmental purse. The Finance Ministry is intimately concerned with the general price level in the economy and with the macrobalances (budget, trade, and foreign exchange). Given their large proportion in the wholesale and consumer price indices, food prices affect inflation; farm subsidies have an impact on the budgetary balances; fertilizer use influences the trade and foreign exchange balance (because a large fraction of the domestic requirement is imported). Finally, demands for loan waiver affect the viability of the credit system, which is of great concern to Finance.

If food prices, farm subsidies, public investment, and loan waivers did not have economywide implications, there would be no clash among these bureaucracies. But because they do, the resolution of these struggles is inevitably political. The cabinet, consisting primarily of elected politicians, ultimately decides how far rural pressures will go. Political considerations point to appeasing farmers; however, that must be balanced against the need to feed people and fiscal realities. As a result, rural power, so visible in Parliament, becomes *refracted*. Although generally more favorable than before, the policy outcomes in the economic realm do not have a one-to-one correspondence with rural demands (Figure I.1). *In other words, the best-case scenarios do not obtain, but the worst-case scenarios are prevented.* Food prices would have collapsed as a result of the food surpluses of the 1980s. Rural power has ensured the prevention of this worst-case outcome.

The argument of this study is developed over eight chapters. Chapter 1 presents a conceptual overview of town–country struggles in the process of development. Chapter 2 begins the empirical investigation, dealing with the Nehru years (1947–64); why an institutional reorganization of agriculture was preferred over other solutions of the agrarian question is explained. Chapter 3 examines why (and how) a shift to a policy of farm-price incentives and higher investments in new technology took place in the mid-1960s. Chapter 4 documents the rise of agrarian power in the political system during the 1970s and traces its impact on economic policy. Chapter 5 analyzes the rise of peasant mobilization over prices, subsidies, and loans in the 1980s. Chapter 6 asks whether or not rural India has lost out. Chapter 7 elucidates why economic outcomes for the countryside lag behind the political gains made by it. The concluding Chapter 8 theoretically explains why India's democratic polity has led to a rise in rural power, self-limited though it may be. It goes on to ask how far rural power will go and projects what would happen if rural power were to overcome its basic internal obstacle, the cross-cutting cleavages in rural identities. At the end, a scenario that might bridge the urban–rural divide is suggested.

1

Town–country struggles in development:
A brief overview of existing theories

It is widely known that as economies develop and societies modernize, agriculture declines. Before the rise of industrial society, all societies were rural. In the advanced industrial societies today, agricultural sectors constitute less than 5 percent of gross domestic product (GDP). Contrariwise, in the poorest economies of the world, agriculture still accounts for anywhere between 30 to 65 percent of GDP.[1] An inescapable irony thus marks agricultural development in the poor economies. Without agricultural development food may not be forthcoming. Agriculture must therefore develop, but it develops sectorally only to decline intersectorally. It is a rare idealist, or utopian, who believes in keeping agriculture and rural communities as they always were.[2] Whether one likes it or not, industrialization requires the eclipse of agriculture.

This irony has given birth to the central question of town–country debates: on what *terms* should agriculture decline, for decline it must. The answer has both economic and political implications. Focusing on the role of agriculture in industrialization, the economic literature deals with how to industrialize and develop agriculture at the same time. The political economy literature examines the conflicts and coalitions that emerge as industrialization gets under way. The economic issues are examined first (Section 1.1), the political issues subsequently (Section 1.2). The distinctiveness of India's town–country struggles will become clear only after the existing economic and political theories have been examined.

1.1 THE ECONOMIC DEBATE

The role of the rural sector is intimately tied up with the question of how to raise resources for industrialization. Particular significance is attached to three kinds

---

1 The World Bank, 1994, *World Development Report 1994*, New York: Oxford University Press, for the World Bank, pp. 166–7.
2 Gandhi, Ruskin, and Tolstoy belong to this category. Also, writing at the time of the industrial revolution, Romantic poets such as William Wordsworth lamented the coming decline of rural life and its simplicities.

of resources: (1) *food* for the increasing urban population; (2) *labor* to man the expanding industrial workforce; and (3) *savings* to finance industrial investment. All three resources may not be simultaneously forthcoming. Worse, maximizing one may minimize the other, which is especially true of food and savings. If, to raise savings for industrialization, agricultural prices are kept low and industrial prices are artificially increased, food production may decline. If, to ensure steadily increasing supplies of food, farm prices are raised, enough savings for industrial investment may not be forthcoming. These dilemmas essentially have led to two kinds of analytical exercises: how to *develop* agriculture and how to *transfer* agricultural resources. Broadly speaking, thinking about the first issue is associated with the microviews of agriculture, and thinking about the second, with the various macroviews. Agricultural production must go up, which requires an understanding of what makes farmers produce. At the same time, agricultural resources should be transferred, but the transfer should be such that it does not hurt agricultural production. Balancing the micro and the macro has been a nagging problem in the economic literature. *Transferring* resources from agriculture has to be distinguished from *squeezing* agriculture. As explained below, the former may benefit farmers as well as the larger society; the latter, under most conditions, will benefit neither.

1.1.1 The institutional and technocratic views in pristine form

At a basic level, economic views about how to develop agriculture can be classified into two broad categories: institutional and technocratic. Several writers have followed the distinction.[3] Let us briefly draw out their respective logics and examine their relationship with the macroviews.

That agrarian structure is central to agricultural productivity is the core of the institutional view.[4] Agrarian structure is basically defined as consisting of two critical elements: size distribution of landownership and tenancy patterns.

The relationship of size to productivity is based on the perceived inefficiency of large holdings in traditional agriculture. Chayanov provided a well-known rationale for why small farms are more productive, measured as output per hectare.[5] Labor is more intensively used on small farms, and since labor is the main input in traditional agriculture, it follows that every additional unit of land transferred from large to small farms will lead to a rise in aggregate production. Farms should not, however, be too small: there is an optimal size – tending

3 For example, Gunnar Myrdal, 1968, *Asian Drama,* New York: Twentieth Century Fund.

4 For a detailed treatment of the institutional view, see Ronald Herring, 1983, *Land to the Tiller: Political Economy of Agrarian Reform in South Asia* (New Haven, CT: Yale University Press), chaps. 8 and 9, and Alain de Janvry, 1981, *The Agrarian Question and Reformism in Latin America,* Baltimore: Johns Hopkins University Press, chaps. 4–6.

5 A. V. Chayanov, 1986, *The Theory of Peasant Economy,* ed. Daniel Thorner, Madison: University of Wisconsin Press.

toward small rather than large – and if agriculture is organized around this optimally small size, aggregate gains will be the largest. Should the land–man ratio, however, make such optimal organizing very difficult – that is, should the land released from transfer above an optimal ceiling make for suboptimally small plots due to population pressure – cooperatives or collectives could be formed to approximate the optimal size.

Tenancy is an inefficient institution, too. Economic critiques of share tenancy go as far back as Adam Smith, but the first systematic treatment of the problem is Alfred Marshall's.[6] The argument is basically about the microeconomic superiority of owner cultivation over share tenancy. In order for the tenant to obtain the maximum output from land, he must apply sufficient working capital and labor. But the tenant does not have the *incentive* to do this, because he receives only a share of the output, not the entire output: work and investment are entirely his, whereas their beneficial outcomes are shared. Moreover, the tenant may also not have the *capacity* to invest. The landlord has the resources which give him this capacity, but he does not have the incentive to undertake the investments required – once again, because the results of such investment are shared. If every tenant produces less than the potential of the land permits, the aggregate outcome will be inefficient. Reforming tenancy patterns – through abolishing tenancy altogether ("land to the tiller") or, less radically, by providing security of tenure to the tenant or statutorily fixing a reduced rent ("tenurial security") – will push up aggregate production.

According to the institutional model, then, institutional reforms in agriculture are defensible on the grounds of both equity and productivity. In the alternative model, prices and technology are considered a more rational and powerful way of increasing agricultural production.[7] While the two may lead to inegalitarian consequences – particularly in the short run – the problem is considered remediable by supplementary policy instruments.[8]

The technological component of the model implies that labor inputs alone (or primarily) can at best have a limited impact on agricultural productivity. Com-

---

6 Modern critiques of Marshall's position began with S. N. S. Cheung, 1969, *The Theory of Share Tenancy*, Chicago: University of Chicago Press. For a review of Marshall and the revisionist neoclassical position, see Mohan Rao, 1986, "Agriculture in Recent Development Theory," *Journal of Development Economics*, June: and Clive Bell, 1977, "Alternative Theories of ShareCropping," *Journal of Development Studies*, July.

7 For a comprehensive treatment, see Peter Timmer, Walter Falcon, and Scott Pearson, 1983, *Food Policy Analysis*, Baltimore: Johns Hopkins University Press for the World Bank; and Peter Timmer, 1987, *Getting Prices Right*, Ithaca, NY: Cornell University Press.

8 Bad distributive consequences result in the short run because, if prices are raised to encourage production, the rural and urban poor suffer. Since over 70 percent of their incomes in the third world are spent on food, their *real* incomes decline when food prices increase. In the long run, however, the employment effect of growth in food production might overpower the income effect. The policy instruments typically suggested to remedy short-run decline are public food distribution programs at a subsidized price and/or food-for-work programs.

bined with technology, however, the same inputs of labor will lead to higher returns. Technology might increase the total costs of agricultural operations (costs per acre), but by increasing yields per acre, it reduces the unit costs (costs per ton). This is a net social gain, not simply that of the individual farmer. Agriculture production, as a result, will be both larger and cheaper.

Prices, on the other hand, affect production, since they determine relative profitability and economic incentives. If the price at which the output can be sold is attractive and a profit can be made, or the relationship between output prices and input costs becomes favorable, a farmer will have the incentive to produce more. Production is affected in another way. Price relationships influence the way a farmer allocates his resources; more resources will be allocated to crops that yield greater return. This, however, does not mean that only the farmer will benefit. The larger society also will.

How society also benefits through the price mechanism is an argument central to welfare economics but, as Arrow and Hahn put it, "it is important to understand how surprising this claim must be to anyone not exposed to the [economic] tradition."[9] In political philosophy, for example, there is a strong tradition, though by no means the only one, originating from Thomas Hobbes, that argues precisely the opposite: if individuals are left free to pursue their self-interest, life will be "nasty, poor, brutish and short." The economic tradition argues differently. Its logic is twofold: (1) the interest of each person is best known to the person concerned; and (2) since the same resource – labor or capital – can be used in alternative ways, the best use of each unit of resources available is to employ it where it yields the best result. Put the first and second elements together, and aggregate gain follows as a syllogism. As a farmer will try to maximize personal gain, resources available for agriculture will be utilized best in a price-induced scenario. The alternative disposition – administrative allocation of resources – will lead to a less than optimal utilization of resources. Since millions of farmers make production decisions, administrators cannot possibly have all the information required to decide what is best for whom. In the absence of that information, administrative methods amount to the requirement that farmers produce according to a social plan, not according to what is best for them. There will be incentive problems and resources will not be fully utilized. The "benevolence" of the farmer, or forcing him to be benevolent, to rephrase Adam Smith, will not produce as much food as the farmer's "regard for his own interest." By ensuring optimal utilization of the resources in the agricultural sector, price signals thus lead to a net social gain.

A price policy aimed at production can, therefore, serve two functions: (1) it will accelerate the growth of agricultural output; (2) it will increase the marketed

9 Kenneth Arrow and Frank Hahn, 1971, *General Competitive Analysis*, San Francisco, CA: Holden Day, p. vi.

surplus. A third function can also be served: by influencing price relationships *among* crops, it can accelerate the growth of certain crops, decelerate others, making it possible to direct the pattern as well as the volume of output.[10]

Once we move beyond this conceptual core and bring in other factors, the neat logic of both approaches partially erodes. First, the arrival of technology in agriculture makes the size advantage of small farms questionable.[11] Tractors cannot be fully utilized on small farms, and fertilizers, along with tubewells and other farm machinery, require resources that small farmers do not normally possess. Second, the problem of incentives in share tenancy is now understood better:[12] if the landlord shares the cost of investments and changes his share of the crop, there is an incentive for him to modernize. Third, it can be shown that price incentives, a powerful mechanism for increasing output of *individual* crops, are less appropriate for increasing *aggregate* production (all crops taken together). The latter is true because even when all agricultural prices are raised, farmers have to choose among competing crops. As a result, only some crops, the more profitable ones, will be chosen, which may then displace the less profitable crops previously sown. Finally, technology can be (partially) decoupled from price, and it can be demonstrated that even if the prices of agricultural output decline, output can go up, provided technological dynamism is generated in agriculture.[13] These complications notwithstanding, the pristine form of the two views remains the bedrock on which even the more complex microviews of agriculture have rested.

1.1.2 Agricultural resources for industrialization: *Toward a macro understanding*

The first economists were pessimistic about agriculture. The "classical pessimism" of the eighteenth and nineteenth centuries (mainly Adam Smith and David Ricardo) stemmed from the belief that, in contrast to industry, agriculture suffered from decreasing returns to scale. This fact led to, as well as called for, a transfer of resources to industry. Later, marginalists like Marshall believed that technical progress was inevitably slower in agriculture. Hence the inevitability

10 Raj Krishna, 1967, "Agricultural Price Policy and Economic Development," in H. M. Southworth and Bruce Johnston, eds., *Agricultural Development and Economic Growth*, Ithaca, NY: Cornell University Press.

11 But certain forms of tenancy can slow down the adoption of technology. See Amit Bhaduri, 1973, "Agricultural Backwardness under Semi-feudalism," *Economic Journal*, March.

12 Pranab Bardhan and T. N. Srinivasan, 1971, "Cropsharing Tenancy in Agriculture: A Theoretical and Empirical Analysis," *American Economic Review*, March; David Newberry and Joseph Stiglitz, 1979, "Sharecropping, Risk Sharing and the Importance of Imperfect Information," in J. A. Roumasset, et al., eds., *Risk, Uncertainty and Agricultural Development*, New York: Agricultural Development Council.

13 Raj Krishna, 1982, "Some Aspects of Agricultural Growth, Price Policy and Equity in Developing Countries," *Food Research Institute Studies*, vol. 28, no. 3.

and desirability of transferring resources from agriculture, given the critical role of technology in economic development.[14]

Ricardo and Malthus. The first famous terms of trade debate took place between two classical economists, Malthus and Ricardo, concerning the Corn Laws in nineteenth-century England. The issue was whether laws limiting grain imports into England should be repealed. If higher imports were allowed, food prices would come down; if they continued to be restricted, food prices would remain high. How would all this affect industrialization in England? Malthus defended the Corn Laws along the following lines. If food imports were increased, terms of trade would turn against agriculture. As food prices came down due to imports, the lords would be faced with a drop in real incomes and would consequently be forced to cut spending. Since the agricultural sector accounted for a large part of the demand for industrial goods, the cut in spending would retard industrial growth.

Ricardo disagreed. To realize gains from trade, he favored repealing the Corn Laws. He also argued that aggregate demand was retarded, not stimulated, by landlords' rents. Land rents ought to come down, not increase, and repeal of the Corn Laws, by making food cheaper and therefore turning the terms of trade against agriculture, would facilitate this process. Modern treatments of this debate suggest that the answer as to whether aggregate demand will go up or come down as a result of food imports and the consequent lowering of food prices depends essentially on how wage earners spend their incomes on goods produced by the two sectors.[15]

In the twentieth century, the issue of agriculture–industry linkages was confronted in a more elaborate and dramatic manner than ever before. The reason was simple. The late developers of the world were unwilling to industrialize in the manner of England and France. Economic processes that took two to three centuries in England and France were now to be telescoped into a few decades. The late developers' desire to industrialize quickly required clarity on the agriculture–industry relationships in the process of industrialization. The economic classics of the twentieth century are the Soviet industrialization debate and W. Arthur Lewis's work on economic development.

The Soviet industrialization debate. The Soviet debate of the 1920s continues to be intellectually important for understanding late industrialization.[16] Commu-

---

14 For a survey of the views of classical economists and marginalists, see Michael Lipton, 1977, *Why Poor People Stay Poor: Urban Bias in World Development*, chap. 4, pp. 89–144.

15 Lance Taylor, 1983, *Structuralist Macroeconomics*, New York: Basic Books, chap. 3. Also see Mohan Rao, "Agriculture in Recent Development Theory."

16 One of the best reviews of the debate is Ashok Mitra, 1977, *Terms of Trade and Class Relations*, London: Frank Cass, and Delhi: Rupa and Co., 1979, chap. 4, pp. 44–68. The page numbers are from the Indian edition.

nism may have collapsed in the 1990s, but for the first Communist country in the world, whether or not a Communist country could modernize its economy faster than its capitalist predecessors was clearly a matter of historic proportions. The issue was how to finance industrialization in the newly born socialist state. The protagonists were Evgeny Preobrazhensky and Nikolai Bukharin, and the debate formed the basis of state policy.

Preobrazhensky argued that the state should turn the terms of trade against agriculture by offering the lowest possible prices for farm products and selling industrial products to the country at the highest possible price.[17] The surplus thus gained would finance industrialization. The context of this argument is important. The farm economy, despite the revolution, was still in private hands: Stalin's collectivization drive started only in 1929. At the top of the agrarian structure was the upper peasantry, the kulaks, who had the bulk of the potential agricultural surplus, and at the bottom – and dependent on the kulaks in various ways – were millions of small and poor peasants. The industrial economy, however, was already state-owned. Preobrazhensky's economic model therefore had a political appeal. The burden of such a price policy, thought Preobrazhensky, would fall almost completely on the kulaks, who were the main producers of agrarian surplus and consumers of industrial goods in the countryside.

Supported by Lenin, Bukharin argued in favor of "equilibrium prices," not "non-equivalent exchange" for agriculture. Economically, food was necessary for industrialization. A temporary truce with the rural sector, still in private hands and dominated by the kulaks, was therefore a political and economic imperative. Preobrazhensky's prescriptions, Bukharin argued, were self-defeating. The kulaks would drastically cut food supply. They would respond to unfavorable terms of trade by producing and/or marketing less. Rural demand for industrial output would contract, as the kulaks, with incomes falling, cut their spending. Bukharin advocated market forces in agriculture along with a state policy encouraging cooperatives for inputs, credit, and farm sales, whose resources and facilities would, however, be especially earmarked for the small peasantry. Cooperatives would reduce unit costs of small peasants. The scale economies, so obtained, would make small peasants much more competitive in the market than the kulaks. Economic rationality would defeat the kulaks as a class and collectivization would dominate the countryside. State-directed market forces would lead to socialism.

Meanwhile, the kulaks did not bless Bukharin's theoretical model with increasing food supplies. Making the argument that parallel lines never meet – the parallel lines being the socialist urban sector and an unyielding, uncollectivized rural sector – Stalin finally embraced Preobrazhensky's model. He solved its intrinsic economic problem – the possibility of the kulaks not providing food

---

17 Preobrazhensky's ideas were developed in his book *New Economics*. An English translation was published by Clarendon Press, Oxford, in 1965.

supplies – by liquidating the kulaks physically and also eliminating a mass of peasants resisting collectivization. Stalin argued that if the state wiped out those who did not provide food for socialist industrialization at reasonable prices, it would end up getting food from the agricultural sector as well as savings – namely, food at low prices. If both savings *and* food from agriculture were required, violence, Stalin concluded, was absolutely necessary.

It turns out that, due to unanticipated economic reasons later understood by economists,[18] Stalin was wrong. So was Preobrazhensky. Even though the investment rate rose from a mere 14.8 percent of GDP in 1928 to 44.1 percent by the end of the First Plan in 1932, this increase was not *primarily* financed by agricultural surpluses. A large part was actually financed by the "forced savings" of the industrial working class. Collectivization did not increase the net agricultural *surplus*, nor did it increase the total agricultural *output*; only the *state procurement* of *wage goods* (especially food) increased. Even more importantly, it did not turn the terms of trade in favor of industry. Rather, the food that could not be procured went into the free ("black") market, and food prices in the free market shot up so much that the overall terms of trade for agriculture in fact improved during the plan period.[19] Inflation was the result. Inflation decreased the real value of the wages being paid to the industrial workers. *Both* the savings thus forced on the urban sector (fall in real wages) and an agrarian surplus, therefore, financed Soviet industrialization under the First Plan (1928–32).

Arthur Lewis and after.   Writing in the middle of the twentieth century, W. Arthur Lewis[20] was sure that a price squeeze on a stagnant agriculture (à la Stalin) would only choke off food supplies and ultimately lead to reckless inflation, thereby hurting industrialization (dependent as it was on increasing food supplies and low wages). Therefore he argued that "industrial and agricultural revolutions always go together" and "economies in which agriculture is stagnant do not show industrial development."[21] At one level, this position is a restatement of Bukharin. Lewis, however, did not stop there. Bukharin's end was somewhat loose, in that he could not discover a profound dilemma inherent in his prescription. If the agricultural sector becomes more productive, "we escape," argued Lewis, "the Scylla of adverse terms of trade," but "we may be caught by the Charybdis of real wages rising because the subsistence sector is more productive."[22] As poor

18 Michael Ellman, 1975, "Did the Agricultural Surplus Provide the Resources for the Increase in Investment in the USSR during the First Five-Year Plan?" *Economic Journal*, December, pp. 844–64.

19 In 1930, 1931, and the first half of 1932, the free market was a black market. The benefits of free-market prices accrued to the peasants and regions that had not yet been collectivized (Central Asia in particular).

20 "Economic Development with Unlimited Supplies of Labor," *Manchester School of Social and Economic Studies*, vol. 22, no. 2, 1954. Lewis won the Nobel Prize for his insight.

21 Ibid., p. 433.

22 Ibid.

economies did not have a high level of savings, low wages, *by increasing profits*, could finance industrial investment. Industrialization was not only dependent on steady food supplies but also on low wages. A productive agricultural sector does not have low but high wages. Labor transferred at high wages to industry would not facilitate accumulation. Thus, both stagnating and prospering agriculture could hurt industrialization.

How should one, then, solve the problem? Taxing *prosperous* farmers was Lewis's solution: "the capitalists' next best move is to prevent the farmer from getting all his extra production. In Japan this was achieved by raising rents against the farmers, and by taxing them more heavily, so that a large part of the rapid increase in productivity which occurred (between 1880 and 1910 . . .) was taken away from the farmers and used for capital formation. . . ."[23] The abiding value of Lewis's model remains precisely in forcefully stating the dilemma and proposing a solution.

Starting with Theodore Schultz in 1964,[24] a *micro*economic orientation, focused more on peasant behavior and raising agricultural production than viewing agriculture as a means to industrial development, came to dominate the economic thinking about agriculture in developing economies. Like Lewis, Schultz argued that for an agricultural revolution to take place, technological investments in agriculture were essential. Unlike Lewis, however, he also argued for price incentives for farmers, for such incentives would be necessary to encourage them to adopt technology. Both price incentives and technological upgrading were required.

Politically speaking, a microeconomic view, reliant as it is on price incentives for farmers, is perhaps the most favorable to the countryside. But a purely microeconomic view leaves a serious economic problem unresolved: how should one raise resources for industrialization? Schultz did not dwell on this question.

In principle, two nonagricultural sources of savings do exist. Minerals or foreign aid (or loans) can step in to provide resources. However, not all countries have rich deposits of minerals, and some can use the income from minerals or oil so recklessly that they end up hurting agriculture through what is known as the "Dutch disease." The examples of Mexico and Nigeria after the oil-price hike in the late 1970s are often cited. Foreign aid can rarely provide all the needed resources. In the early stages of development, countries typically aim at a 15 percent investment rate but save only 5 percent of their income. Only in exceptional cases does foreign aid make up such a large shortfall (American aid to Israel and South Korea in the 1950s comes to mind). A slow pace of industrialization, if chosen, may also reduce the burden on agriculture, but very few poor countries choose to be slow industrializers.

It is not surprising, therefore, that a microeconomic view alone would not be

---

23 Ibid., pp. 433–4.
24 *Transforming Traditional Agriculture*, Chicago: University of Chicago Press, 1964.

feasible. Later developments in economic theory recast the microposition by linking it with the macroproblem of resources for industrialization. In this reconstructed vein, Peter Timmer argues that a Schultz-induced productivity in agriculture "creates a surplus, which . . . can (then) be tapped directly through taxation . . . , or indirectly, through government intervention into the urban–rural term of trade."[25] This position is a marriage of Lewis and Schultz.

Recent empirical research has thrown further light on how resources are generated and transferred in the process of industrialization. It turns out that the *extent* of agricultural contribution has generally been overestimated, though agriculture does provide resources – in some cases a very large part.[26] The contribution of the agricultural sector has typically been overwhelmingly large in countries with a large export agriculture sector, which makes it easier for the government to tap agricultural resources. This argument does not mean that leaders of developing countries have not tried to force the price scissors on the countryside; rather, even when they have done so, the objective economic consequences of their actions have led to inflation financing *part* of the investment through a fall in urban wages – that is, in real terms industrial wages fell, this fall financing investment objectively. Only in the presence of cheap food imports in adequate quantities could this result – squeezing of the food sector without inflationary consequences – be avoided. An export-oriented agricultural sector is typically more readily exploitable. In much of Africa and also Southeast Asia, therefore, agricultural exports may have contributed heavily to the modernization of economies.

These works help us categorize the various ways in which agriculture has intertwined with the process of industrialization. Late developers seem to have followed one of the following four paths to industrialization:

1. squeeze agriculture (à la Stalin);
2. extract a surplus from the export agriculture sector but do not squeeze the entire agricultural sector;
3. extract a surplus from minerals or rely on foreign resources for funding industrialization;
4. make agriculture productive (via technological investments) but transfer resources through taxation or terms of trade.

By now, it is clear that route 1 is self-defeating (much of Africa seems to have followed this option). Options 2 and 3 are not available to all countries: not all of them have big export agriculture sectors or great mineral deposits; neither do foreign resources easily come in such large magnitudes. Option 4 remains the best for those low-income countries still in the early industrializing phases.

25 Peter Timmer, 1988, "The Agricultural Transformation," in Hollis Chenery and T. N. Srinivasan, *The Handbook of Development Economics*, Amsterdam and New York: North Holland Press.
26 M. A. R. Quisumbing and Lance Taylor, 1990, "Resource Transfers from Agriculture," in Kenneth Arrow, ed., *The Balance Between Industry and Agriculture in Economic Development*, London: MacMillan, 1990.

It should also be noted that the institutional approach to agricultural modernization, *if* it can indeed generate productivity, produce a food surplus, and release manpower, is by far the most attractive option for an industrializer. If the institutional approach is unable to increase productivity, the technocratic approach to agricultural transformation is willy-nilly the best choice. The industrializing planner will have to allocate resources to agriculture, for price incentives and technological upgradation, quite obviously, consume economic resources. Option 4 is essentially a marriage of the technocratic approach and a concern for industrialization.

1.1.3 The Indian case

India seems to fall either into the fourth category or, more likely, constitutes a possible fifth – namely, making agriculture productive via price incentives and technology but finding it impossible to impose a tax on the countryside or manipulate the terms of trade, due to political pressures emanating from the countryside. A study by Raj Krishna showed that for the period 1950/1–1973/4, a net transfer of resources *into* agriculture took place.[27] That was also the time, as I will argue later, when the countryside was actually less powerful in the polity than it has been in the period since then. It is likely that the Krishna result also applies to the two decades since the early 1970s. If future econometric work further corroborates this hypothesis, it would establish, perhaps beyond doubt, that the resources for Indian industrialization have primarily come from the urban sector, supplemented by foreign aid. Agriculture may not have contributed a significant amount of savings to the industrial sector. It may also partly explain India's slow industrial growth rate until the late 1970s.[28]

1.2 THE POLITICAL ISSUES

Economic theories may suggest the obvious truth that agriculture declines in the process of modernization. The political tangles, however, remain. Why should the peasantry accept a plummeting fate? After all, what helps the society at large may not benefit the villages. At any rate, the social benefit at time T, which may improve the lot of the rural folk in the end, may not help them at time T-1. Doesn't the peasantry fight the march of history? If not, why not? If yes, why doesn't it succeed?

27 Raj Krishna, 1982, "Trends in Rural Savings and Capital Formation in India, 1950–51 to 1973–74," *Economic Development and Agricultural Change*, vol. 30, no. 2, January.
28 The debate on industrial growth (with the partial exception of K. N. Raj and Sukhamoy Chakravarty) has virtually ignored agriculture–industry linkages. See Ashutosh Varshney, 1984, "Political Economy of Slow Industrial Growth," *Economic and Political Weekly*, September 1.

1.2.1 "No bourgeois, no democracy." "Yes peasants, no democracy"

In *The Eighteenth Brumaire of Louis Bonaparte*, Karl Marx provided the initial formulation of why the peasantry was powerless when confronted with the larger forces of history:

[T]he great mass of the French nation is formed by simple additions of homologous magnitudes, much as potatoes in a sack form a sack of potatoes. . . . In so far as there is merely a local interconnection among these smallholding peasants, and the identity of their interests begets no community, no national bond and no political organization among them, they do not form a class. They are consequently incapable of enforcing their class interest in their own name, whether through a parliament, or through a convention.[29]

Barrington Moore's well-known classic carried the argument further.[30] Moore identified three political routes to a modern (that is, industrial) society: democratic (England, the United States, France), fascist (Germany and Japan), and communist (Russia and China). In all cases, the peasantry is sooner or later subdued.

Moore also pointed to the correlation that "by and large, the elimination of the peasant question through the transformation of the peasantry into some other kind of social formation appears to augur best for democracy."[31] Emergence of the first democracies was premised upon a liquidation of the peasantry, not physically but as a class. Over a period of two centuries, enclosures in England swept aside the peasantry. Of the other early democratic cases, the United States never had a peasantry, only a commercial farmer class.[32] On the face of it, this historical conclusion is a paradoxical one: democracy requires the elimination of the subaltern, the weakest class. Why must it be true?

Moore is more explicit about why *industrialization* is preceded by, or leads to, a taming of the peasantry, but not so clear on why *democracy* may require the elimination of the peasant. However, he did hit upon an obvious truth, not fully appreciated before his work, that modern democracies emerged *in the process of* European and American industrialization. Applying economic theory to Moore's ideas, the linkage between the peasant question and democracy can be pushed further.

Historically speaking, both industrialization and democracy were unprecedented transformations. Democracies subverted the hereditary principle of rule;

---

29 As cited in Theodore Shanin, ed., 1987, *Peasants and Peasant Societies*, New York: Basil Blackwell, p. 332.

30 Barrington Moore, Jr., 1966, *Social Origins of Democracy and Dictatorship: Lord and Peasant in the Making of the Modern World*, Boston: Beacon Press, esp. chaps. 6–8.

31 Ibid., p. 422.

32 And as for France, though the landed aristocracy was eliminated by the French Revolution, "the instability of French democracy during the 19th and 20th centuries is partly due to [the] fact" that the Revolution did not "eliminate the peasant question" (Moore, p. 426). Even, "in smaller client democracies of Scandinavia and Switzerland, the peasants have become part of democratic systems by taking up fairly specialized forms of commercial farming, mainly dairy products, for the town markets" (p. 422).

and industry transformed what had been essentially rural societies. Two historical correlations therefore appeared. The better-known first correlation goes by the dictum "no bourgeois, no democracy"; and the somewhat forgotten second dictum can be called "yes peasants, no democracy." Both are necessary. The logic behind the first dictum is self-evident: in order for industrialization to take place, there ought to be a bourgeoisie (or what is functionally equivalent, a state that performs the functions of the bourgeoisie). But the emergence of a bourgeoisie can directly bring about industrialization, not democratization. The latter also depends on what happens to the countryside in the process of industrialization: or, as Moore put it, on whether or not agriculture is commercialized, and how.

What is the link between commercialized agriculture and democracy? Economic theories surveyed above provide an answer. If a society is predominantly rural, as all societies are in the early stages of industrialization, then the *surplus* necessary for industrialization, or a large part of it, must of necessity come from the rural sector. A commercialized, as opposed to a stagnant, agriculture can provide the necessary surplus: labor surplus, food surplus, and a savings surplus. Stagnant agriculture can not provide these surpluses without coercion. It cannot produce enough food for both the rural sector and towns, making food transfer to towns dependent on coercion. Lacking technology, it cannot produce food at low (per unit) costs, making cheap pricing of food also dependent on coercion. Finally, unproductive agriculture cannot release as many people for towns as commercialized agriculture can, without coercion. If productivity does not go up, n people will produce s quantity of output, whereas commercialized agriculture can produce the same s units of output with $n-m$ people, releasing thereby m people. In the absence of commercialization, it follows, m people will have to be coerced out of the rural sector to act as workers and the remaining $n-m$ people will also have to be coerced to produce s quantities of food output, and probably more.

Thus, industrialization in the face of a stagnant agriculture requires coercion of the countryside, where most people live. It may call for an authoritarian state, not a democratic one. Real-life examples of this logic are plentiful: Stalinist dekulakization in the Soviet Union, or African parastatals forcing the peasantry to part with their product are the most well known.

Peasant revolutions of the twentieth century were the only cases, according to Moore, when peasants were not an object but a subject of history. But peasant-based revolutions, he added, did not lead to a consolidation of peasant power after the revolutions. "Twentieth century peasant revolutions have had their mass support among the peasants, who have then been the principal victims of modernization put through by communist governments."[33] Peasants thus suffer no matter how the political system is constructed.

Moore's argument about peasant revolutions did have a significant impact

33 Moore, *Social Origins*, p. 428.

later. For Moore, whether or not peasants would revolt depended on three factors: (1) whether peasants had strong links with the lords; (2) whether peasants had a strong tradition of solidarity; (3) whether links with urban classes against the lords were established. Investigating conditions under which peasants revolted, Scott further developed the first two insights, and Popkin's work emerged as a counter to Scott and developed the third insight fully.[34] During the 1960s, in the Vietnam War context, the rebellious capacity of peasants became an article of faith.

1.2.2 Urban bias and Brechtian forms of class struggle

About the same time, another argument emerged. Known as the "urban-bias" view and associated in varying shades with Michael Lipton, Theodore Schultz, and Robert Bates, this argument holds that the power structure of the third world is marked by an "urban bias," and the overriding concern of the city is cheap food.[35] Artificially low food prices result from this, amounting to a tax on the countryside. In the polemical but influential words of Michael Lipton:

the most important class conflict in the poor countries of the world today is not between labor and capital. Nor is it between foreign and national interests. It is between rural classes and urban classes. The rural sector contains most of the poverty and most of the low-cost sources of potential advance; but the urban sector contains most of the articulate-ness, organization and power. So the urban classes have been able to win most of the rounds of the struggle with the countryside; but in so doing they have made the develop-ment process needlessly slow and unfair. Scarce land which might grow millets and beansprouts for hungry villagers, instead produces a trickle of costly calories from meat and milk, which few except the urban rich (who have ample protein anyway) can afford. Scarce investment, instead of going into water pumps to grow rice, is wasted on urban motorways. Scarce human skills design and administer, not clean village wells and agri-cultural extension services, but world boxing championships in showpiece stadia. Re-source allocations, within the city and the villages as well as between them, reflect urban priorities rather than equity or efficiency. The damage has been increased by misguided ideological imports, liberal and marxian, and by the town's success in buying off part of the rural elite, thus transferring most of the costs of the process to the rural poor.[36]

There are of course many consequences of urban bias that would reflect in

---

34 James Scott, 1976, *The Moral Economy of the Peasant*, New Haven, CT: Yale University Press; and Samuel Popkin, 1979, *The Rational Peasant*, Berkeley and Los Angeles: University of California Press.

35 Lipton and Bates are discussed below. As for Schultz, here is a representative quote: "[T]here is a 'political market.' Even though the rural population in low-income countries is much larger, the political market strongly favors the urban population at the direct expense of rural people. Politically, urban consumers and industry demand cheap food. Accordingly, it is more important politically to provide cheap rice in Bangkok than to provide optimum price incentives for rice farmers in Thailand . . . ." *Distortion of Agricultural Incentives*, Bloomington: Indiana Univer-sity Press, p. 10.

36 Lipton, *Why Poor People Stay Poor*, p. 13.

many policy areas – investment, taxation, and not simply prices – but food prices are absolutely critical. Whatever else might happen, food must remain cheap. Indeed, the "basic conflict" in the third world boils down to one, says Lipton, between "gainers from dear food and gainers from cheap food."[37] All urban classes are interested in cheap food: the industrialist, because that will keep wages low; the worker, because that "makes whatever wages he can extract from the boss go further"; and the salaried middle classes, because they will have to allocate less for food in their relatively tight household budgets. Conversely, "the whole interest of the rural community is against cheap food." The surplus farmer gains from expensive food because he can get more for what he sells; the deficit farmer, because he can supplement his income from more employment and/or higher wages that result from the surplus farmer hiring more workers when food is more costly. Rural craftsmen gain because rural carpenters and ropemakers get more work when their patrons are rich; and landless agricultural laborers – generally starved of work – also find employment if patrons are richer. The surplus farmer, however, is bought off by the city, says Lipton, through agricultural subsidies. In the end, he doesn't lose from low food prices. His acquiescence to cheap food, however, is purchased to urban advantage and to the great detriment of the countryside.

Theories of collective action have led to a further development of this argument. Lipton's theory did not allow for differential state treatment of distinct crops, nor was it clear what elements of his analytical structure would explain the overvaluation of agriculture in the developed world. Was it because of a rural bias, or was a theory different from the one relevant to the developing world required? In his work on African agriculture, Robert Bates offered an integrated explanation of why urban bias exists in the predominantly agrarian societies of the developing world and, paradoxically, why in the West, farmers manage to exercise considerable power.[38] Bates's argument moves in three steps. First, to extract resources for the treasury, city, and industry, African states set prices that hurt the countryside. Second, by selectively distributing state largesse (subsidies and projects), African states divide up the countryside into supporters that benefit from state action and opponents who are deprived of state generosity, and are frequently punished. Such policy-induced splits preempt a united rural front. Third, independently of the divisive tactics of the state, rural collective action is difficult because (*a*) the agricultural sector is very large, with each peasant having a small share of the product, and (*b*) it is dispersed, making communication difficult. The customary free-rider problem in such situations impedes collective action. Industry, on the other hand, is small and concentrated in the city, and the share of each producer in the market is large, making it worthwhile for each producer to organize.

37 Ibid., p. 67. The remaining quotations in this paragraph also come from this page.
38 Bates, *Markets and States in Tropical Africa*, Berkeley: University of California Press, 1981.

The urban-bias argument is not simply academic. Since the late 1970s, the international development agencies, too, have been expressing a great deal of concern about the agricultural price policies of the developing countries. Rational price regimes, according to the World Bank, are essential to the success of development strategies.[39] But agricultural prices, it argues, are highly distorted in the third world, partly because of the urban-dominated politics in these countries. A series of World Bank studies sought to document the claim about price distortions in agriculture.[40]

Finally, the theme of the relative powerlessness of the peasantry has surfaced elsewhere, too. Earlier celebrating the revolutionary potential of the peasantry, James Scott, in an influential work, has moved from Mao to Brecht:

[T]he emphasis on peasant rebellion was misplaced. Instead, it seemed far more important to understand what we might call *everyday* forms of resistance – the prosaic but constant struggle between the peasantry and those who seek to extract labor, food, taxes, rents, and interest from them. Most of the forms this struggle takes stop well short of collective outright defiance. Here I have in mind the ordinary weapons of relatively powerless groups: foot dragging, dissimulation, false compliance, pilfering, feigned ignorance, slander, arson, sabotage, and so forth.[41]

We thus have a long line of scholarship on the powerlessness of the countryside in the process of development, a powerlessness escaped only by the landlord class, and that too not always.

1.2.3 The Indian case

The literature discussed above raises two important political issues for India. First, India remains a predominantly peasant land, but it is a democracy, defying the "yes peasants, no democracy" dictum. How do peasants and democracy coexist? Second, if rural power accounts for the difficulty entailed in transferring resources from the countryside, how exactly does rural power operate?

As already indicated, the standard argument – made by Marx, the Soviet antagonists, and Moore as well as several others in the vast literature on the peasantry – that a peasant by definition produces for home consumption, not for the market, is becoming increasingly irrelevant. Due to enhancements in productivity brought about by the green revolution, most peasants now participate in market exchanges, and peasant agriculture is no longer the stagnant agriculture it used to be. While the distinction between farmers and peasants is thus disappearing, peasantry as a class is not. A combination of factors – technology, crop

---

39 *World Development Reports*, 1982, 1986, and 1988, New York: Oxford University Press.
40 See the five-volume series on the political economy of agricultural pricing policies, edited by Anne Krueger, Maurice Schiff, and Alberto Valdes. A synthesis of the five volumes is available in Anne Krueger, 1992, *The Political Economy of Agricultural Pricing Policies*, Baltimore: Johns Hopkins University Press for the World Bank.
41 James Scott, 1985, *Weapons of the Weak: Everyday Forms of Peasant Resistance*, New Haven, CT: Yale University Press, p. 29.

choices, farm size, and agrarian infrastructure (water, extension, inputs) – is turning some peasants into surplus producers and making others self-sufficient. Indeed, the green revolution has raised agricultural productivity to such an extent that India, widely viewed as "a basket case" in the 1950s and 1960s, has had a veritable food surplus right through the 1980s (relative, of course, to effective demand). The green revolution, by producing a food surplus, may have blunted the customary contradiction between industrialization on the one hand and the existence of the peasantry on the other.

That nonetheless leaves the first twenty years of India's democracy unresolved; the green revolution, after all, arrived only in the late 1960s. Under Nehru's leadership, India did initiate a heavy industrialization program in the 1950s. From where did the resources for industrialization come? What role did the rural sector play? These issues are discussed at length in the next two chapters. A brief summary here can put the Indian experience in perspective.

While initiating the Second Plan (1956–61), which laid the foundation of heavy industry, Nehru and his planners struggled with the issue of how to finance the plan. Nehru tried to persuade his party cohorts of the necessity of a food surplus and of savings transfer (that is, food transferred at cheap prices):

next to food production, the question of the price of foodgrains is of vital importance. Indeed, the two are intimately connected. If the price of foodgrains goes up, . . . the whole fabric of our planning suffers irretrievably. How can we keep the price of foodgrains at reasonable levels? . . . It is well known that the moment the government goes into the open market, prices shoot up. The only other course, therefore, is for government purchases of foodgrains to take place compulsorily at fixed and reasonable prices. . . .[42]

Nehru proposed two more ideas for the generation and easy tapping of an agrarian surplus: nationalization of foodgrains trade and turning small peasant farms into cooperative farms (to reap economies of scale). After the views of the chief ministers and the party were relayed to Nehru, the first proposal was dropped, and the proposal to build up a "large stock" of food procurement bought "compulsorily at fixed and reasonable prices" was substantially modified. The state chief ministers were closer to the rural world than Nehru in everyday political dealings, and therefore knew its political realities better; state legislatures were already rural to a great degree; and even in Nehru's cabinet in Delhi, the Food and Agriculture ministers always represented the state lobby in the Congress party organization.[43] If the party's wishes had to be taken into account for policy measures, Nehru's agrarian proposals could not be pushed through. *One could not give suffrage to rural India and at the same time procure food from it beyond a point against its wishes.* The democratic constraint required making a deal with rural India, whatever its consequences for industrial development.

---

42 *Fortnightly Letters to Chief Ministers*, vol. 4, dated August 1, 1957, Delhi: Oxford University Press, 1989.

43 Ajit Prasad Jain and S. K. Patil were the longest-serving Ministers for Food and Agriculture in Nehru's various cabinets.

By not forcing the issue, the Congress party, implicitly, did make that deal. Essentially, procurement from the countryside became a modest operation. American wheat surpluses, supplied under Public Law 480, filled a critical food gap in the crucial decade of industrialization (1956–65), a gap closed indigenously only after the green revolution.[44] Supplying five to eight million tons of wheat annually in the mid-1960s, American – not Indian – farmers were feeding a large part of urban India. It was a relationship that became extremely troublesome for both countries and was resolved only when domestic surpluses emerged.

Finally, instead of settling primarily for Brechtian forms of resistance, India's peasantry has graduated to active exertions of power. As argued later, it has penetrated political parties and state institutions and has sustained mobilization on an impressive scale. But the class of landless agricultural laborers has been left out of the rural mobilization. It is this class which may well embody all the Scottian expressions of collective and individual weaknesses, not the entire peasantry. Owning roughly between 5 to 10 acres of land, the so-called middle peasantry has become especially assertive since the green revolution. And the small peasantry (2.5 to 5 acres) has also vigorously participated in organized political action.

44 A participant's observations of the PL-480 supplies are available in W. David Hopper, 1976, "A Perspective on India's Food Production," *Coromandel Lecture*, Madras: Coromandel Fertilizer Company, January 5. Retiring as vice president of the World Bank in 1990, Hopper spent several years in India in the 1950s with The Ford Foundation and USAID, both of which were involved with India's agricultural policy.

2

Nehru's agricultural policy: A reconstruction (1947–1964)

At the time of India's independence, the agricultural situation was bleak. During the four decades preceding 1946–7, India's foodgrain output grew by a mere 12 percent, whereas the population increased by over 40 percent, resulting in a decline in the per capita availability of foodgrains.[1] Foodgrain yields had remained constant over this period. Yields for rice, India's main crop, accounting for close to one-half of its foodgrain output, had in fact dropped. In 1947, only about 15 percent of the cultivated land was under irrigation; the rest was dependent on the proverbial vagaries of the monsoon.[2] Moreover, agriculture in many underdeveloped parts of Asia had moved ahead. Java, through labor-intensive methods, had managed to increase food output to match its population growth.[3] Paddy yields in China were twice as high as average yields in India. Thus, the task of transforming agriculture was daunting and urgent. As a reminder of what could happen, one of the century's worst famines had already taken place in Bengal a few years back – in 1942 – when a million people died.

What strategy should India adopt for transforming agriculture? Political leaders of independent India went through a long and intense debate. There was agreement on the production objective. A substantial increase in food production was essential, new areas had to be brought under cultivation, and yields had to go up. The choice of strategy, however, involved a series of fundamental and contentious questions: what place agriculture should have in the larger development strategy, what the resource allocation between industry and agriculture should be, what role the government had to play in agriculture, what means were appropriate if government involvement was essential, and whether landownership patterns had to be changed in order for agriculture to grow.

At stake was not only what the leadership should do here and now; decisions were likely to have an abiding impact on the future as well. To understand why

---

1 For details, see George Blyn, 1966, *Agricultural Trends in India, 1891–1947*, Philadelphia, PA: University of Pennsylvania Press, p. 96.

2 Ibid., pp. 219–24.

3 Clifford Geertz, 1963, *Agricultural Involution, the Processes of Ecological Change in Indonesia*, Berkeley and Los Angeles: University of California Press, pp. 28–38 and 77–82.

this was so, it is necessary to outline India's agrarian structure in the initial years of its independence.[4] An acute land scarcity coexisted with profound inequalities in landownership. The land–man ratio in rural India was .92 acre (per capita), considered very low by comparative standards. About 22 percent of rural households were landless. Another 25 percent owned less than one acre. Slightly above this mass of the landless or the near-landless stood those who owned between 1 to 2.5 acres (one hectare or less). Their numbers constituted about 14 percent of the rural households. Over 60 percent of rural India, thus, was landless or owned holdings below 2.5 acres. Taken together, the "subalterns" owned less than 8 percent of the total cultivable land. In contrast, those owning holdings of more than 10 acres constituted 13 percent of the total rural households and accounted for 64 percent of the area.[5] Of these, 5 percent (of the total) owned 20 acres or more, comprising 41 percent of the (total) area. Less than 1 percent of the rural households had holdings over 50 acres. In all size groups, holdings were further subdivided into noncontiguous plots, some spread over villages. Inequalities were thus overlaid with irrational subdivisions.

Tenancy further complicated the picture. Different parts of India had different tenurial patterns. It would be an awesome task to describe the existent patterns in their entirety.[6] For our purposes here, description of some modal characteristics will suffice. In the Northeast, an elite class – the *zamindars* (roughly, "absentee landowners") – created by the British to collect land revenue for the government, hardly tilled the land. The zamindars were from high castes. They lived mostly in the cities, leasing out their lands to tenants, and the leases were often oral. Some of the larger tenants – the "substantial tenants" – subleased these lands, mostly to small landowners. The whole system thus had complex layers of ownership, lease, and tilling. In the Northwest, the elite zamindar class did not exist and the incidence of owner cultivation was higher. In the South, West and in central India too, there were variations – regional and, in some places, even subregional. Generally speaking, the incidence of tenancy was higher in the rice growing areas and owner cultivation marked the wheat belt.

How should production be increased in this variegated agrarian structure? Moreover, given profound inequalities, should equity be considered an objective?

The answers given by India's political leaders and the strategies suggested fall into two separate packages. Those who favored reforms in the agrarian structure

4 Detailed data on landholdings in India were first collected in 1954–5, later published in *National Sample Survey*, no. 10, *First Report on Landholdings, Rural Sector* (Delhi, 1958).

5 This also means that about 26 percent of households owning between 2.5 and 10 acres were "middle peasants." They accounted for 28 percent of the area. In the terminology used in later years, the size categories came to be known as follows: less than 2.5 acres, "marginal"; between 2.5 and 5 acres, "small"; 5 to 10 acres, "middle"; and the rest "upper" (with various further subdivisions).

6 A survey of the variety can be found in P. C. Joshi, 1975, *Land Reforms in India: Trends and Perspectives*, Bombay: Allied.

as a way of increasing production and reducing inequalities asked for an *institutional* strategy. Those who thought agrarian reforms could at best reduce inequalities but would not solve the problem of production were more in favor of a *technocratic* strategy, a shorthand term for a price- and technology-based strategy, as already explained (Chapter 1). The first group won the political battle in the beginning, leading to the adoption of an institutional strategy. By the mid-sixties, this strategy was in crisis. The second group then managed to change India's agricultural strategy. Their policy design continues to this day.

2.1 THE POLITICAL CONTEXT

The Congress party emerged from independence as an umbrella party. It represented many political tendencies, each with powerful protagonists, though none as powerful and charismatic as Nehru. Nehru and the *left-of-center* group made the institutional argument. The *right-of-center* faction was lukewarm toward land reforms, hostile to cooperatives, and sympathetic to a technocratic strategy, calling for greater outlays on agriculture and farm incentives. Their resistance was not entirely due to an alternative, coherent worldview. Some were merely opposed to what they considered a pernicious attempt to usher in communism through land reforms and cooperatives – an attempt, they thought, Nehru orchestrated with the help of intellectuals in the Planning Commission. Nehru wanted the Planning Commission to have a privileged place in the economic decision making of the country. The right of center was more entrenched in the party organization. Known as the "state bosses," these leaders had a strong base in their respective states.[7]

Agricultural policy was intertwined with the power struggle within the ruling Congress party. Two types of power were involved: power based on a hold over the electorate and power stemming from a hold over the party. If the same faction had been preponderant in both senses, a stable equilibrium for pursuing policies would have resulted. A divergence between the two led to an unstable equilibrium characterized by much pushing, pulling, and compromising. Nehru was the supreme leader of the masses, but his authority within the party was challenged by the "state bosses," who differed with Nehru on economic policy (as well as some other policies). The state bosses had independent political bases in their states, knew the local political configurations, and were organizational stalwarts. Nehru, therefore, had to accommodate this faction in the power map in Delhi. Typically, the state bosses would obtain ministries that had routine dealings with the states. Agriculture mostly went to them: Planning, Industry, and Finance did not. However, in and of themselves, the state bosses could not win national

---

7 The important leaders of this faction and their respective states were: Morarji Desai, Gujarat; Atulya Ghosh, West Bengal; Sanjiv Reddy, Andhra Pradesh (at that time part of Madras); S. Nijalingappa, Mysore; C. Rajgopalachari, Madras; Y. B. Chavan and S. K. Patil, Maharashtra; and G. B. Pant and C. B. Gupta, Uttar Pradesh; and Mohan Lal Sukhadia, Rajasthan.

elections. They, in turn, required Nehru's national stature and supreme popularity.[8]

This chapter deals with the institutional strategy adopted by India when Nehru was alive, and the next chapter with the technocratic strategy. The logic and elements of India's institutional strategy are analyzed first; why this strategy excluded price incentives and its implications for technology in agriculture are then discussed; and, finally, the failure of the institutional strategy addressed. It will be shown that ideas derived from theories and ideologies intermeshed with the struggle for power in complex ways, both at the level of policy making and policy implementation.

2.2 NEHRU'S INSTITUTIONAL STRATEGY: LOGIC AND ELEMENTS

Nehru's agrarian model was a synthetic one.[9] Agricultural productivity was not simply an economic matter; it depended on a political, economic, and social transformation of India's rural life. The model had three constitutive elements. India's agriculture could be transformed with (1) land reforms, (2) farm and service cooperatives, and (3) local self-government at the village level.[10] By setting a ceiling on holdings (ceiling reform), by securing tenancy rights (tenancy reforms), or by restoring land to the tiller (abolishing tenancy), land reforms would provide incentives to the actual tiller to produce more. Cooperatives would bring economies of scale: service cooperatives would bring economies for inputs such as credit, seeds, water, manures, and mechanical implements; and by joining together small plots of land, distributed via land reforms, farm cooperatives would facilitate rational land use. Local self-government – the *Panchayati*

---

8 The only national-level, charismatic leader who shared the beliefs of the "state bosses" and could have conceivably replaced Nehru, Sardar Patel, had already died in 1950.

9 In reconstructing Nehru's model, I have drawn freely upon his writings, speeches, and biographies: Jawaharlal Nehru, 1946, *Discovery of India*, New York: John Day; Government of India, 1963–8, *Jawaharlal Nehru's Speeches*, vols. 1–5, Delhi: Publications Division, Ministry of Information and Broadcasting; S. Gopal, 1977, 1979, and 1984, *Jawaharlal Nehru: A Biography*, vols. 1–3, Cambridge, MA: Harvard University Press; J. Nehru, *Fortnightly Letters to Chief Ministers*, 1947–63, Delhi: Oxford University Press, for the Nehru Memorial Museum and Library.

10 Conceptually, all three elements of the model – land reforms, cooperatives, and local self-government – existed right since the mid-1940s. See, for example, Nehru's autobiography, *Discovery of India*, pp. 533–5. As actual policy matters, however, they were chronologically separated. Land reforms came first, cooperatives and local self-government (*panchayats*) later. It is not clear why Nehru did not go for all three simultaneously. The only plausible reason seems to be that, given the opposition to some of his views in an important faction of the Congress party, his commitment to the democratic principle, and the complexities of building institutions in a newly independent country, he wished to push his vision gradually, starting with what was less controversial first. Land reforms in the late forties were less controversial than today. The other two elements were fervently pushed by Nehru in the mid-fifties when he realized that progress toward structural transformation at the grass roots was unsatisfactory due to the power exercised by the landed elite and the biases and sloth of the local bureaucracy. See S. Gopal, *Jawaharlal Nehru*, vol. 3, chap. 1.

Raj[11] – was a new element introduced by Nehru in the ideal typical institutional model (Chapter 1). Local self-government, in his view, was necessary to ensure that land reforms were implemented and cooperatives were run according to the collective interests of the village, not according to those of the privileged few. Given the local power structure, complicity between the erstwhile landed oligarchy and the local bureaucracy, some of whom actually came from the landed upper classes, was easily conceivable. Bureaucracy alone could not be entrusted to implement the strategy. Principles of universal suffrage and majority vote would enable the poor to translate their numerical strength into political power, thus ensuring that their rights were respected and measures intended to benefit them were actually implemented.

The model had two supplementary elements as well: (1) introducing scientific practices into India's traditional agriculture (which would increase production directly); and (2) incorporating villages into a modern education system (which would do it indirectly).[12] Added to the institutional thrust, these two elements would help India achieve the full potential of its countryside, its people, and its lands.

2.2.1 Ideology and rationality in Nehru's model

It is often claimed that Nehru's unwillingness to seek a solution within the existing agrarian structure was due to his ideological commitment to equality and socialism.[13] There is a ring of truth in this assessment, but in itself it does not capture the multiple logic of Nehru's model.

It would be helpful to recall that in the intellectual climate of the 1950s, socialists were not the only defenders of land reforms. Those on the right defended them on the ground of political stability, those on the left for equity gains;

11 In policy terms, the Community Development Program, a variant of local governance, chronologically preceded the Panchayati Raj, but by the mid-fifties, it was not working. In 1957, the Balwant Rai Mehta Committee, appointed by Nehru, identified excessive bureaucratization and lack of popular initiative as its main failing. Nehru then returned to his earlier insistence on panchayats. These were, however, simply different means of achieving the same purpose – raising agricultural productivity through a complete institutional transformation of the countryside. For an appraisal, see S. C. Dube, 1969, "Community Development: A Critical Review," in A. R. Desai, 1969, *Rural Sociology in India*, Bombay: Popular Prakashan. For details of change in strategy, see S. Gopal, *Nehru*, vol. 3, pp. 167–9, and also pp. 15–16.

12 These are supplementary elements, for, Nehru's commitment to science notwithstanding, his willingness to push science and technology in agriculture, as discussed later, was not as wholehearted as in industry. Education as a *separate* element was added consciously only as late as 1959, when it became clear to him that his institutional model would not function effectively unless the poor were educated and able to develop a sharper consciousness of their rights. A famous speech was made at the 1959 Congress session in Nagpur, called "Three Basic Institutions," *Nehru's Speeches*, vol. 4, p. 129. The three institutions were the cooperative, the panchayat, and the village school.

13 E.g., Myron Weiner, 1987, "The Indian Political Tradition and the Shaping of the Ideological and Institutional Features of Indian Modernity," in S. N. Eisenstadt, ed., *Patterns of Modernity: Beyond the West*, New York: New York University Press.

while both sides could make arguments about production gains as well.[14] Nehru explicitly denied that his commitment to socialism was the *sole* basis for his insistence on land reforms:

We have said that our objective is a socialist pattern of society. I do not propose to define precisely what socialism means in this context because we wish to avoid any rigid or doctrinaire thinking. Even in my life I have seen the world change so much that I do not want to confine my mind to any rigid dogma. But, broadly speaking, what do we mean when we say "socialist pattern of life"? We mean a society in which there is equality of opportunity and the possibility for everyone to live a good life. Obviously, this cannot be attained unless we produce the wherewithal to have the standards that a good life implies. . . .

There is good deal of talk these days about (land) ceilings, and one naturally tends to agree with it because one wants to remove disparities. But one has always to remember that the primary function of a growing society is to produce more wealth; otherwise it will not grow, and one will have nothing to distribute. *If in the process of fixation of ceilings or in any other method of producing some kind of equality, you stop this process of wealth accumulation, then you fail in your objective.* Therefore, whether it is in industry or agriculture, the one and the primary test is whether you are adding to the wealth of the country by increasing production. . . .[15]

A similar logic could be applied to cooperatives in agriculture, which, in the 1950s, were as a matter of fact in place not only in a socialist country like China but also in Israel. It is often said that Nehru was very struck by Chinese cooperatives. It has hardly been noticed that he also sent a team of experts to Israel to study the working of cooperatives so that India could learn from the Israeli experience.[16] In an effort to explain the rationale for cooperatives, Nehru explicitly refuted the charge that ideology, not production considerations, underlay his notion of cooperatives:

For some odd reason the word "cooperative" rather frightens some people. . . . It has been said that this leads to something terrible – communism. . . . Communism has nothing to do with this. Whether communism is good or bad, you can argue. But to bring in this kind of thinking and confuse the issue seems to me quite amusing.[17]

He explained the rationale:

By forming cooperatives the peasants pool their resources for providing credit and getting their supplies of seeds, implements, fertilizers etc and can organize the sale of their produce. The cooperative removes the moneylender and the middleman. That is why all over the world farmers have formed themselves into *service* cooperatives.[18]

---

14 For links between political stability and land reforms, Samuel Huntington, 1967, *Political Order in Changing Societies*, New Haven, CT: Yale University Press, pp. 374–96. For a comprehensive review of all the existing views – both from the left and right – on land reforms, see Ronald Herring, *Land to the Tiller*, Chaps. 2, 8, and 9.

15 Emphasis added. From Nehru's speech initiating the debate on the Second Five-Year Plan in the Lower House of Parliament, May 23, 1956, reproduced in *Nehru's Speeches*, vol. 3. p. 96.

16 Nehru's memorandum to A. P. Jain, Food Minister, May 21, and to S. K. Dey, Minister for Community Development, July 2, 1959, cited in S. Gopal, *Jawaharlal Nehru*, vol. 3, p. 117.

17 Speech in Lok Sabha (Lower House of Parliament), August 22, 1960, reproduced in *Nehru's Speeches*, vol. 4, p. 141.

18 Speech in Madurai, April 15, 1959, in *Nehru's Speeches*, vol. 4, p. 130.

Farm cooperatives, too, had a production logic:

What is the future of our peasantry? A great number of them have barely one or two acres of land to cultivate. . . .

. . . How will the peasant function with his small patch of land? It is not possible for him to take advantage of modern techniques or the facilities offered by new methods unless he works in cooperation with others of his kind. Cooperation is the key to his future growth and the cooperative movement thus must spread all over the country and comprise all the villages and peasants of this vast land.[19]

Production, in fact, had to be a non-negotiable objective, for, over and above its desirability in a country of low food output, Nehru's ambitious industrialization program *required* agricultural surpluses.

The ideology of equality thus did not sidetrack considerations of production in Nehru's model. Maximization of both objectives – production and equality – was built into his strategy. One can even argue that he wanted to maximize another objective. The agrarian model had to be such that democracy was maintained. Nehru rejected nationalization or collectivization of land, for he was "too much of an individualist and believer in personal freedom to like overmuch regimentation."[20] Instead of collectivization, he chose elected local government as a means through which the numerically preponderant rural poor would be empowered to make the other two elements of the model work. Moreover, membership in the cooperatives was voluntary, not compulsory.

Why did Nehru exclude price incentives and the profit motive from his model? What about science and technology? What was the view of Nehru's planners? How did Nehru and his planners deal with the technocratic predilections of the right-of-center group? The right of center may not have had Nehru's stature, but it did have arguments and it did speak up. A. P. Jain, Food minister between 1953–7, for example, argued:

There is . . . a school of thought in this country consisting of economists and persons confined to their rooms. They think that you can finance the Plan by depressing the agricultural prices. Some of them go to the length of saying: "fix the price of wheat (at a very low level) and the price of rice and other agricultural commodities compulsorily in the market and that will solve the problem of prices. Wages will not go up and the Plan will progress smoothly." These people seem to forget that there is some such thing as agricultural sector in our economy and that it all forms part of the Plan. . . . If we adopt any policy of low prices for agriculture, it is a regressive policy. If our policy does not give any incentive to the farmer, he is not going to produce and if the Plan fails it will wreck on the policy of depressing agricultural prices.[21]

Were the state bosses wrong? Were price incentives and investments in technology not suited to the three objectives Nehru had in mind?

There are three answers to these questions: (1) Nehru's normative assessment of the profit motive and whether it cohered with the cultural traits of Indian

19 "Cooperative Farming," *National Herald*, October 3, 1957.
20 Nehru, *Discovery of India*, p. 17.
21 *Lok Sabha Debates*, 2d ser., vol. 4, July 30, 1957, p. 6066.

society; (2) the dominant economic view of peasant behavior and traditional agriculture in the 1950s, which guided economic planning; and (3) the logic of Nehru's overall development strategy, in which industrialization was accorded the highest priority.

Nehru was convinced that strategies based on price incentives and profit maximization were unsuited to the communitarian Indian character.

It would be absurd to say that the profit motive does not appeal to the average Indian, but it is nevertheless true that there is no such admiration for it in India as there is in the West. The possessor of money may be envied but he is not particularly respected or admired. Respect and admiration still go to the man or woman who is considered good and wise, and especially to those who sacrifice themselves . . . for the public good. The Indian outlook, even of the masses, has never approved of the spirit of acquisitiveness.

. . . [C]ommunal undertakings and cooperative efforts . . . [are] . . . fully in harmony with old Indian social conceptions, which were all based on the idea of the group. The decay of the group system under British rule, and especially of the self-governing villages, has caused deep injury to the Indian masses, even more psychological than econom-ic. . . . But still the village holds together by some invisible link, and old memories revive. It should be easily possible to take advantage of these age-old traditions and to build up communal and cooperative concerns in the land. . . .[22]

When challenged by his opponents on price incentives, he argued: "Incentives are necessary; I agree. But there are many types of incentives, some incentives that are good for society and some that are bad. . . . I do not want to encourage acquisitiveness in India beyond a certain measure."[23]

Nehru thus fluctuated between positing that the profit motive did not have a significant place in Indian society and saying that the profit motive was undesir-able, a trespassing from the positive to the normative. There had to be other, more compelling, reasons for pushing the institutional strategy and excluding price incentives. The enormously powerful and technically sophisticated planners pro-vided those reasons. In their formulation of plans, the planners were guided by the economic theories of the time. Nehru's ideas and the planners' theories came together. The right of center had virtually no support in the technocratic and intellectual community in Delhi. Their arguments could easily be dismissed as ideological, whereas Nehru's ideas were "scientific."

2.3 ECONOMIC THEORY AND AGRICULTURAL PRICES: THE VIEW OF THE 1950s

Over the last decade and a half, agricultural prices have come to occupy a central place in policy and academic discussions about agricultural production. In the 1950s, however, this was not the case. Food production was not considered to be

---

22 Nehru, *Discovery of India*, p. 554.
23 Speech in Lok Sabha, discussion on the Draft Outline of the Third Five-Year Plan, August 22, 1960, in *Nehru's Speeches*, vol. 4, p. 140. Also, his earlier speech delivered at the All-India Congress Committee meeting in January 1957, entitled "Away from Acquisitive Society," in *Speeches*, vol. 3, pp. 51–3.

responsive to higher prices. Agricultural prices were viewed more in a macro-economic framework: how they affected industrial development and economy-wide prices. Moreover, the other macroeconomic question considered important today – namely, the impact of exchange rates on agricultural development – was also absent (see Appendix).

Economic theory in the 1950s viewed peasants as price-unresponsive. Peasants had a backward-bending supply curve, not an upward-sloping one: that is, in response to higher prices, they would cut production instead of increasing it. Why? Given that consumption patterns in these economies were "tradition-bound," farmers would go for a *level* of income that satisfied the traditional consumption requirements, not for *maximization* of income. Since income is equal to price times output, higher prices would reduce output. Even if all farmers do not behave in this manner, "at least a segment of the agricultural population is likely to act perversely in this regard, diluting any positive effect in regard to other sectors of agricultural population."[24]

In commercialized agriculture, on the other hand, farmers are price-responsive because (1) purchased inputs like fertilizers are used heavily, which are both yield-increasing and make farmers conscious of output–input price ratios; (2) the flow of labor resources is much higher between farm and nonfarm sectors, which makes it possible to allocate labor in response to price changes; and (3) return to labor is higher, which encourages inputs of labor at the expense of leisure.[25] In commercialized agriculture, then, the production response of the farmer will be that of a maximizing economic agent. Recall what a normal, "rational" supply curve looks like in the textbooks. It is upward-sloping, not backward-bending: the response to higher prices is higher production.

The economic theory outlined above guided the planners' microview of agricultural prices.[26] Starting with the early to mid-sixties, the economic view would start to change. Village-level microstudies done by two economic anthropologists – David Hopper, who studied economic behavior in a village in eastern India while living there for about two years, and Sol Tax, who did a similar study in a Guatemalan village – and careful statistical estimates of farm-supply response made by Raj Krishna for Punjab showed that peasants were price-

---

24 John Mellor, 1966, *The Economics of Agricultural Development*, Ithaca, NY: Cornell University Press, p. 203.

25 Ibid., pp. 203–4.

26 Cf. I. G. Patel, "On a Policy Framework for Indian Agriculture," *Coromandel Lecture*, Delhi, December 18, 1980, p. 7; John Mellor, 1977, *The New Economics of Growth; A Strategy for India and Developing World*, Ithaca, NY: Cornell University Press, p. 26. An early exposition of the price-unresponsive behavior of peasants was provided by Sir Manilal Nanvati in "Problems of Indian Agriculture," *Proceedings of the Sixth International Conference on Agricultural Economics*, London: Oxford University Press, 1948, pp. 265–77. John P. Lewis, a USAID administrator in India in the late 1950s and 1960s, states that S. R. Sen was perhaps the only high-placed economist in the government willing to make arguments about price incentives for agriculture. See John P. Lewis, "Essays in Indian Political Economy," unpublished manuscript, 1990.

responsive.[27] What caused a shift in economic thinking was the subsequent argument made on the basis of these studies by Theodore Schultz, later a Nobel Laureate in Economics. In his influential book, *Transforming Traditional Agriculture*, Schultz argued that farmers in the third world were "poor but efficient":[28] what constrained their productivity was not price unresponsiveness but the low level of technology in developing agriculture. Government investments in material (technological upgrading) and human (how to use the new technology) capital would transform traditional agriculture.[29] In other words, changing the *attitude* of the peasant was not the issue; changing his *environment* was.

The existing macroview of agricultural prices also militated against price incentives for farmers. At the center of the macroview of the 1950s lay the terms of trade issue – the role of *relative* intersectoral prices in development. As explained earlier (Chapter 1), agriculture is potentially a source of several surpluses for the development process: food, savings, labor, and sometimes foreign exchange. Food surplus is required because (1) the urban population increasing under the impact of industrialization must be fed; (2) given the low base of consumption, rising incomes resulting from industrialization lead to an increase in demand for food; and (3) a rise in food prices, which will come about if food is in short supply, must be moderated so that wages can be kept low to facilitate industrialization. A savings surplus is required because industrialization must be financed; a labor surplus, because it is necessary to build an industrial labor force and industrial wages must be kept low. And, finally, foreign exchange being generally a bottleneck, lack of food imports (or agricultural exports) could ease that constraint. How agricultural prices (relative to industrial prices) affect these various surpluses, and how that in turn affects industrialization, are issues with which every economy on its development path has to contend. An ideal scenario would obtain if somehow all or most of these surpluses could be procured on cheap terms: that is, without having to pour substantial resources *into* agriculture. Nehru's industrial strategy was essentially premised upon this logic.

---

27 David Hopper's Ph.D. dissertation, "The Economic Organization of a Village in North Central India" (Cornell University, 1955) remains unpublished, but a paper based on it was later published as "Allocation Efficiency in Traditional Indian Agriculture," *Journal of Farm Economics*, August 1965. Sol Tax's *Penny Capitalism* was originally published in 1953, but remained unnoticed until Schultz popularized it and the University of Chicago Press republished it in 1963. For Raj Krishna, see his "Farm Supply Response in India-Pakistan: A Case Study of the Punjab Region," *Economic Journal*, September 1963. While the coefficients in the Krishna were not very large, they were significantly positive: i.e., the upward slope of the supply curve might not be steep, but a backward-bending supply curve certainly seemed out of place.

28 Chicago: University of Chicago Press, 1964. See especially chap. 3.

29 Not all aspects of Schultz's argument were acceptable. There was a great debate on whether or not the marginal productivity of labor is zero in traditional agriculture. See the exchange between Amartya Sen and Theodore Schultz in *Economic Journal*, March 1967.

2.4 INDIA'S INDUSTRIAL STRATEGY AND ITS AGRICULTURE–INDUSTRY LINKAGES

Nehru's industrial strategy had three main characteristics: industrialization had to be rapid; it had to focus on heavy and basic industries; and, while private enterprise would exist in many sectors, the basic and heavy industries – "the strategic points" of the economy – were to be in the public sector.[30] Eventually, the trio of steel, power, and machines became the centerpiece of India's industrial strategy.[31] These industries required large investments and had long gestation periods. On this ground, the private sector was neither expected to take them up nor was it willing to.[32] Public resources had to be found for making these large investments.

India's Second Five-Year Plan (1956–61) embodied Nehru's view. A target growth rate of 5 percent per annum was considered desirable for the economy during the plan period. India's savings rate at that point, however, was a mere 5 percent. In order to generate an investment rate that would make it possible to achieve the target growth rate of 5 percent, foreign savings had to be tapped to supplement domestic savings.

Industrialization also required increased food supplies. An increasing labor force in industry (and increasing population) had to be fed. Given the foreign-exchange constraint, it was not possible to import food in large quantities commercially. Domestic production of food had to go up. Heavy public outlays in industry required for steel, power, and machines, however, were a serious constraint on how much the government could invest in agriculture. The total outlay for agriculture and irrigation in the Second Plan dropped from 34.6 percent in the First Plan to 17.5 percent in the Second. Since the Second Plan was much larger than the First, absolute investment levels in agriculture did not drop. But in the total agricultural outlay, compared to the First Plan, absolute expenditures on irrigation (and other schemes that increased production directly) did decline. Resources had also to be allocated for scientific research in agriculture, its dissemination through extension service, building of rural roads, community projects, etc. The problem of resource mobilization was so serious that even after additional taxation, mobilization of concessionary foreign savings, and

30 Nehru articulated the logic behind this strategy: "It seems to me obvious that if we want to industrialize India quickly, we have to pay special attention to basic and heavy industries. Unless we have the basic and heavy industries, we remain dependent. If we want to have more steel in India, as we do, we must produce our own steel. What is more, we must produce the plant which makes steel. Then only we lay the foundation of steel industry. This applies to a number of other basic industries." Address to the UN Seminar on Management of Public Industrial Enterprises, Delhi, December 1, 1959, in *Nehru's Speeches*, vol. 4, p. 132. The strategy based on this logic had come into existence with the Second Five-Year Plan in 1956. See ibid., vol. 3, pp. 90–105.
31 Speech in the Lower House of Parliament, August 22, 1960, *Nehru's Speeches*, vol. 3, p. 136.
32 In the Bombay Plan conceived in 1944, India's industrialists had already expressed a preference for state investment in these sectors after independence.

maximum deficit financing considered "safe," the plan was still left with a "resource gap."

The logic of this development strategy for the agricultural sector was clear. A stable increase in food production was required, but an effort had to be made to bring about this increase with small capital investments. Labor-intensive methods had to be the mainstay. From the viewpoint of public finance, cooperatives and organizational restructuring of agriculture seemed to be a rational policy design for increasing production. Providing farm machinery, mechanized irrigation, and chemical fertilizer to innumerable peasants required heavy capital investments. Ideally, Nehru and his planners would have liked to invest in both agriculture and industry, but faced with a choice between making capital investments in agriculture or industry, they preferred the latter for (*a*) they believed that labor-intensive ways of increasing production were possible in agriculture but not in industry, and (*b*) that capital investments in industry would bring in greater returns.

In addition to the need for surplus food, the resource gap, as already mentioned, had also to be filled. It required additional savings. For some time, the idea of nationalizing foodgrains trade was seriously pursued as a way of mobilizing savings from agriculture. Mahalanobis, the architect of India's Second Plan, commented that "if additional Government profits are to be raised, it might be necessary for the State to enter into the field of trading or production of consumer goods."[33] The nationalization plan, however, had to be ultimately abandoned when serious opposition from within the Congress party emerged. That it was impossible to supervise the market transactions of 60 million peasants was the argument with which the trade nationalization plan was opposed.[34]

The industrialization strategy also had implications for food-price policy. Larger food supplies were essential, but the price of food had to be low. The overall price level in the economy, acutely sensitive to food prices in a developing country, was not to upset the *real* value of planned investments. Nehru, as already indicated, argued:

next to food production, the question of the price of foodgrains is of vital importance. Indeed, the two are intimately connected. If the price of foodgrains goes up, then the whole fabric of our planning suffers irretrievably. How can we keep the price of foodgrains at reasonable levels? The only course appears to be to have a large stock of foodgrains at every time. . . . It is not possible to maintain large stocks if the Government has to buy them in open market. It is well known that the moment the Government goes into the open market, prices shoot up. The only other course, therefore, is for Government purchases of foodgrains to take place compulsorily at fixed and reasonable prices . . . I see no way out except this way.[35]

---

33 P. C. Mahalanobis, "Extracts from the Second Five Year Plan," chap. 3, reproduced in his *The Approach of Operational Research to Planning in India*, New York: Asia Publishing House, 1963, p. 130.

34 For the struggle over state takeover of foodgrains trading, see Francine Frankel, *India's Political Economy*, chaps. 4 and 5. Ultimately, foreign savings and additional deficit financing filled the resource gap.

35 *Fortnightly Letters to Chief Ministers*, dated August 1, 1957.

To sum up, price controls rather than price incentives marked Nehru's agricultural strategy. The normative and the positive came together. Price incentives and the profit motive were undesirable, thought Nehru, in the Indian cultural setting; economic theory ruled them out for his planners; and the development strategy rendered them impossible in agriculture because using prices to raise production would "irretrievably" upset the plan. Instead, the microeconomic setting within which Nehru visualized maximizing behavior was that of a peasant liberated from his earlier socioeconomic bondage of tenancy and having his own plot of land; a peasant who therefore had an incentive to produce more, for he could keep the output of his labor; a peasant who would join others in forming service cooperatives, since that would bring down the costs of inputs and would ensure that proceeds from the sale of output came to him and were not appropriated by middlemen; a peasant who finally would join his plot of land with that of others so that scale economies could be exploited and the full productive potential of agriculture realized.

2.4.1 Implications for technology in agriculture

The imperatives of Nehru's development strategy also make his view of the role of science and technology in agriculture intelligible. Nehru did not see prices *and* technology as an inseparable policy package. They could be separated. He disapproved of price incentives, not science and technology: "If I have to say in one word what is wrong with agriculture, I would say it is the complete lack of anything that might be called scientific agriculture."[36] The First Plan (1951–6) had a clear bias in favor of major irrigation projects. Four major river-valley projects were undertaken and the large dams and canals, in a famous speech, were called "temples of the new age."[37]

Modern agricultural technology in the developing world has come to be known as the seed–water–fertilizer technology, a shorthand formula that captures the *biochemical* core of the green revolution. There are two more sides to the science involved in agriculture: (1) *mechanical* inputs represented by farm machines such as tractors and threshers; and (2) *research and extension*, which stand for innovations, their adaptation to specific environments, and the transmission of this knowledge to farmers.

These elements were accepted by Nehru in varying degrees. Research and extension were enthusiastically welcomed. India's collaboration with American agricultural science started as early as 1951.[38] It included setting up institutions of agricultural science that were entrusted with soil surveys, seed development, field

---

36 Cf. S. Gopal, *Nehru*, vol. 3, p. 19.
37 *Nehru's Speeches*, vol. 3, pp. 1–4.
38 Uma Lele and Arthur Goldsmith, 1989, "The Development of Agricultural Research Capacity: India's Experience with the Rockefeller Foundation and Its Implications for Africa," *Economic Development and Cultural Change*, January.

demonstration of technologies, and training of cadres for extension work. A large part of the expenses for research and extension was borne by aid givers, particularly the U.S. foundations. Their contribution enhanced the degrees of freedom Nehru had with domestic resources. Without the external funds, it is unclear how far Nehru would have gone ahead with his commitment to science in agriculture.

Mechanical and biochemical inputs were more problematic: they were highly capital-intensive, and in the case of chemical fertilizers foreign exchange was required. Of the three biochemical elements, the high-yielding variety of seeds had of course not been discovered at that point – science produced them only in the early sixties. Nehru was ambivalent toward the other two elements: water and fertilizer. His ambivalence becomes intelligible only in the context of his industrial strategy. Nehru and his planners went for "major irrigation" (large dams and canals) but not for chemical fertilizers. Both required heavy outlays of investment, which were made for dams but not for chemical fertilizers. The reason was that dams were also important to the industrial strategy, since they could create hydroelectric power, which, along with thermal power, was the main source of electricity in India.[39] Power was one of the pillars of Nehru's strategy. Expensive river-valley projects – the "temples of modern age" – were commissioned. Fertilizers, however, consumed both capital and foreign exchange and had little use beyond agriculture. They were unacceptable.

Thus, while American collaboration in science went forward, the concern of the U.S. Agency of International Development about the very low fertilizer usage in India went unheeded.[40] So did the suggestion often made in domestic circles that fertilizer use be stepped up, larger quantities imported, and investments made in domestic capacity. Nehru wrote to the state chief ministers:

We know it for a fact that some other countries have rapidly increased their food production in the last few years without any tremendous use of fertilizers. How has China done it? Chinese resources in this respect are not bigger than ours. China is at the same time laying far greater stress on industrial development and heavy industry than we are. Yet, they are succeeding in increasing their agricultural production at a faster pace than we are. Surely, it should not be beyond our powers to do something that China can do.[41]

To sum up, a general commitment to science and technology notwithstanding, Nehru's concept of science and technology for agriculture was subject to his industrialization strategy. Capital intensity in agricultural technology was acceptable only if it served industrial purposes as well. A more rational organization of the agrarian structure coupled with affordable science, Nehru thought, was sufficient for agricultural transformation.

---

39 By 1954, hydroelectric power accounted for about one-third of the energy produced in India, with the remaining two-thirds coming from thermal stations. Figures taken from P. C. Mahalanobis, *The Approach of Operational Research to Planning in India*, p. 13.
40 Arthur Goldsmith, 1988, "Policy Dialogue, Conditionality and Agricultural Development: Implications of India's Green Revolution," *Journal of Developing Areas*, vol. 22, no. 2, January.
41 *Fortnightly Letters to Chief Ministers*, vol. 4, August 12, 1956, p. 394.

2.5 FAILURE OF THE INSTITUTIONAL STRATEGY

By the early sixties, India's agricultural strategy was in disarray. After the first round of land reforms, which essentially removed the revenue-collecting land-lords (zamindars), no further progress could be made on ceiling or tenurial reforms. Cooperatives could not expand on the scale envisaged by Nehru. Instead of the poor capturing local governments by virtue of their numbers, panchayats became yet another source through which the local "notables" exercised power. This was precisely the class that, according to the institutional model, was to be dislodged from power.

Moreover, and this is critical, India's food production remained more or less stagnant in 1960–1 and 1961–2, and then declined in the next two years (Figure 2.1). In 1956–7, the planners had expected an increase of about 30 percent in food production over the Second Plan period. An increase of this magnitude was considered necessary for the country's food needs. By that yardstick, output should have been about 90 million tons by 1961–2. At 82 million tons, the food output, however, was far behind, and it stagnated there for the next two years. Worse still, the output increase over the entire period since 1949–50 was not primarily due to *yield* increases but to *acreage* expansion, as more land came under cultivation.[42]

In a country of low tolerance for inflation, wholesale price increases of over 6 percent annually, led by a food-price rise, also concerned planners. Increases in food imports from the United States were unable to moderate the uptrend in food prices. Of particular concern was the increase of more than 9 percent in food prices within six months in 1962. In addition, there was pressure on the balance of payments and resources to finance the Third Plan were not coming through. A final coup de grace was delivered by China's attack on India in 1962. Nehru was especially fond of quoting Chinese successes of the mid-1950s as a model of labor-intensive agriculture. India's humiliating defeat in the war with China embarrassed Nehru on several fronts, including that of agriculture.[43]

Nehru's speeches about his agricultural strategy in the last year of his life, 1963–4, are marked by irritation, helplessness, and a sense of failure. Showing signs of cognitive dissonance, he sometimes blamed his strategy and, at other times, the "unchanging Indian peasant."

"I am . . . naturally disappointed," he told Parliament, "at many things, more especially our performance in agriculture. . . . You may of course apportion blame between the Planning Commission, the Government of India, myself and

---

42 Dharm Narain, 1977, "Growth of Productivity in Indian Agriculture," *Indian Journal of Agricultural Economics*, January–March.
43 Nehru had spent such a large proportion of public resources on development that Indian defense was ill-prepared. Now, among other things, additional resources for defense had to be found.

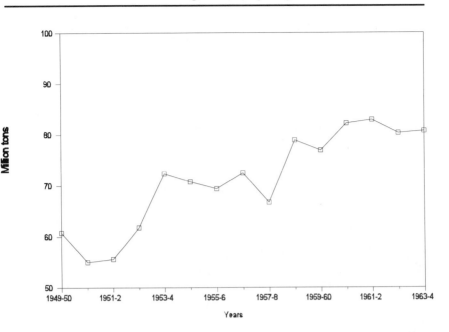

Figure 2.1. India's foodgrain output, 1949–50 to 1963–4. *Source:* Government of India, 1990, *Agricultural Statistics at a Glance,* Delhi: Directorate of Economics and Statistics, Ministry of Agriculture, p. 6.

the State Governments. It is not because of the blame that I am saying this, but ultimately the solution depends upon the farmer, the actual cultivator."[44] He had earlier explained what he meant: "the basic problem facing India is that of the peasant. How do we change his mental outlook, . . . and get him out of the rut in which he has been living since past ages?"[45] A little later, however, Nehru castigated the government strategy, not the peasant: "Though we all know that agriculture is essential and basic, it has been rather neglected. I say neglected in the sense that people hope that crops will grow by themselves and not by much effort on our part."[46] At various places and times, he admitted that all the elements of the strategy – land reforms, cooperatives, panchayats – had failed.

Why did the institutional strategy fail? The weather, of course, did not help in some years, but two structural causes were central: factional struggle at the top

44 Debate in the Lower House, December 11, 1963, in *Nehru's Speeches*, vol. 5, p. 123.
45 Speech on the No-Confidence Motion against the Government, Lower House, August 22, 1963, in ibid., p. 83.
46 Speech in New Delhi at the Conference of Ministers of Irrigation and Power, January 3, 1964, in *Nehru's Speeches*, vol. 5, p. 138.

levels of the Congress party; and the contradiction between the policy logic pushed from above and the quotidian reality at the grass roots.

2.5.1 Factional struggle over agriculture in the Congress party

As already indicated, the Congress party was an umbrella party. Its right-of-center faction, led by the "state bosses," was opposed to Nehru's center-left leanings and plans. Nehru had to accommodate the state bosses because they were in control of the party organization. The state bosses, in turn, could not displace Nehru because he was the ultimate election winner. Unlike Nehru, the state bosses, as the term implied, had regional, not national, stature.

Unable to displace Nehru, the state bosses went for the second-best strategy. They would try first to get Nehru or the Planning Commission to water down their policy proposals, by throwing their weight in debates within the Congress party.[47] If that did not happen (and even if proposals were watered down), they would subsequently dilute or subvert the implementation of unwelcome proposals by using their alliances at the state level. In the process, Nehru would essentially win the battle for policy formulation; he would, however, lose the battle for policy implementation.

Throughout his tenure as Prime Minister, Nehru's Food ministers continued to disagree with him: K. M. Munshi dissented in 1952, A. R. Kidwai and A. P. Jain after him; and S. K. Patil, quite vociferously, after 1959. Patil's view was unambiguous: "Whether it was Russia, America or India, experience has shown that any increases in agricultural production could be brought about only through incentives to the individual."[48] Some of these ministers resigned over differences on agricultural policy. Despite disagreements and resignations, the Food ministers were unable to subdue the combined power of Nehru, left of center, and the Planning Commission.

The state governments introduced another level of complication. In the constitutional distribution of power, unlike industry, agriculture was a state subject. The state governments were critical to the implementation of agricultural policies adopted by the party at its highest level. The struggles over land reforms that emerged between the left of center and the right of center in the various state legislatures are by now well documented.[49]

Political analysts have remarked that for land reforms to succeed without a revolutionary transformation of society it is necessary that "concentrated power" from above be applied. Nehru's official biographer, S. Gopal, made a similar observation when he attributed Nehru's failures in agriculture to "nobility with-

---

47 For details, see Frankel, *India's Political Economy*, chaps. 4 and 5.
48 *The Hindustan Times*, January 9, 1964.
49 For Bihar, see F. Thomassan Januzzi, 1974, *Agrarian Crisis in India: The Case of Bihar*, Austin: University of Texas Press; for Kerala, see Herring, *Land to the Tiller*.

out force, statesmanship without strength," arguing that "it would have been far better" if Nehru, had pushed ahead with "drastic measures."[50] In a democratic system, it is unlikely that such "drastic measures" could have been taken. An ideological conversion of the opposing faction through argumentation, or a center-left control of the party organization, were Nehru's best options. In the absence of both, power that came from above turned out to be fractured and weak, not concentrated.

2.5.2 The policy logic above and the quotidian logic below

The world from below is also worth considering. What were the power relationships at the local level, and how were they supposed to change in the institutional model?

The tenant and the poor peasant were dependent on the landlord not only for cultivation contracts (tenancy, given a large pool of potential tenants, could always be rotated), but also for consumption loans (given the lack of rural credit markets, the landlord was the main source of credit). The landlord, in addition, was the peasant's link to the world outside – to the town and the bureaucracy. Finally, landlords came from higher castes in India's hierarchical social structure, whereas the peasants were mostly from lower castes.

The lord–peasant link was both "moral" and "rational." It was moral because this nexus did form a patron–client regime marked by reciprocal norms of conduct, as social anthropologists and political sociologists have often pointed out. The institutional model assumed that, encouraged by the government, the tenant would revolt and report to the government the "truth" about how long he had been a tenant and what rents he had paid. A revolt against the normatively laden patron–client linkage was difficult. Moreover, if the peasant did revolt, local power was on the landlord's side. The state in Delhi might not have been a preserve of landlord power, but the state machinery as it existed at the local level had few mediations between the landlord and the state. The local police and village-level bureaucracy often came from the high castes, shared the biases of a hierarchical social structure, and tilted in favor of the high castes and against the lowly peasants. Thus, there was considerable "rationality in tenant quiescence."[51]

For land reforms to succeed in such an agrarian structure, there had to be significant political mobilization by the ruling party in favor of the intended beneficiaries of the strategy at the local level, so that power countervailing that of the landlord could be made available and the tenant could feel secure in the event of a showdown. Both concentrated pressure from above (policy) and pressure

---

50 In Gopal, *Nehru*, vol. 3, pp. 301 and 295.
51 Ronald Herring, 1981, "Embedded Production Relations and Rationality of Tenant Quiescence in Tenure Reform," *Journal Of Peasant Studies*, January.

from below (mobilization) were required. The institutional model, in other words, lacked political microfoundations.[52]

Nehru was aware of the necessity of exerting pressure from below. Local governments (panchayats), the third pillar of his model, were supposed to do this. Instead, local governments were captured by the local "notables." How this happened is explained by the imperatives of "party building in a new nation."[53] The lower wings of the Congress party – the district and *taluka* (subdistrict) levels – came under the control of landlords and substantial landowners. These groups saw the advantages of entering the party in power. Nehru could not displace them, for, being educated, wealthy, and from higher castes, they were the local "influentials." A note written in 1953 by Dr. Sampurnanand, Chief Minister of the State of Uttar Pradesh, to his top state party colleagues explained:

It comes to this, that we have antagonized every class which has so far possessed education, wealth, social status and consequently, influence. . . .

The classes to which I have referred above belong, in general, to the Brahmin, Rajput, Bhumihar, Kayastha and Vaishya communities, namely the . . . "higher castes." The measures which we have adopted and apparently intend soon to adopt, have had the definite tendency of affecting adversely the interests of the higher castes who, it must be remembered have, in general, been the people from whom the Congress has derived the greatest measure of support in the past. They have been culturally affiliated to our leadership and we have come to office literally on their shoulders.[54]

Contrariwise, due to their educational, social, and economic backwardness, the intended beneficiaries of the institutional strategy had few leaders from their own castes and communities. If the Congress party were to reach far and wide, the local leaders and locally powerful groups had to be used, at least in the short run. However, if Nehru's economic model were to succeed, it was precisely these groups which had to be defeated. After its emasculation from above, this contra-

---

52 After Nehru's death, land reforms were successfully implemented in the South Indian state of Kerala in a democratic framework, not by the Congress but by an elected communist government. With the exception of West Bengal in the 1970s and 1980s, Kerala's was the only case of successful land reforms in India. A micromanipulation aided the tenants in Kerala. Instead of the law requiring the tenant to prove in court that the land he tilled had been under his cultivation for a given number of years, which would qualify him for entitlement, the landlord was required to prove that he had actually been cultivating, failing which the tenant would automatically get the benefits of legislation. This struck directly at the constraints of the peasant's microsetting. See Herring, *Land to the Tiller*, chaps. 2 and 5.

53 Myron Weiner, 1968, *Party Building in a New Nation: The Congress Party of India*, Chicago: University of Chicago Press.

54 Confidential note, cited by Paul Brass, 1984, "Division in the Congress and the Rise of Agrarian Interests and Issues in Uttar Pradesh Politics," in John R. Wood, ed., *State Politics in Contemporary India*, Boulder, CO: Westview Press. Brass has been able to get access to the personal files of Charan Singh, whose political career, from the early fifties to the early seventies, included cabinet posts and chief ministership in the state government of Uttar Pradesh. Singh's personal records from the 1950s have shed clearer light on the gap between the reality in the states and Nehru's views.

diction between Nehru's political and economic imperatives destroyed whatever local force the institutional agrarian strategy might have had.

Could the strategy have succeeded had it been implemented? This counterfactual question cannot be answered conclusively – it is after all counterfactual. Chinese successes of the mid-1950s suggest a positive answer, but Chinese reverses in the early and late sixties also suggest that, beyond the first phase of increases in productivity, an institutional strategy quickly reaches a plateau. There are limits to how much productivity can be increased by labor intensity alone. Even *after* organizational restructuring, investments in technological upgrading, public expenditures for the dissemination of new technology, and credit subsidies facilitating the adoption of new technology are typically required.[55] If both organizational restructuring and technological upgrading can be done simultaneously, we achieve the ideal outcome: productivity goes up while equity objectives are also satisfied. Constraints on resources, however, do not easily allow the pursuit of both policy tracks, making a choice necessary. Whatever the fate of Nehru's strategy might have been in the event of its implementation, its political difficulties ultimately turned out to be formidable. The structure finally prevailed over the efforts to change the structure. And ideas collapsed on the bedrock of interests.

---

55 For an early critique on these lines, see John P. Lewis, 1962, *Quiet Crisis in India*, Washington, D.C.: Brookings Institution, chap. 6, esp. pp. 146–66.

3

Policy change in the mid-1960s

Between 1964 and 1967, India's political system suffered two exogenous shocks. Nehru died in May 1964. And two successive droughts brought food production down to the level of 1956–7, creating near-famine conditions and leading to doomsday predictions about India's economic future. After a mere eighteen months in power, Nehru's successor, Lal Bahadur Shastri, also died, and a weak and uncertain Mrs. Gandhi was elected to India's highest office.

Politically, this period in India has been described as an era of the "passing of the tall men":[1] there were no charismatic leaders from the national movement left and none of equal stature had emerged to replace them. Economically, according to many in the West, it was the beginning of India's long famine, something akin to what one normally hears about sub-Saharan Africa these days. Using an analogy from the battlefield, a "popular" book of the mid-1960s argued that those wounded in the battle were of three types: the slightly wounded, who could be cured with small degrees of medical attention; the more seriously wounded who required surgery but could be saved; and those so gravely wounded that they were generally left to die, for it was pointless to attend to them.[2] India belonged to the third category: "no matter how one may adjust present statistics . . . it will be beyond the resources of the United States to keep famine out of India during the 1970s."[3]

Between 1967–8 and 1970–1, however, India's food output continued to rise. In 1965–6 and 1966–7, its output had been 72.3 and 74.2 million tons, respectively. In 1967–8, food production reached 95 million tons; and by 1970–1, it was 108.4 million tons, one and a half times higher than the output achieved in 1965–6. Almost wholly dependent upon 10 million tons of American wheat supplied under Public Law 480 in 1965–6, India's public foodgrain reserves

1 Rajni Kothari, in *Politics in India*, 1970, Boston: Little, Brown, and Delhi: Allied.
2 William and Paul Paddock, 1967, *Famine 1975! America's Decision: Who Will Survive?* Boston: Little, Brown.
3 Ibid., p. 217.

had 8.1 million tons of domestically procured supplies in 1971. In the same year, India unilaterally terminated the imports of American wheat. Still later, by 1986–7, public stocks of foodgrain had soared to 30 million tons. Largely as a result of these stocks, the drought of 1987–8, one of the worst in the century, did *not* lead to a famine.

The performance of the food economy is not without blemish. India's distributional record is unremarkable. Ecological problems have emerged in the green revolution areas. Still, food production over the last three decades and India's ability to feed itself are economic achievements that few had thought possible in the mid-1960s. Of particular note has been the source of output increase. Although, at 2.9 percent per annum, the trend growth rate of foodgrain production between the mid-1960s and 1991–2 has been only slightly higher than between independence and the mid-1960s, *yield increases* have been the primary source of output increase after the mid-1960s, as opposed to *acreage expansion*, which largely accounted for production gains before that. With the expansion of arable land virtually exhausted by the mid-1960s, production, in the absence of yield increases, would have remained stagnant, as indeed it had between 1960/1– 1966/7. Since population was growing at 2.3 percent per annum, stagnation in food production would clearly have caused enormous difficulties for the Indian economy and polity.

What accounts for India's agricultural turnaround? A decisive shift in public policy – a change in the form of state intervention in the agricultural economy – is by now widely accepted as the main reason. Over a period of three years between 1964 and 1967, India's agricultural strategy was fundamentally changed from one that was based on an institutional reorganization of agriculture to one that accepted the existing institutional structure as given but sought to increase production through price incentives and technical change.

This chapter analyzes the political economy of policy change in the mid-sixties. The central question addressed is: what forces led to the change in state behavior? The argument will be that the primary sources of policy change lay within the state. Organized interest groups or social classes did not push the government toward a price- and technology-oriented strategy. *Price-based interest groups appeared on the political scene much after the policy change.* However, to say that the social groups played no role at all would also be incorrect. The state governments in India were heavily influenced by the landed upper classes, and these classes, by the mid-1960s, had more or less frustrated the efforts of the central government to transform rural India via land reforms and cooperatives. A strategy that could secure the cooperation of state governments as well as increase food production in the country was needed. These classes, however, had no proposals about what the new strategy should be.

The international actors – the World Bank, the U.S. government, and some private U.S. foundations – were also involved in the process of change. They were not responsible for the *conception* of the new alternative; but without their financial support, *implementation* of the new agricultural policy would have been more difficult than it actually turned out to be. The external actors leaned against an open door; they did not force the door open.

The argument is developed as follows. Since the policy originated in the state, I first examine struggles within the state institutions and ask: who made policy, with what institutions, allies, ideas, and motivations? Then, I take the next step and ask: What forces outside the state were involved with, or affected by, the decisions of the state? Were those affected also the initiators of those decisions? Did these forces emerge from within India or from the international system? Both documentary evidence and extensive interviews with decision makers are used as building blocks for the argument.

3.1 THE POLITICAL CONTEXT

In the previous chapter, the origins and evolution of India's institutional strategy were analyzed in terms of two types of "policy actors": political leaders, particularly those of the ruling party; and bureaucrats, particularly those in the Planning Commission. The political leadership provided the *design*; the planners fashioned the *details* of the design. Political leaders operated with two sets of considerations: ideologies and interests. Decision makers in the economic bureaucracy operated with the economic theories of the time and, one should also suppose, with a regard for what could preserve or expand their newly created power under Nehru. The dominant economic theory of development in the 1950s – with its emphasis on planning, the industrial "big push" driven by public investment in capital goods, and institutional change in agriculture – meshed well with a Fabian socialist worldview of the political leadership, just as the dominant Keynesian economic theory of the 1950s mingled neatly with a social democratic political design in the West.

It was also shown that factional conflict within the ruling party was, inter alia, over economic designs for the country. Nehru's institutional view, represented in the Planning Commission, was opposed by his adversaries in the ruling Congress party. A side-effect of this struggle was that many of Nehru's opponents were resentful of the power over economic policy given to the Planning Commission. The Commission was presided over by the Prime Minister himself, and its members, not elected by the people but nominated by the leader, were given ministerial and quasi-ministerial ranks.

There were, thus, two kinds of conflicts over economic policy: inside the state institutions, particularly between the Planning Commission and the Food and Agriculture Ministry; and within the ruling party, especially between the left of center, which dominated policy making in New Delhi, and the right of center, which had substantial control over the party organization at the state and lower levels.

After Nehru's death, the institutions and men that made economic policy, and the ideology that underlay their functioning, changed significantly. It was a brief moment of change, as Shastri, Nehru's successor in June 1964, himself did not live beyond January 1966. In a matter of eighteen months, however, decisive shifts in India's economic policy took place. A technocratic view came to replace the earlier, institutional view in agricultural policy.

Shastri's political background had a significant bearing on the struggle over agricultural policy. He was chosen because "minimax," as it were, was the dominant strategy of the main actors: compared to Nehru, he was not "tall," but he was well enough known in the party to be presented as a head of the government and weak enough to be considered malleable by the organizational stalwarts. Moreover, Shastri was uncontroversial enough to be acceptable to both the center right and the center left. The potential candidate from the right of center, Morarji Desai (who eventually became Prime Minister in 1977), was unacceptable to the left of center. At the same time, Desai was also considered too independent by other important members of the right-of-center faction.[4]

Once elected, however, this background determined Shastri's political maneuvers. Two characteristics stood out: a relatively small political stature and a tenuous ideological anchorage. The former meant that he had to consolidate his power; the latter ensured that his key bureaucratic appointments were not driven by considerations of ideological conformity. Nehru's top bureaucratic personnel, particularly those he appointed to the Planning Commission, had shared his Fabian socialist worldview – men such as V. T. Krishnamachari, Professor Mahalanobis, Tarlok Singh, and Gulzarilal Nanda.

These two characteristics had a decisive impact on economic policy. Shastri launched a remarkable but quiet assault on the Planning Commission. He redefined procedures and administrative rules hitherto governing the Commission. First, members of the Planning Commission were now to have a fixed term; under Nehru, they enjoyed an indefinite tenure. Second, the office of the Cabinet Secretary – the top bureaucratic office in the country to which secretaries of all the ministries were accountable – was detached from the Planning Commission; under Nehru, the Secretary of the Planning Commission also served as Cabinet Secretary, which gave the Commission a unique position in the bureaucracy. Finally, Shastri created a Prime Minister's Secretariat with its own team of experts on economic policy (as well as other policies). The Prime Minister's Secretariat had two important political effects: on economic policy, it weakened the supremacy of the Planning Commission; and on policy matters in general, it created an alternative source of policy advice, reducing Shastri's dependence on the cabinet where some of the powerful state bosses were present as ministers. The Prime Minister's Secretariat introduced a quasi-presidential feature into a parliamentary form of government. It increased the power of the Prime Minis-

---

4 For details, see Francine Frankel, 1978, *India's Political Economy*, Princeton, NJ: Princeton University Press, pp. 240–50.

ter's office over all other offices in the country. A strong man like Nehru did not need such bureaucratic strengthening; his charisma and political stature ensured that de facto. A weak man like Shastri, however, had to ensure it de jure.

The ideological amorphism of Shastri had significant effects too. As his Principal Secretary, the head of the Prime Minister's Secretariat and, therefore, the top bureaucrat in the country, Shastri appointed L. K. Jha, a senior civil servant and a trained economist, who was more inclined toward the market mechanism than was customary for economic bureaucrats in those days. At the same time, Shastri did not fundamentally alter the composition of the Planning Commission. Ashok Mehta, appointed the head of the Planning Commission under Nehru in 1963 and a respected socialist thinker, continued to hold his position. However, since the authority of the Planning Commission had been greatly reduced, the view prevailing in the Prime Minister's office became more decisive in the conduct of economic policy. The amorphous ideological setting and political flux led to an open-ended policy battle that, in the past, had always been overwhelmed by Nehru's ideological certitude and political stature.

Shastri might not have been a leader with a powerful ideological *vision*, but he did have *instincts* and *predilections*. Compared to Nehru, he had greater political experience of party functioning at the state and local levels. Moreover, in contrast to Nehru's urban, aristocratic and Oxbridge background, Shastri had rural origins and pro-agriculture instincts. His political experience had also made him sensitive to the operational realities of Congress politics, dependent as it was on landlord support at the local levels. The way this background influenced the policy parameters is interesting. Because of his political stature and ideology, Nehru thought he could change India; Shastri, on the other hand, had to work toward his own political consolidation rather than toward changing India by championing deeply held policy designs. However – and this is critical – if the policy struggle was more or less evenly matched, he as Prime Minister could tilt the scales. Shastri's leanings could thus be decisive in situations of stalemate and near-stalemate. As we shall see below, this indeed turned out to be the case.

3.2 CHANGE IN AGRICULTURAL POLICY

If Nehru was the inspiration behind India's institutional strategy, C. Subramaniam, India's Food and Agriculture Minister between 1964 and 1966, was the architect of policy change. In the state politics of Tamil Nadu, Subramaniam had developed a reputation for efficient administration and for emphasizing science and technology in policy. In 1962, Subramaniam was brought to New Delhi by Nehru himself. His technocratic inclinations were used in the Ministry of Steel and Heavy Industries, a policy area where Nehru especially valued technocratically inclined colleagues.

Upon Nehru's death, the first personnel decision made by Shastri was to invite Subramaniam to head the Food and Agriculture Ministry. Once in charge of the

Food Ministry, however, Subramaniam saw the same connections between science and agricultural production as between science and steel production:

If I were to tell one of you who is manufacturing, say, a product out of steel, that I will give you only a limited quantity of steel, you will come back and say that with that quantity of steel, only a specified quantity of output is possible. Those who administer the economic laws of our managed economy will not question your judgment but will cock a snook at the poor agriculturist who asks for more fertilisers. To produce more food with less fertiliser is as impossible a task as to produce more steel with less iron ore or more cloth with less cotton, given the current state of technology. . . . Better seeds for agriculture are as crucial as better machine tools for industry. . . . Better water management is as essential as gasoline for your vehicle but nonetheless it is surprising how many levels of authority we have to convince. This is really a problem of attitudes.

Subramaniam provided a powerful rationale for an alternative policy design. He did not, however, singlehandedly bring about the transformation. His task was facilitated by the new political and ideological constellation: the taming of the Planning Commission and the rise of the Prime Minister's Secretariat; within the Congress party, the rise of the state bosses after Nehru's death; the ideological shift toward a right-of-center view; and, finally, the pro-rural instincts of the Prime Minister. Earlier Food ministers, even when they made arguments more or less similar to Subramaniam's, though never with the same tenacity, were unable to overpower Nehru and the Planning Commission.

3.2.1 Subramaniam's agrarian model

Subramaniam's agrarian model[5] can be divided into three components: the economic, the technological, and the organizational.[6] His economic view was that price incentives would motivate farmers to produce more because it would be profitable to do so; technology was required, as acreage expansion had reached its limits, making production increases dependent on yields per acre; and organizational effort was needed, because in order for the first two components to work,

5 I have abstracted Subramaniam's model from two books and my own interview with him in Madras, December 14, 1984. The two books I have used have more or less similar titles but offer different ways of getting inside the world of policy. The first, *A New Strategy in Agriculture: A Collection of the Speeches by C. Subramaniam* (New Delhi: Indian Council of Agricultural Research, 1972), comprises his speeches *during* his tenure as a Food minister between 1964 and 1966. The other, *The New Strategy in Agriculture* (New Delhi: Vikas, 1979), reproduces the lectures Subramaniam later gave at the Australian National University in 1978. Here, Subramaniam offers important insights into the political battles over policy, whereas the earlier work, as could be expected, was more a statement of intent. Hereafter I shall refer to the first book as *Speeches* and the second as *The New Strategy*.

6 A methodological note is in order here. The quotes I shall use in the main text to make the case that these three components constituted Subramaniam's model are not all taken from 1964–5, i.e., the year the seeds of new policy were planted; I have also used speeches from 1965–7. The quotes are chosen on the basis of how well they express the new approach and how forcefully they contrast with that of Nehru. I would not claim that Subramaniam saw all the elements of the new approach with utmost clarity right from the start: although it did come into being right from his first year, its details were developed over time. I am collapsing three years of time for the sake of logical clarity.

institutions had to be created for the purpose of determining what the level of prices should be and how to implement them. Also required was a research and administrative structure that would generate or adapt yield-increasing technologies and transmit them to farmers.

Price incentives. The first paper Subramaniam prepared for the Cabinet was on price policy:[7] he explained how his understanding evolved:

My move from steel and heavy industries to agriculture was a big change as far as the nature of the work and job was concerned, but perhaps this in itself was an advantage because I was able to look at agriculture with a completely new perspective. For example, in industry, no industrial unit can progress and succeed unless it is a profitable concern. If it is a losing concern, no industry can prosper. I looked at agriculture from a similar point of view and, after study and analysis, came to the conclusion that Indian agriculture was a losing concern for the farmer. He did not receive a return commensurate with his labour, or with the investment he was prepared to make. This was mainly because of the price policy which had been adopted since independence. . . .[8]

Contrast this with Nehru's position. Nehru also considered food prices important, but for reasons of planning and industrial production, not for food production: ". . . next to food production, the question of foodgrains is of vital importance. . . . If the price of foodgrains goes up, then the whole fabric of our planning suffers irretrievably."

Subramaniam was conscious of the need to keep food prices in check, but keeping the consumer prices of food under control, according to him, was not equal to keeping the producer prices down. Nineteen sixty-four was a year of food-price inflation. After conceding that "we are in the midst of a rising spiral in the prices of foodgrains," and after supporting retail price controls, Subramaniam maintained that price controls could only be a short-run response, for "in the long run, increased production is the only answer to scarcity."[9] High food prices could thus be brought down only by long-run increases in food production, for which price incentives to producers were necessary in the first place. A rise in producer prices would increase production, and higher production would eventually bring consumer prices down.

To say that the producer should be given price incentives, however, was not enough. What the incentive levels should be, how they would be implemented, and what impact producer incentives would have on consumer welfare were also important issues. According to Subramaniam, the government should intervene in the foodgrain market to ensure incentive prices for producers, but should do it in a way that *stabilized* prices at reasonable levels. Stabilization was required because sharp price rises (which would take place in the event of harvest failures), only to be followed by sharp price falls (which would happen in the event of good harvests), would not motivate farmers to invest in farming and produce

7 *The New Strategy*, p. 5.

8 Ibid., p. 4.

9 "A National Distribution-cum-Price Policy," speech at the State Chief Ministers' Conference, June 24, 1964, New Delhi, *Speeches*, p. 187.

more. A stable price that lay somewhere between an otherwise natural peak and trough was the solution:

An affluent country can afford to keep its consumer prices of foodstuffs relatively high; the average level of incomes is high and individuals spend relatively smaller parts of their incomes on food. But in a poor economy like ours, the consumers spend a substantial part of their incomes on food, and high food prices create complications in the economic situation. At the same time, the farmer lives on the very margin of subsistence and he has also to pay high prices for most of his inputs. We have, therefore, to reconcile the dilemma of compensating the farmer adequately and maintaining a reasonable price level for the consumer. . . .[10]

For this formula to work, two institutions were also needed: one that calculated what prices were reasonable to producers, and another that bought up surpluses from producers at those prices. The Agricultural Prices Commission (APC) and the Food Corporation of India (FCI), were thus born as two institutional hubs of the price strategy, the former to make price recommendations and the latter to buy and sell grains at the recommended price.[11]

Technology policy. Science and technology were the second critical component of the new strategy. Subramaniam launched a critique of the traditional agricultural practices prevalent in India:

Most of the practices as well as tools employed in agriculture have their genesis in the inventive genius of our ancestors dating back to the *Vedic* age. Our main farm implements, viz. the country plough, the simple hand-hoe and sickle, were developed at that time and it is a measure of our stagnation that they still dominate the rural scene. . . . if we wish to obtain yields from our crop plants of an order which could not be conceived earlier, we have to radically alter the whole set of agricultural practices. . . . There is nothing derogatory to the prestige of our ancestors or of our present-day farmers if we emphasize the need to discard outdated ideas and outmoded tools in agriculture.[12]

New, biologically developed seeds – "the miracle seeds" – had changed the nature of agriculture in the mid-twentieth century:

The crux of the new approach is the introduction of intensive cultivation using new high-yielding varieties of seeds backed by more and better plant nutrients – effective plant protection and adequate water supply. Some experts, not geneticists [but other scientists] have expressed doubts as to the feasibility of the high yields which have been obtained by the new varieties. It is strange that these experts should admit that while such high yields [are] possible in other countries they are not possible in ours. . . . What other countries can do we can also do.[13]

---

10 "Increasing Food Production," inaugural address delivered at the Seminar on Increasing Food Production in Coimbatore, Tamilnadu, November 28, 1964, in *Speeches*, p. 24.

11 Speech in Coimbatore, November 28, 1964, in *Speeches*, p. 24.

12 Convocation address delivered at the Indian Agricultural Research Institute, New Delhi, December 28, 1965, in *Speeches*, p. 141. Subramaniam had expressed similar ideas in one of his first speeches after taking over as the Food minister; see *Speeches*, p. 9.

13 Speech in Kanpur, February 2, 1966, in *Speeches*, p. 40. An earlier statement about the centrality of seeds is available in Subramaniam's speech, delivered on January 1, 1965, to the National Development Council. See *Speeches*, p. 31.

Notice the package introduced; High Yielding Variety (HYV) seeds, plant nutrients (chemical fertilizers), plant protection (pesticides), and controlled water (irrigation). The most controversial element in this package were chemical fertilizers, due to their foreign-exchange implications. That is why Nehru had found chemical fertilizers unacceptable. If anything, the foreign-exchange situation was even tighter in the mid-sixties, the per-acre fertilizer requirement of the new seeds higher, and India's domestic production of fertilizers considerably short of the quantities required. Nevertheless, convinced that without fertilizers adequate increases in production were not possible, Subramaniam called them indispensable:

> The king-pin of agricultural development in the modern age has been adequate fertilization of the soil. I am aware that there are two schools of thought on this: some people feel that we should resort increasingly to the use of organic manure. I do not disagree that whatever the inputs of fertilizers, we have to use our available organic manure also in the most efficient way possible. It is, however, true that the history of other countries is standing evidence of the fact that revolutionary breakthroughs in agricultural productivity have come about mainly by . . . increased use of fertilizers. It is important to note this factor because, taking the country as a whole, India uses today roughly 2 to 3 tons of fertilizers . . . per thousand hectares of arable land. This compares with the world average of 7.86 tons, Japan's 124 and our neighbour Ceylon's 6.25. . . . Our position still remains low down in the scale.[14]

Just as implementing the new price policy required the APC and the FCI, so the science and technology policy also had its institutional requirements. Subramaniam placed the highest emphasis on research and extension. Whereas his first cabinet paper was on price policy, his second[15] was on the importance of strengthening scientific research institutions and of giving "financial inducements" to agricultural scientists "so that proper men of quality [are] attracted to these professions."[16] In the event, research institutions were reorganized, a new agricultural research service was established,[17] collaboration with international agricultural research institutes was strengthened,[18] and the salaries of agricultural scientists were increased.[19] Finally, to make sure that the results of new research reached farmers, the extension service was restructured. Under Nehru, the extension agent, the so-called Village Level Worker, was expected to play multiple roles: inform farmers about education opportunities and teach them health care, plant care, and sanitation, as well as spread new scientific research. Subramaniam deemphasized the "generalist" role of extension agents, emphasized their technical training in agricultural universities, and increased their numbers so that villages could be adequately covered.[20]

14 Speech in Coimbatore, November 28, 1964, in *Speeches*, p. 21.
15 *The New Strategy*, p. 12.
16 "A New Deal For Agricultural Scientists," speech, July 17, 1964, *Speeches*, p. 11.
17 For details, see "Need for a Dynamic Research Programme," in *Speeches* (pp. 63–71) and "The Reorganization of Agricultural Research" in *Speeches* (pp. 76–84).
18 See, e.g., "International Cooperation in Rice Research," in *Speeches*, pp. 264–71.
19 See "A New Deal for Agricultural Scientists."
20 *The New Strategy*, pp. 40–41.

In short, whereas Nehru's agrarian model was institutional in that agricultural productivity in his model was a function of nothing less than a political and social restructuring of India's rural life, Subramaniam's model was essentially technocratic (or "ecotechnocratic," if technocratic is held to cover only the technological aspects). Subramaniam was not opposed to institutional change in principle, but he was convinced that the institutional strategy had little chance of success. On land reforms, he argued: "Unfortunately one could not wait until the land reform legislation was implemented effectively. We had been trying for this over the last ten years but owing to political and other factors it had not proved possible to implement it properly. . . ."[21] On cooperatives, the second key component of Nehru's strategy, his argument was: "Where cooperation is not in a position to deliver the goods, shall we wait indefinitely for the cooperatives to become effective instruments?"[22] Subramaniam believed that in the context of the mid-1960s, the institutional approach amounted to "mere slogan shouting," stressing that a "pragmatic approach" was needed. The choices were clear: "Would you like to have . . . high production and attain self-sufficiency within the country . . . or would you prefer to continue dependence upon food imports indefinitely?"[23] The institutional approach would lead to the latter; his own approach would usher in food self-sufficiency.

The exponents of the institutional approach, however, did not relent. Fierce political battles within the state institutions ensued. Those supporting Subramaniam thought he was correcting an anti-agriculture bias in India's development policy. His political opponents believed that their ideological designs were superior – designs that were now being devalued. In the end, the structure of post-Nehru power politics, a skillful strategy by Subramaniam, and the serendipity of weather produced a victory for the technocratic policy design. By the late sixties, the new agricultural strategy had irreversibly come to stay. The intervening struggles, however, were fought with remarkable seriousness; the main contours are reviewed below.

3.3 STRUGGLES WITHIN THE STATE INSTITUTIONS

The most intense policy struggle took place between the Food and Agriculture Ministry on the one hand and the Finance Ministry and the Planning Commission on the other. Also involved were the Prime Minister's Secretariat and the Congress party. This struggle can not be understood in purely political terms. Part of the battle was driven by the "technical" parameters within which these ministries or bureaucracies customarily operate. Food prices and investments in agricultural technologies intersect with the respective concerns of these bureaucracies in

21 In ibid., p. 28.
22 Subramaniam's speech to the Agricultural Committee of the National Development Council, printed in full in Appendix 1 of the Ministry of Food and Agriculture, *Agricultural Development: Problems and Perspective*, New Delhi: Government of India, 1965.
23 *The New Strategy*, p. 28.

significant ways. I outline below the logical structure of these competing concerns. Having done so, I shall move on to an empirical account of these struggles and of how they were resolved.

3.3.1 The logic of interbureaucratic politics

To the Finance Ministry, the general price level in the economy and macro-balances (budget, trade, foreign exchange) are matters of great concern.[24] Food prices have economywide implications. First, they can be highly inflationary for the economy, since they weigh heavily in the various price indices. Second, they affect budget balances and the level of deficit financing, for if raising producer prices for food cannot be passed on entirely to consumers, a food subsidy is inevitable. Moreover, to induce farmers to adopt new technology, if it is necessary to subsidize fertilizer use or capital investments on the farm, then another level of subsidy is created. Third, if the agricultural strategy is heavily fertilizer-based, then fertilizer imports affect the trade balance and involve foreign-exchange outlays. These expenditures can presumably be met if revenues can be raised.[25] If resources cannot be adequately raised but new programs must be run, deficit financing becomes necessary, which may, in turn, cause inflation. One can make the connections even more complex, but let us stick with our simple model. The simplest way of saying all this is that the Finance Ministry is the ultimate housekeeper: it has to pay the government bills.

Food prices are of concern to the planners, too.[26] First, due to their effect on the price level in the economy, they determine the *real* value of the planned investments even when nominal magnitudes stay the same. Second, by affecting

24 Based on personal interviews with the various Finance Ministers, Finance Secretaries, and Chief Economic Advisers (CEAs) since 1965. Those interviewed include L. K. Jha (Finance Secretary in the fifties; interview in Delhi, December 23, 1986); Ashok Mitra (CEA, mid-sixties, also later Chairman of the Agricultural Prices Commission; interview in Calcutta, December 25, 1984); Manmohan Singh (CEA, early seventies; later Governor of the Reserve Bank of India and Deputy Chairman of the Planning Commission; currently Finance Minister, interview in Bombay, December 7, 1984); Mr. V. B. Eswaran (Expenditures Secretary, early eighties; interview in Delhi, November 22, 1984); and Dr. Bimal Jalan (CEA, early eighties; interview in Delhi, December 22, 1984). Also interviewed were three Finance Ministers: Pranab Mukherjea (1980–4; interview in Delhi, January 21, 1987); H. M. Patel (1977–9; interview in Delhi, December 2, 1986); and Madhu Dandavate (1989–90; interview in Delhi, January 7, 1990).

25 By imposing an income tax or user levies on those benefiting from the state-subsidized new technology, but in order for that to happen, the subsidy must be provided to begin with; by imposing higher income taxes in urban sectors or increasing indirect taxes (excise, sales, customs), which may or may not be difficult; and by increasing exports, which may or may not be difficult.

26 Interviews with deputy chairmen and members of the Planning Commission at various points: Dr. D. T. Lakdawala (Deputy Chairman, 1977–9, interview in Ahmedabad, December 9, 1984); Professor Raj Krishna (Member, 1977–9; interview in Delhi, January 23, 1985); Professor Hanumantha Rao (Member; interview in Delhi, November 23, 1984), Professor Sukhamoy Chakravarty (Member, early seventies; interview, August 17, 1984).

the real incomes of the population, food prices determine the effective demand in the economy which, in turn, directly feeds back into the growth rates of various consumer industries. Third, food prices affect wages, hence profitability in industry. Finally, in the early stages of development, resource transfers from agriculture are expected to finance industrialization, but raising food prices and financing new technology in agriculture may entail an investment shift away from industry and toward agriculture, including the possibility that a surplus from other sectors might have to be raised to finance agricultural development.[27]

The Food and Agriculture Ministry has its considerations.[28] If prices and technology are considered critical for increases in food production, then clearly an intersectoral view of food prices, typical of Finance and Planning ministries, can not be the perspective of the Food and Agriculture Ministry. It is typically an intrasectoral and microview that links increases in producer prices with increases in food production. Besides, if technological investments are also required in agriculture, then whether these entail a shift away from industry is not the primary concern of the Food and Agriculture Ministry: its primary task is to increase food production. An interbureaucratic struggle is built into the very logic of the price and technology strategy. In terms of economic theory, this is essentially a clash between the micro- and macroviews of agriculture, with the latter represented in the Finance and Planning ministries.

Which of these views would prevail cannot simply be a "technical" matter. If the *political* heads of these bureaucracies – that is, the respective ministers – share a particular ideological worldview (let us say, the institutional view of agriculture), some moderation of tensions will automatically take place. If that is not the case, the responsibility of resolving these differences, in a parliamentary system of government, rests with the Prime Minister.

Consider the various bases upon which a Prime Minister could formulate his position: his own worldview, political calculations, financial implications, or a mixture of all these. Take the ideological side first. If the Prime Minister is inclined toward an institutional position, the Food and Agriculture Ministry will have to accommodate Planning and Finance. If he is convinced of a price and technology vision, the Planning and Finance ministries will have to accommodate Food and Agriculture.

---

27 Raj Krishna and G. S. Raychowdhry claim that the urban sector has been making a net contribution to capital formation in Indian agriculture. See their "Trends in Rural Savings and Capital Formation in India, 1950–51 to 1973–74," *Economic Development and Cultural Change*, vol. 30, no. 2 (January 1982).

28 Interviews with Mr. C. Subramaniam; Rao Birendra Singh, Food and Agriculture Minister, 1980–6, Delhi, September 18, 1986; C. Sivaraman, Agriculture Secretary, 1965–7, Madras, December 13, 1984; G. V. K. Rao, Agriculture Secretary, 1977–9, Delhi, November 6, 1984; S. P. Mukherjea, Agriculture Secretary, 1982–4, Delhi, December 20, 1984; B. C. Gangopadhyay, Food Secretary, early to mid-eighties, Delhi, December 21, 1984.

The Prime Minister may also have some power considerations in mind. He may go with a minister who is more powerful regardless of where his sympathies lie; he may think of how his party would react to the decision, or how the larger society would react. The decision may also depend on certain political exigencies – for example, how close the elections are and whether the decision would have any electoral impact. A final set of considerations may be the financial implications of the decision. Is a price and technology strategy, even if desirable, affordable? If expensive but desirable, what readjustments in the current financial priorities of the government could possibly be made?

What this array of choices indicates is how crucial the role of the leadership can be to policy changes. There is no special reason for the Prime Minister to accept what is presented as a "technical" economic matter by Finance or Planning. He has his own worldview. He has to contend with the importance of factions if they exist in the party. He also has to think of larger social considerations. Moreover, leaving aside these political considerations and speaking purely technically, there are two versions of rationality competing here: the macrorationality of Finance and Planning and the microrationality of Food and Agriculture. An agricultural strategy considered ill-suited and expensive, even dangerous, for the rest of the economy by Finance and Planning might be considered necessary by Food and Agriculture. Even technical correctness thus has no uniquely acceptable definition.

How was the abstract logic of interbureaucratic politics played out in India? How were the clashes resolved? With what consequences?

3.3.2 Toward an empirical account

The actual process of agricultural policy change can be divided into three parts: (1) the formulation of strategy (1964–5); (2) the battle for resources and political support required to implement the strategy (1965–6); and (3) the implementation (1966–7). Competing technical issues outlined above kept surfacing, their intensity depending upon the ideological vision of the protagonists and their political stature.

Conception: Putting ideas and institutions in place. The Finance minister was the first to raise objections when Subramaniam introduced his ideas on price policy: "there was a heated debate in the cabinet . . . with particular opposition from Finance Minister, T. T. Krishnamachari. He argued the other side; how could we afford to increase food prices, particularly for industrial labour and for the urban population? It would lead to much discontent. . . ."[29]

Shastri's pro-agriculture instincts helped Subramaniam. One of Shastri's first policy problems – barely a week after taking over as Prime Minister – was to make a decision on the perspective presented by the Planning Commission for

29 *The New Strategy*, p. 5.

the Fourth Plan, originally scheduled for 1966–71. Shastri instructed the Planning Commission to give the highest priority to agriculture, to produce a "common man's plan," and, in the rural sector, to concentrate on minor irrigation, fertilizers, and small-scale industry.[30]

Aware of the opening provided by the Prime Minister but conscious at the same time of the opposition of the Finance Ministry, Subramaniam's strategy was to generate larger support for his ideas. Shortly after the cabinet meeting in which the Food and Finance ministers clashed, Subramaniam presented his price-oriented analysis to the state chief ministers.[31] Then he sought the support of experts, particularly those holding powerful positions in the economic bureaucracy. He also wanted to get a professional view on what prices to recommend in the current agricultural year (1964–5). In a dexterous move, he asked the Prime Minister to appoint a committee with his own Principal Secretary, L. K Jha, as chairman. The committee would look into foodgrain producer prices for 1964–5 as well as formulate the terms of reference for an agency that would investigate prices on a continual basis. The purpose was to present the Finance Minister with the recommendations of a high-powered, expert body. Subramaniam knew Jha's economic views.[32] Jha was more inclined toward a technocratic than an institutional position. He was also well suited and well placed for Subramaniam's purposes;[33] he had been a senior officer, a Finance Secretary, and, with his current position as head of the Prime Minister's Secretariat, he could be a bridge between Subramaniam and the Prime Minister, between the central government and the state chief ministers, and could exercise considerable influence on the economic bureaucracy. Cooperation of state governments was important, because implementation of agricultural policy is, under India's constitution, within the purview of states. Policy is made by the central government, not implemented by it.

The Jha Committee was constituted on August 1, 1964. Its composition reflected the interbureaucratic dimension of the problem. Chaired by the head of Prime Minister's Secretariat, it had high officials from not only the Ministry of Food and Agriculture, but also from Finance and Planning, and had a leading academic agricultural economist.[34] On September 24, the Jha Committee submitted its report to the Prime Minister. It was accepted. The Committee argued: ". . . one of the most important problems facing the national economy is that of

---

30 *The Times of India*, June 24, 1964.

31 "A National Distribution-cum-Price Policy," *Speeches*, pp. 187–92.

32 Interviews, C. Subramaniam and L. K. Jha.

33 Interview, L. K. Jha. Also see Frankel, *India's Political Economy*, pp. 257–9.

34 Besides Jha, the other high-ranking members of the committee were T. P. Singh (Secretary, Planning Commission), B. N. Adarkar (Additional Secretary, Ministry of Finance), and S. C. Chaudhri (Economic and Statistical Adviser, Ministry of Food and Agriculture). M. L. Dantwala was the academic economist. Dantwala went on to chair the first Agricultural Prices Commission (APC).

augmenting agricultural production in a big way. This could be brought about mainly through the adoption of improved technology and additional investment required for this purpose. To the extent that the price policy can assist this process, it should be its major objective to do so."[35]

The immediate recommendation of the committee about producer prices in the year 1964–5 was even more supportive of Subramaniam. The committee took the average of the *wholesale* prices of paddy over the preceding three years, 1961–4, and recommended a *minimum support* price for producers that exceeded that average by 10 to 20 percent in most states.[36]

The committee also recommended that in the normal course of things the government should compete in the market as a buyer; there should be no compulsory procurement. Finally, the committee suggested that a separate governmental agency for determining producer prices every year be created to "provide incentive to the producer for adopting improved technology to the widest possible extent and for maximizing production," without, however, losing sight of the "likely effect of the price policy on the rest of the economy, particularly on the cost of living, level of wages, industrial cost structure etc."[37] Until Nehru's time, the latter macroconsiderations had overwhelmed the former microconcerns; the committee stressed both. The Prime Minister accepted its recommendations.

Subramaniam made some more key bureaucratic changes. He found the economic bureaucracy in the Agriculture Ministry still steeped in old thinking. The

---

35 Government of India, 1965, *Report of the Foodgrains Prices Committee* (henceforth the Jha Committee), p. 17. Notice that this position is in fact only a partial confirmation of Subramaniam's view. It gave priority to technology and a secondary place to prices, though Subramaniam had argued for both in the same vein. The committee was, as a matter of fact, even more explicit about this prioritization: "We have been unable to go along with the view that a mere increase in producer prices will serve the objective of maximizing production . . . up to a point, higher prices can help in encouraging the adoption of better techniques of food production and greater use of inputs provided the facilities in the shape of fertilisers, water, better seeds etc are there and all that the farmer needs is a better price to make full use of them . . ." (p. 5). This statement needs to be clarified. If the policy choices are (1) an institutional strategy or (2) a price *and* technology strategy, then the stated precedence of technology over prices is not a critical rebuttal of Subramaniam's view. If, however, the institutional position has been set aside and the issue is whether prices *or* technology should be the central pillar of policy – as it has become in the current discussions of agricultural policy – then it is critical to make this distinction. In fact, then one will have to make three distinctions: a purely economic view arguing that "getting prices right" is all that is necessary – technological development is a function of price relationships; a purely technological view arguing that public investments in science and technology would drive agricultural growth even if relative prices for agriculture fall; and a view that argues for a mix of prices and technology since new technology will not be adopted if prices are not favorable. Such complications arise only once the debate is internal to the price and technology strategy, not between it and the institutional strategy. In the mid-1960s, the latter was the case. That is why it is widely believed that the Jha Committee vindicated Subramaniam's view.
36 Jha Committee Report, p. 23.
37 Jha Committee Report, pp. 20–1.

Agriculture Secretary, the *bureaucratic* head of his ministry, was a senior civil servant, but he could see agriculture only "in the files." Subramaniam, as the *political* head of the ministry, replaced him with another civil servant who was a specialist in agriculture, and who shared Subramaniam's views on prices and technology.[38] Subramaniam also reorganized the Indian Council of Agricultural Research (ICAR). Piqued that the highest policy-making body in agricultural research was headed by a generalist civil servant, whereas its counterpart in industry – the Council of Scientific and Industrial Research (CSIR) – was headed by a scientist, he appointed a scientist, noted for his work on rust in wheat, as director general of the ICAR.[39] Finally, upon the acceptance of the Jha Committee report, the Agricultural Prices Commission (APC) and the Food Corporation of India (FCI) came into being in January 1965.

By the end of 1964 – within seven months of assuming charge – Subramaniam had thus "set his house in order," received the support of the Prime Minister and his Secretariat, created the institutions required for his policy design, and gotten the proposal for policy shift accepted *in principle* by the cabinet. Policy details were still to be worked out. The response of the Congress party and the financial implications of the new strategy were also to be ascertained.

Struggle for party support and financial resources.[40]   Factional struggle within the Congress party once again came to the fore. The party met at Durgapur for its annual session in January 1965. A new agricultural policy had not yet been laid out in detail; only the portents of change were present. The debate was therefore pitched at a general level: whether socialist principles were being abandoned, whether the goal of equity was being sacrificed over a concern with production. The more radical fringes of the center left, now organized as the Congress Forum for Socialist Action, mounted an attack on the new directions and called for a return to Nehru's ideals. Their vociferousness was, however, met by the state

38 *The New Strategy*, pp. 51–2. Also interviews with Subramaniam and Sivaraman. C. Sivaraman was appointed secretary. As a career civil servant in Orissa, he had specialized in agricultural programs and problems.

39 *The New Strategy*, pp. 13–14. Dr. B. P. Pal, the director general, was the first scientist to head the ICAR.

40 This section builds upon Frankel's *India's Political Economy* (Chaps. 7 and 8). Between 1963 and 1967, the Fourth Plan outline presented by the Planning Commission went through so many changes – concerning the size of the plan, its sectoral break-up, and how to finance the proposed investment – that, left on their own, these documents are very nearly opaque. However, once one systematically relates them to the various stages of the political battle over economic policy, as Frankel has done, the changes begin to make sense. While building upon her painstaking research in this period, I should record two points of disagreement. First, I find Frankel's view of Subramaniam's role and positions unacceptable: she believes that he was simply acting under the influence of the Ford and Rockefeller foundations and had no worthwhile positions of his own. Frankel did not research what drove the Food and Agriculture Ministry as minutely as she did the Planning Commission. Second, Frankel believes that the change in agricultural policy was bad for the country. I do not share this view.

chief ministers and the state bosses. The new agricultural proposals had already been accepted by the state chief ministers; they had been consulted extensively by the Jha Committee.[41]

In his address, the president of the Congress party, Kamaraj, attacked the Planning Commission. A state boss himself, Kamaraj argued that in view of the food situation in the country, some rethinking about investment priorities was essential, and instead of relying on deficit financing or foreign aid for public investment, the planners should think of private investment as a source.[42]

Ultimately, a compromise resolution was passed. The party reaffirmed the goal of a socialist society but recognized the need for stepping up the pace of production, both agricultural and industrial. This was convenient political rhetoric for saying that there were sharp divisions in the party.

Meanwhile, Subramaniam decided that his strategy should be tried on a pilot basis so that the seed–water–fertilizer package could be tested. A National Demonstration Program was thus born, with the 1965–6 season as its starting point. A small amount of new seeds – 200 tons – would be imported from Mexico. A thousand plots with good irrigation would be identified. Seeds and fertilizer would be distributed to the farmers owning these plots. No farmer would be asked to sow the entire crop with the new inputs; rather, "in the midst of traditional agriculture, . . . two hectares [would be] cultivated with the new technology."[43] The risks would not be high, and if the farmer took a loss, the government would recompense him.

Subramaniam's short-run political problems, however, worsened with the involvement of foreign agencies in the country's economic policy. Faced with India's increasing demand for foreign aid to support its investment effort, the World Bank started a six-month-long expert evaluation of the entire Indian economy in January 1965. The country was also beginning to feel the effects of a monsoon failure (as it turned out, in 1965–6 food production dropped from 89.3 to 72.3 million tons). India's dependence on American wheat was likely to increase, but the four-year PL 480 agreement concluded under President Kennedy was to run out in June, and President Johnson's attitude was not very clear. Section 3.4 will examine the role of external actors during policy change in detail. It will suffice to note here that external involvement, in India's charged political atmosphere, only increased the level of controversy over policy. Subramaniam was now being accused of promoting an American idea.

Battle for resources.   Later in the year the full financial implications of the new strategy were laid on the table. Two issues became clear. The agricultural pro-

---

41 Subramaniam himself presented his views a second time to the state chief ministers on January 1, 1965, at a meeting of the Committee on Agricultural Production in the National Development Council. He had earlier done so, in June 1964.

42 For details, see Frankel, *India's Political Economy*, pp. 266–7.

43 Ibid., p. 48.

posals implied that (1) the agriculture–industry balance of plan allocations would have to change drastically, and (2) because of the finances required, particularly foreign exchange, India's development strategy would have to be ideologically reformulated. A greater role for private investment, both domestic and foreign, and a larger reliance on the world market would be necessary. Less attention would have to be given to the short-run equity goals.

In August 1965, as the last stages in the preparation of an approach paper to the proposed Fourth Plan (1966–71)[44] drew near, the Food and Agriculture Ministry released its comprehensive outline of the new strategy. To price incentives and new technology was added a "betting on the strong" approach.[45] The new inputs would not be spread around evenly; that would be suboptimal. Rather, "a few areas with assured rainfall and irrigation" would be chosen for a "concentrated application" of the new inputs, so that maximum production results could be realized. This was directly opposite to the Nehruvian attempt to develop backward areas, especially through public investment.

The foreign-exchange component[46] of the new strategy over the five-year-plan period (1966–71) was projected to be Rs 1,114 crores (Rs 11.14 billion, that is, about \$2.8 billion at the existing official exchange rate). This was over *six times* the total amount allocated to agriculture during the preceding Third Plan (Rs 191 crores). The three largest imports were going to be fertilizers, seeds, and pesticides.[47]

For such a large allocation to take place, foreign exchange for industry, it was clear, would have to be drastically cut. Further, to expand domestic capacity in fertilizers, pesticides, and seeds, foreign and domestic private investment seemed to be the only practical source, for the state simply did not have enough resources of its own. Fertilizers were especially troublesome. Until 1965/6, fertilizers were more or less completely a public-sector monopoly. At the initiative of Subramaniam, foreign investors had already been consulted early in the year. Bechtel International, an American company, was prepared to set up five large factories in collaboration with the Government of India, but, given India's import substitution thrust and the insistence of Bechtel on complete managerial and technical control, India's Finance Minister had rejected the proposed arrangement.

The proposals of the Agriculture Ministry, therefore, required a severe cut in

44 Partly because of the political struggles over planning, the Fourth Plan, originally scheduled for 1966–71, could not come into being until 1969.
45 Details in Ministry of Food and Agriculture, 1965 *Agricultural Production in the Fourth Five-Year Plan: Strategy and Programme*, New Delhi: Government of India, pp. 1–3.
46 The financial magnitudes here and in the following paragraphs are taken from Frankel, pp. 277–8. I shall not repeat this source in the footnote unless a different source is available.
47 The projected consumption of nitrogenous fertilizer was 2,400,000 tons by the end of plan. In 1965–6 India was producing 450,000 tons, and by 1971 the domestic production of nitrogen was expected at best to reach 1,800,000 tons. India did not have a modern seed industry; all new seeds, thus, were to be initially imported. And, as against the installed capacity of about 26,000 tons in 1966, the requirement of plant-protecting pesticides was expected to be 76,000 tons.

investment in the planned industries and an ideological reformulation of the import substitution strategy. A major policy proposal of this kind, under Nehru, would have gone first to the Planning Commission, which was the sole arbiter of economic policy. It was a sign of the times that the Agriculture Minister chose to disregard the Planning Commission and elected to make a policy proposal on his own. The Planning Commission found the proposal unacceptable. It proposed a cut of 46 percent in the outlay projected by the Agriculture Ministry – with fertilizers receiving a 58 percent cut.

The planners had once again created a plan that ran into the by now customary – and to some, highly irritating – financing problems. To accommodate the wishes of the political masters, investment for the agricultural sector had indeed been increased from 21.8 percent of the total public outlays (in the 1964 proposal) to 22.8 percent (in the new 1965 proposal), and industrial investment was reduced from 21 percent to 19.8 percent, respectively. But the proposed changes hardly loosened the two big constraints: domestic savings and foreign exchange. The plan had a "savings gap" of Rs 3650 crores. Only a large increase in public savings could fill this gap. Convinced that new urban taxes were not possible any more, the planners demanded that one-fourth of the "gap" be filled by taxing the rural sector, which had contributed barely 2.6 percent of the total tax revenues of the last three plans. This was exactly the opposite of what the Agriculture Ministry was proposing: it was arguing for a larger investment in agriculture, not higher rural taxes.

The foreign-exchange constraint was even more serious. A "foreign-exchange gap" of Rs 1550 crores existed,[48] even before the demand of the Food and Agriculture Ministry for Rs 1100 crores' worth of foreign-exchange came. This demand, if accepted, would push the *current* expenses deficit to Rs 2650 crores. Finally, if the foreign-exchange component of *investment* expenses was also included, external assistance worth Rs 4000 crores was required. Essentially, this meant that foreign aid would have to go up from its Third Plan level of $1.1 billion per annum to $1.7 billion per annum. The foreign-exchange and domestic-savings gap together constituted nearly half of the total financial requirement for the Fourth Plan.

The Planning Commission therefore made it clear that the only affordable way to increase food production was to return to Nehru's model: to "concerted and well-coordinated efforts of the Community Development organization, Panchayati Raj institutions and cooperatives."[49] The Finance Minister supported this view.[50]

48 Exports for the plan period were expected to reach Rs 5100 crores, but maintenance imports (imports to keep the earlier investments going or to meet other current requirements) and debt servicing required Rs 6650 crores.

49 Planning Commission, 1965, *Fourth Five-Year Plan – Resources, Outlays and Programmes*, New Delhi: Government of India, p. 28.

50 For details, see Frankel, *India's Political Economy*, pp. 270–80.

Resolution of the struggle and policy implementation. Both proposals – of the Agriculture Ministry and the Planning Commission – were presented to the National Development Council, where the central government and the state chief ministers were to pass their judgment on the plan. The views of the state governments were known to be pro-agriculture.

Three months later, Shastri resolved the policy battle via realpolitik. Instead of asking Finance Minister Krishnamachari to resign on policy grounds, Shastri essentially secured his resignation on personal grounds. In a somewhat mysterious way, an old case of suspected corruption against the Finance Minister abruptly surfaced again – and with particular virulence.[51] The Prime Minister instituted an inquiry, upon which Krishnamachari himself submitted his resignation. One of the strongest opponents of a policy shift and a strong proponent of Nehruvian economic policies in the Cabinet thus made an unceremonious exit from power, not on grounds of ideology and policy but to save himself from further personal ignominy. Within a day of Krishnamachari's resignation, a "pliable" Finance Minister, Sachindra Chaudhri, was appointed.[52]

Subramaniam's victory was even more complete later that year. Upon Shastri's sudden death barely two weeks after Krishnamachari's resignation, Mrs. Gandhi was elected by the Congress party on January 19, 1966 to head the government. The logic that accounted for Shastri's rise to the prime ministership is also considered to have led Congress men to elect her: she was well enough known to be presented as a leader but, without a significant base of her own, she was weak enough to be dependent on the party bosses.

Mrs. Gandhi did not disturb the cabinet composition significantly. But one of her first acts facilitated Subramaniam's task. In addition to his current responsibilities as the Agriculture Minister, Subramaniam was also made a member of the Planning Commission. He had "by-passed the Planning Commission till early 1966,"[53] which led to controversies and conflicts. Now, he was a member of it. The interbureaucratic tension was resolved and the results were dramatic. In September 1965, planners had asked for a return to community development, panchayats, and cooperatives. A year later, in August 1966, with Subramaniam in the Planning Commission, the new draft outline of the Fourth Plan read as follows:

If our dependence on imported foodgrains has to cease, it is necessary to make far greater

---

51 Krishnamachari was accused of misusing his office to grant special favors to a firm managed by his sons. How this case became politically important in December 1965 is still not clear. The usual hypothesis is that the timing was politically intended.

52 Chaudhri, a Member of Parliament from West Bengal, was a political lightweight. He was considered knowledgeable on company law but had absolutely no experience in public finance. It was hard to avoid the impression that the Prime Minister wanted to put an end to the recalcitrance of the most important economic ministry in the country; the left-of-center faction could not defend Krishnamachari due to the uproar over suspected corruption.

53 *The New Strategy*, p. 50.

use of modern methods of production. . . . A new strategy or approach is needed if we are to achieve results over a short span of time. During the last four years as a result of the trials conducted in several research centers in India on exotic and hybrid varieties of seeds, a break-through has become possible. . . . The long term objective is to organise the use of high-yielding seeds together with a high application of fertilisers over extensive areas where irrigation is assured.[54]

And specifically on chemical fertilizer, the planners' bête noire, the draft outline read:

The intensive programme for high yielding varieties in particular will require a large supply of fertilisers. Unless special steps are taken, supplies are likely to be a major impediment. It would be essential to make arrangements for the speedy establishment of the requisite number of factories with sufficient capacity to produce as much fertiliser as possible indigenously. Import from abroad would have to be arranged to make good the shortage of indigenous supply.[55]

The planners also accepted the price component of the strategy: "A . . . factor which contributed to slow growth in agricultural production was the absence of an effective price policy. Price support policy in the past was aimed at eliminating distress. But this did not provide the incentive needed for dynamic agricultural growth. . . ."[56]

Meanwhile, the National Demonstration Program – the two hectares cultivated with new seed–water–fertilizer technology "in the midst of traditional agriculture" – started to bear fruit. Although, due to a second successive drought in 1966–7, the foodgrain production at 74.2 million tons was barely up from 72.3 million tons in 1965–6, the islands of two hectares were doing rather well: "Farmers used to come there as on a pilgrimage to see this new wonder and finally, when the harvesting was being done, everybody was amazed that this level of productivity could be achieved on their own land."[57] For 1966–7, the Food and Agriculture Ministry had planned to import 5,000 tons of wheat seed, but "demand picked up so much" that ultimately India ended up importing 18,000 tons of wheat seeds.[58]

The fertilizer expenses were also met. The changed Finance Minister was only too willing to comply: "I approached the Finance Minister for resources for the import of fertilizers. At the time of the controversy, the Finance Minister had been very much opposed to the use of scarce foreign exchange for the import of fertilisers for these new varieties, but by the time I made my approach another Finance Minister had been appointed who was more open to influence. We thus secured the foreign exchange and mounted an import programme for fertilizers."[59]

---

54 Planning Commission, 1966 *Fourth Five-Year Plan: A Draft Outline*, Delhi: Government of India, p. 175.
55 Ibid., p. 189.
56 *Fourth Five-Year Plan*, p. 174.
57 *The New Strategy*, p. 48.
58 Foreign exchange for the additional quantities came from the Rockefeller Foundation; ibid., p. 48.
59 *The New Strategy*, p. 37.

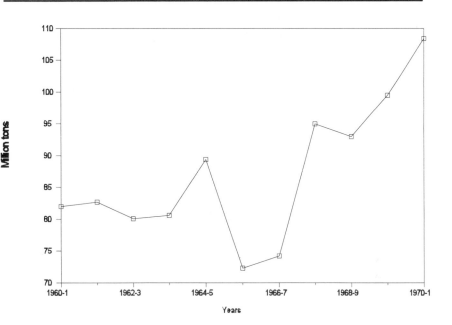

Figure 3.1. Foodgrain production in India, 1960–1 to 1970–1. *Source:* Ministry of Agriculture, 1990, *Agricultural Statistics at a Glance,* Delhi: Government of India.

The first year of the implementation of new strategy was 1966–7. Out of a total of 130 million hectares under crops, 2.4 million hectares were to come under new seeds in 1966–7.[60] The projection was that by the end of 1970–1, 2.4 million hectares would expand to 13 million hectares. For self-sufficiency, a production increase from an average of about 80–85 million tons to 105–10 million tons was required. Assuming an additional output of 2 to 2.5 tons per hectare with the new seeds, 10 to 13 million hectares were sufficient to meet this requirement.

Were these targets met? India's foodgrain output rose substantially from 74.2 million tons in 1966–7 to 95 million tons in 1967–8. Two successive droughts are never followed by a third bad year in India. In 1967–8, rains were overdue, and the monsoon did return. But even the most unsparing critic of the new strategy could not have attributed a rise of 20 million tons in a year to the weather alone. By 1970–1, India was indeed producing 108.4 million tons. The area under HYV seeds, starting with 1.9 million hectares in 1966–7, had gone up to 15.4 million hectares in 1970–1, which was higher than expected. The new technology had caught the fancy of farmers in the irrigated belt. A green revolution had arrived.

The new agricultural strategy survived even the absence of Subramaniam in the government. Subramaniam lost his parliamentary seat in the 1967 general

60 The *projected* figures in this paragraph are from *The New Strategy*, p. 45; the *actual* figures, from *Fertilizer Statistics*, 1985–6, pp. II-33 and II-107.

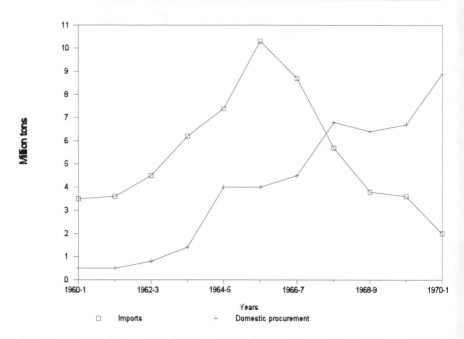

Figure 3.2. Imports and domestic procurement, 1960–1 to 1970–1. *Source:* Ministry of Agriculture, 1990, *Agricultural Statistics at a Glance,* Delhi: Government of India.

elections.[61] The growth in foodgrain output after the new strategy stood in such dramatic contrast to the earlier stagnation that the success of Subramaniam's approach was transparently obvious (Figure 3.1). Also, consider what happened to imports (Figure 3.2.): between 1960/1 and 1965/6, food imports, mostly American wheat, rose, while domestic procurement lagged far behind. After the policy change, domestic procurement rose to exceed imports, and by 1970–1 the equation had completely reversed.

3.4 DID THE INDIAN STATE ACT AUTONOMOUSLY?

An explanation of state policy in terms of struggles within the state is methodologically incomplete. The state, after all, operates in a context: the civil society and the international system. Did the forces outside the state influence its actions or did the state act independently? How does one define independent state action? I take up first the more often cited source of India's policy change: the pressure exerted by the West. Then I move to its domestic correlate: the dominant class in Indian agriculture.

61 The language issue – Hindi versus Tamil – consumed most Congress politicians in the state of Tamil Nadu in the 1967 elections. Policy performance hardly made a difference.

3.4.1 The role of external actors

Three external actors were involved in India's agricultural policy: the World Bank, the United States government, and the private U.S. foundations (Ford and Rockefeller). Did they *cause* the policy change? Or did they merely *facilitate* the policy change already under way? Did the external actors "lean against an open door," or did they force open a door that was closed?[62]

It is widely believed in the left circles in India that the policy change in the mid-sixties was a result of Western and/or American pressures. This belief is not confined to the left, however. The external actors themselves have made that claim. Consider the following statement by the World Bank:

Changes began in 1966. A number of foreign experts working in India for the Rockefeller and Ford Foundations began *pressing* the Indian government to import high-yielding wheat varieties. . . . The Indian government decided that the potential of the [new] technology far outweighed its risks . . . IDA [soft-loan window of the World Bank] was closely involved with this decision. It had carried out a massive study of Indian agriculture in close collaboration with the government of India. . . . *As a result of this study*, an Agricultural Prices Commission was established to set prices at which the government would purchase crops from farmers; the favorable mixture of grain and fertilizer prices it set encouraged farmers to produce more. The Food Corporation of India was created to buy up grain in the good years to store for the lean. Largely as a result of this organizational effort India now maintains comfortable stocks of rice and wheat. (Emphasis added)[63]

The World Bank.   The Bell Mission of the World Bank reviewed India's economic policy in the mid-sixties. It is sometimes held to be responsible for the change in India's agricultural strategy.

The central thrust of the Bell Mission's critique of Nehru's agricultural policies was as follows: "While additional labor does add to production, increased labor alone will not add enough to keep pace with the needs of a growing population. . . . There must be steps to . . . provide price incentives, to back incentives with adequate supplies of needed imports and to promote the credit basis for investment by large and small farmers alike."[64] The "needed imports" were mainly fertilizers, pesticides, and farm machinery.

The Bell Mission was particularly severe on India's price policy. It argued that:

1. Producer prices should be "high enough to make investment in increased inputs profitable. . . . the Government cannot carry consumer interests to the point of offering disincentive to farm production."[65]

2. There should be institutions to support this price policy: "While not being a

---

62 The metaphor is from L. K. Jha, 1973, "Comment: Leaning Against Open Doors?" in John P. Lewis and Ishan Kapur, *The World Bank Group, Multilateral Aid, and the 1970s,* Lexington, MA: D. C. Heath and Company, p. 97.

63 The World Bank, 1983, *IDA in Retrospect,* p. 44.

64 The World Bank, 1965, *Bell Mission Report to the President on India's Economic Development Effort,* vol. 2, Agricultural Policy, October 1, p. 37.

65 Ibid., p. 47.

monopoly buyer or seller (the government) must try to command the market situation at pre-determined low and high points. To eliminate fluctuations by curbing both extremes, it must command stocks and some assured inflows such as imports. . . ."[66]

No different from Subramaniam's approach, these recommendations were given in October 1965. Even if it is argued that only the formal recommendations were given in October 1965 and the Mission had started its work in January 1965 (therefore its views must have been known), the fact remains that these policies and institutions had already been proposed *before the Bell Mission started its work*. Subramaniam's price-policy paper to Indian cabinet was submitted in June 1964; the Jha Committee was appointed on August 1, 1964; its recommendations were accepted in October 1964; and, on the basis of the Jha Committee and Subramaniam's views expressed as early as June and July 1964, the FCI (and APC) had already come into existence in January 1965.

Moreover, as was pointed out in the previous chapter, India's Food and Agriculture ministers since 1952 had been arguing for price incentives and technological investments in agriculture. They could not defeat Nehru's institutional view, which was also supported by the economic bureaucracy. A more favorable political context in the mid-1960s made a remarkable difference.

Thus, both in terms of ideas and institutions, a causal case in favor of the World Bank cannot be made. That "the changes started in 1966," as the World Bank argues, is a claim that an internal political reading of economic policy does not substantiate. Changes had already started in 1964.

The role of the U.S. government.   The American involvement was of two kinds: that of the government and that of private foundations, especially the Ford and Rockefeller foundations.[67] No less a figure than President Lyndon B. Johnson himself claimed that the shift in India's strategy was "the first important direct result of our new policy."[68] What was the "new" American policy and how did it develop?

Figure 3.3 shows India's dependence on imports (predominantly American

66 Ibid., p. 51.
67 The written materials cited below have been supplemented by several interviews. The most important for this section are: John P. Lewis (Administrator, USAID in Delhi in the 1960s; interview at Princeton, NJ, March 25, 1991), and W. David Hopper (Ford and Rockefeller foundations in Delhi, 1950s and 1960s; retired as vice president, the World Bank, interview in Washington, D.C., March 3, 1991). Professor Lewis also shared his manuscript, in which he has put together an account of the policy interaction between the U.S. and Indian governments during the 1950s and 1960s.
68 Lyndon B. Johnson, 1971, *The Vantage Point*, New York: Holt, Rinehart and Winston, p. 225. Those who have formed judgments only on the basis of the archives from the Johnson presidency have been led to a similar conclusion. An example is Carlyn Castore, 1982, "The United States and India: The Use of Food to Apply Economic Pressure – 1965–67," in Sydney Weintraub, ed., *Economic Coercion and the US Foreign Policy*, Boulder, CO: Westview Press.

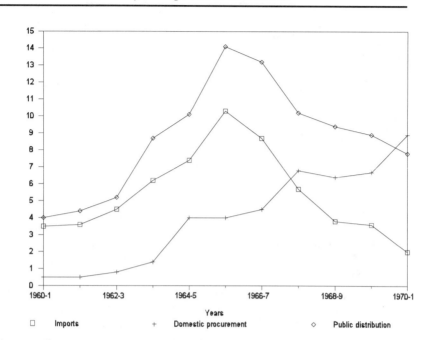

Figure 3.3. Imports, domestic procurement, and public distribution, 1960–1 to 1970–1. *Source:* Ministry of Agriculture, 1990, *Agricultural Statistics at a Glance,* Delhi: Government of India.

wheat) for its public distribution requirements in the 1960s. India and the United States had signed the first of their many agreements under Public Law (PL) 480 in 1957. The United States undertook to supply wheat to India at concessional terms, which included the provision that part of the payment could be made in rupees. The agreement represented a marriage of convenience. Given India's foreign-exchange constraint, full payment in dollars would have been very difficult. Moreover, compared to Indian wheat, American wheat was very cheap. Wheat imports thus provided a means to circumvent the political difficulties associated with procuring food domestically at low procurement prices. For the United States, exports to India, a large country with a large need, offered a way to reduce its accumulating wheat surpluses.

In 1956, the United States started with 3.1 million tons of wheat exports. Over the next decade, however, the exports rose to reach a peak of 8, 10, and 8 million tons in 1965, 1966, and 1967, respectively. Imports from the United States were never a large proportion of India's overall production, for even quantities as high as 8 to 10 million tons constituted only between 12 to 15 percent of the total output. However, the public distribution system for the cities by the mid-sixties became almost completely dependent on wheat imports from the United States.

Trouble began in 1965. As India's dependence mounted with the first big drought in 1964, the United States reserves entered a period of decline. In 1961, the American wheat stocks stood at 38.4 million tons; by 1965, they had declined to 22.2 million tons. Moreover, the prediction for the 1966 crop was bad; production was expected to fall sharply.[69] In the autumn of 1965, faced with declining stocks at home and increasing demand from India, President Johnson himself took charge of wheat exports. He put wheat supplies on a "short tether." Wheat under PL 480 would be supplied, but shipments would be released on a month-to-month basis. The Government of India would submit an estimate of its food needs every month and President Johnson's clearance would depend upon a reform in India's agricultural policy: giving price incentives to producers, increasing fertilizer production under private auspices, and bringing more acreage under irrigation. These demands were communicated to the Indian government in the fall of 1965.[70] It is noteworthy that Subramaniam had already moved in this direction a year before, and the Food and Agriculture Ministry had also prepared its detailed policy proposal for the consideration of the National Development Council by August 1965.

The outbreak of the Indo-Pakistan War in October 1965 led to the suspension of U.S. aid. Later, resumption of aid was made conditional upon policy reform that went on to include economic policy in general instead of agricultural policy only. The changes recommended were: a greater role in the economy for domestic and foreign private capital and a devaluation of the currency. Two kinds of aid thus became entangled: economic aid and food aid. A second year of drought followed, putting both under greater stress.

By the spring of 1966, the State and Agriculture departments were arguing that agricultural policy reforms in India were already in place. Moreover, a second crop failure, these departments argued, might lead to conditions of famine: therefore, a short-tether policy was inappropriate.[71] Whatever the presidential response toward economic aid, the short tether on food aid, they pleaded, ought to be lifted. The White House, however, remained uninfluenced.[72] In June 1966, India finally devalued the rupee by 36.5 percent, a decision that led to countless

---

69 For a detailed account of the Indo–U.S. food-aid relationship, see Robert Paarlberg, 1985, *Food Trade and Foreign Policy: India, the Soviet Union and the United States*, Ithaca, NY: Cornell University Press. Also, James Bjorkman, 1980, "Public Law 480 and the Policies of Self-Help and Short-Tether: Indo-American Relations, 1965–68," in Lloyd Rudolph and Susanne Rudolph, eds., *The Regional Imperative*, Atlantic Highlands, NJ: Humanities Press. The figures are from Paarlberg, p. 146.

70 Paarlberg, *Food Trade and Foreign Policy*, p. 148.

71 Ibid., pp. 151–7.

72 "I stood almost alone, with only a few concurring advisors, in this fight to slow the pace of U.S. assistance. . . . This was one of the most difficult and lonely struggles of my life." Lyndon B. Johnson, *The Vantage Point*, p. 225.

political difficulties for Mrs. Gandhi's fledgling government.[73] Johnson resumed U.S. aid but still "kept the short tether on. No one would starve because of our policies. India would receive the grain it needed but on a month-to-month basis rather than a year-to-year basis."[74] The short tether was not relaxed even after Subramaniam declared in November 1966 that without 2 million tons of immediate shipment, the food stocks in India would be completely exhausted by mid-January.[75] The short-tether policy remained intact until the spring of 1967. At that time, with the return of good weather and a record crop, the crisis resolved itself. Dependence on U.S. wheat thereafter continued to decline until India unilaterally terminated the PL 480 agreement on December 31, 1971.[76]

What can we infer about policy change from this chronology of events? Change can be said to have been caused by external actors only if the preferences of decision makers were different from those of the external agents. Of the various policies involved, it is clear that Indian leaders did not want to devalue the currency on their own. The two ministries concerned with such a decision, Finance and Commerce, had rejected it outright. Devaluation, in other words, took place in the face of *counterpreferences* of Indian decision makers; it was a result of the combined pressure from the United States and the World Bank.

What of agricultural policy? Let us look at Subramaniam's account first:

Johnson always had a sense of self-importance. If anything good or important was happening in the world, it should be a Johnson initiative . . . he thought the . . . Indian farmer, the Indian minister and the Indian scientist were not adequate, and that he should take a hand in the initiation of this strategy. He reiterated in speeches that India should adopt this new technology, which, as a matter of fact, created problems for me in India. The speeches gave ammunition to those who were attacking me on the grounds that I was following American advice. . . . *We had already announced and taken these steps and I had to tell people that President Johnson was telling us nothing new. . . . The fact that we had to send our requirements of foodgrains to (President Johnson) every month created many difficulties*, not only among the communists but amongst people who were sympathetic to America. Unfortunately, it has to be recognised that America gives generously but does not know how to give. I reached the conclusion that they would give and still create a feeling of enmity. . . . (Emphasis added)[77]

---

73 Domestic criticism cut across ideological lines. The *mildest* criticism was that it was neither "sound economics, nor honourable politics." Trenchant criticisms were more characteristic. Devaluation also figured in the 1967 elections and contributed to the unpopularity of the Congress party.

74 Johnson, *The Vantage Point*, p. 229.

75 Food in quantities required by India *at concessional rates* was not available from other sources. Requests for wheat went to Canada, Australia, France, the Soviet Union, Mexico, and Argentina.

76 However, "in a curious turn of events in the spring of 1968, it suddenly became in the US interests to expand food aid shipments; wheat production was up, farm prices were down. Accordingly, the Department of Agriculture and the State Department approached the Indian government to suggest that India take more PL 480 wheat than it had already requested" (Paarlberg, p. 156).

77 C. Subramaniam, *The New Strategy in Agriculture*, pp. 53–4.

Readers of this account and of the chronology outlined above might wonder what exactly motivated the White House policy during 1965–7. Devaluation took place in June 1966, but the short-tether policy continued until a year later. Other key policy suggestions, such as greater private initiative in the fertilizer sector, had also been accepted by mid-1966. While firm conclusions must await a future historian's judgment when more hard evidence is available from both sides, it is hard to escape the *inference* that reform in agricultural or economic policy was not the sole, or the main, U.S. objective. The short-tether policy continued till the spring of 1967, *by which time agricultural reforms were already close to three years in existence and had completed one year of full implementation.* Paarlberg documents the fact that many objectives got mixed up – agricultural policy, economic policy, foreign policy – and argues that ultimately what kept the short-tether policy going was India's opposition to U.S. policy in Vietnam. Indeed, as American pressure grew, the domestic criticism of the Indian government for its failure to defend national autonomy became increasingly strident – which in turn made it necessary for the Indian government to criticize U.S. policy in Vietnam even more strongly. Paarlberg comments that "it was in some ways surprising that Johnson did not understand this."[78] Chester Bowles, the U.S. ambassador to India, was also convinced that agricultural policy was not the main reason for the continuance of short tether; India's foreign policy was.[79]

However, does this mean that the United States played no role in the evolution of India's agricultural policy? It is necessary to make another distinction: between the origins of the new agricultural policy and its implementation. Whereas the *origins* of the new agricultural policy were not affected by the U.S. government since it was already in place, its *implementation* was. The new agricultural policy was foreign-exchange-intensive. To recapitulate, according to the planners, India's export income was expected to go up by Rs 5100 crores between 1966–71, but the foreign exchange required for implementing the plan was Rs 9100 crores. The country, as it were, was expected to live 180 percent beyond its means.

It is here that the World Bank and the United States stepped in. Without enough foreign exchange, the implementation of new agricultural policy would have been *much slower*. It would not have been *impossible*, for, given the policy struggle in the changed political context, it is unlikely that the Planning Commission would have been able to force the Agriculture Ministry to cut its outlay without the commission cutting its own industrial outlays simultaneously. In the end, the primary role of the United States and the World Bank consisted in

---

78 Paarlberg, *Food Trade and Foreign Policy*, p. 166. It is also surprising, one should add, that Indian planners did not anticipate some arm-twisting while preparing a plan with a huge savings and foreign-exchange gap.

79 Chester Bowles, 1971, *Promises to Keep*, New York: Harper and Row, pp. 534–58.

facilitating the implementation of the new agricultural policy by providing resources for importing fertilizers and other inputs upon which the success of the new policy depended. They did not cause the change itself.

The role of the Ford and Rockefeller foundations. Since 1954, the Rockefeller Foundation had taken the lead in setting up institutions of agricultural sciences in India, supported later by the Ford Foundation. As a result, India had developed a substantial pool of agricultural scientists and qualified manpower by the mid-sixties.[80] A large infrastructure for conducting research and verifying the results of the new HYV seeds was thus in place as Subramaniam took over. When the potential of the HYV seeds, particularly those developed by Norman Borlaug, was brought to Subramaniam's notice by the Rockefeller Foundation in Delhi, he was impressed by the scientific evidence presented. Tests under laboratory conditions in India seemed to confirm these results.[81] Next, it was a matter of testing the new seeds on actual farms. The Rockefeller Foundation also provided the foreign exchange to import the new seeds when Subramaniam was faced with foreign-exchange difficulties.[82]

What conclusions can we draw? There is no doubt that hybrid seeds were an entirely new element in the production package in the mid-sixties. However, without the political context in which Subramaniam worked, this fact in itself would have been of little consequence. To repeat, minus the new seeds (which were not available before the mid-sixties), India's Agriculture ministers had been asking for a strategy based on prices and technology since the mid-1950s. They were unable to change Nehru's view. A Ford Foundation study published in 1959 had supported the view of the Agriculture ministers.[83] Yet a change in agricultural policy the Ford Foundation could not secure. Instead, the outcome was a small pilot project, known as the Intensive Agriculture District Program (IADP), covering only thirteen districts. Moreover, the mixed results of this program did not unambiguously support the idea of concentrating fertilizers and organizational effort on areas with assured irrigation.[84] The difference in the mid-sixties was that a crusading Agriculture minister had taken charge, the political context had changed, and the agricultural crisis was more severe.

80 For a detailed treatment, see Uma Lele and Arthur Goldsmith, 1989, "Building Agricultural Research Capacity: India's Experience with the Rockefeller Foundation and Its Significance for Africa," *Economic Development and Cultural Change*, January.
81 C. Subramaniam, *The New Strategy*, pp. 22–3.
82 "For 1966–67, . . . with the foreign exchange provided by the Rockefeller Foundation, the team was able to buy 18,000 tons of wheat seeds" (ibid., p. 48).
83 Government of India, 1959, *Report on India's Food Crisis and Steps to Meet It*, by the Agricultural Production Team of the Ford Foundation, Delhi: Ministry of Food and Agriculture and Ministry of Community Development and Cooperation.
84 See D. K. Desai, 1969, "Intensive Agricultural District Programme," *Economic and Political Weekly*, June 28.

3.4.2 Rural society and public policy

This brings us to the role of the groups in India's countryside. Two questions are involved here. How organized were the social groups in the countryside? And what was their relationship to agricultural policy per se?

Examining the relationship between agrarian demands and public policy, the first study of interest groups in the Indian polity, by Myron Weiner, concluded:

(Agricultural) Policy is debated – often hotly debated – within the Ministries of Community Development and Cooperation, and Food and Agriculture, the Planning Commission, and the Congress Party. Other political parties, intellectuals in general, have heatedly discussed the relative merits and defects of ceilings on landholdings and, most recently, proposals for cooperative farming. But one could write the history of the postwar agrarian policy in India, and of the political struggles which have entered into making such policy, with little or no reference to farmer organizations.[85]

Weiner studied the big landlords on the one hand and the small peasantry and the landless on the other. Neither group had any impact on policy formulation. As for policy implementation, the landlords were unorganized but powerful enough to defeat *full* implementation. The small peasants and the landless were not organized enough: they affected neither policy formulation nor policy implementation.

Landlord influence, effective at the local level, progressively eroded as one moved up the hierarchy, from the local setting to the central government in Delhi. At the local level, the lords were effective not because they were "organized." They belonged to many castes, and even when, in a given area, they came from a single caste, there were intense internecine conflicts. Moreover, calling landlords oppressors, the left nationalist factions in the Congress party had destroyed the ideological legitimacy of any landlord groups that might have formed to fight the government. In the circumstances, a microstrategy – that is, *individual* and *discrete* as opposed to group- *orchestrated* and *organized* – appears to have been adopted by most landlords. Rather than fighting the Congress party as an organized interest group or class, they simply infiltrated the party to protect their interests. They were helped in this endeavor by the fact that the party needed these "men of power and prestige" to reach out to the countryside. The declared oppressors were also the "natural leaders" at the local level. However, the state capitals were the uppermost layers of landlord power. New Delhi was virtually devoid of any significant landlord influence.

The sources of landlord power were thus structural: their position in the local power hierarchies enabled them to beat back the legislative pressure locally and manipulate it at the state level. Failed policy implementation was an aggregate effect of such discrete microstrategies, not of collective action or political organization.

---

85 Myron Weiner, 1962, *The Politics of Scarcity: Public Pressure and Political Response in India,* Chicago: University of Chicago Press, p. 149.

What about the small landowners and the landless? Many organizations had attempted to organize the peasantry, including the ruling Congress party. The process started with the emergence of many, loosely knit Kisan Sabhas (peasant associations) in 1926–7.[86] A confederation of these associations, All-India Kisan Sabha (AIKS), came into existence in 1936–7. Ideological differences kept splitting the AIKS. First, there was a split between Marxists and Gandhian socialists in 1942. Then a split among the Marxists took place in 1944, with a breakaway group led by Swami Sahajanand Saraswati, a respected peasant leader. Finally, when the Communists launched an insurrectionary movement to overthrow the Indian government after independence, they were banned until their strategy changed from violent insurrection to an acceptance of electoral means. These various bodies had their pockets of influence, but there were no effective nationwide peasant organizations. In areas where the peasant organizations were strong, they had some impact on policy *implementation*: for example, land reforms were better implemented. Elsewhere, they had little influence. In any event, they were not strong enough to have an impact on policy *formulation*.

Given the dependence of peasants on landlords and the structure of landlord power, the peasants could have become a powerful force if a political party had mobilized them to counter the power of landlords and provided them with protection. The most powerful party, however, turned out to be dependent on landlord support. This vicious circle could not be broken, except in the two states of West Bengal and Kerala, which came under Communist influence.

3.5 SUMMARY

The sources of change in policy lay within the country. The external actors facilitated the implementation of the strategy through financial support or by supplying information to decision makers in a political climate that was more conducive to a policy change than before. They could not bring about the change in the face of counterpreferences – that is, when the *key* decision-making elite in India had a view different from that of the external actors. Only when the elite changed substantially, the counterpreferences turned weak in the political structure, and new preferences close to the view of the external actors emerged with a domestic base of their own did a new strategy come into being.

Similarly, mobilized interests (groups or classes) in the civil society did not lead to a change in India's agricultural policy. Interests in the Indian countryside were not organized enough in the 1950s and 1960s. This does not mean, however, that the civil society did not have *any* impact on state policy. It was clear that the institutional strategy was not succeeding and had little chance of success: the classes that the institutional strategy aimed to defeat were precisely the classes that the Congress party needed to reach in the countryside. Evolving a

---

86 For details, see A. R. Desai, 1968, *Social Background of Indian Nationalism*, Bombay: Popular Prakashan, pp. 188–94.

more pragmatic alternative to the institutional strategy, therefore, seemed increasingly necessary as the years under Nehru passed by. What this alternative should be was left unspecified by the classes that held power in India's villages. The battle for policy was essentially fought within the state institutions by political leaders who had different visions of the agrarian economy and who, along with their bureaucratic allies, led different factions of the ruling party.

4

The rise of agrarian power in the 1970s

The 1970s were a turning point for rural India. Until the late 1960s, the power of dominant agrarian groups was confined to state politics. As argued in the last two chapters, these groups had the capacity to defeat the implementation of agricultural policy but little control over its formulation, which remained a function of intragovernmental struggles and factional battles within the top echelons of the Congress party.

By the end of the 1970s, a new agrarian force had emerged in national politics. On the one hand, this force was dramatically represented in the personality and ideology of Chaudhary Charan Singh, one of the most powerful peasant leaders in post-independence India, who came to occupy important ministerial positions in the central government and brought his peasant-based party into the uppermost strata of the power structure. On the other hand, new ideologies of rural political mobilization began to take root. Agricultural prices increasingly came to replace land reforms as the major element in agrarian unrest. This was a development with major political implications, because land reforms had mobilized only the subaltern rural classes against the landlords, never the rural sector as a whole. Agricultural prices, as the decade closed, began to emerge as a sectoral, as opposed to a class, issue which, to the great surprise of urban intellectuals, attracted small farmers too. A battle cry of rural versus urban India, not tenants versus landlords, made its entry into the ideological discourse of Indian politics.

What were the key moments in the rise of agrarian power during the 1970s? What impact did rising rural power have on agricultural policy, and how? These are the two central questions addressed in this chapter. The emphasis will be on agricultural prices, especially food prices, which are – politically – the most contentious aspect of India's agricultural policy.

For most of the decade, there was a clash between the economic and political arguments for agricultural prices. The economic bureaucracy, basing its arguments on accepted canons of economic theory, had to contend with the steady rise of agrarian power. While not denying the role of prices in stimulating food production, the economic bureaucrats kept emphasizing the macroeconomic implications of food prices: their impact on inflation, on budgetary subsidies, and on welfare levels of the poor. On the other hand, while not completely ignoring the implications for the rest of the economy, the politicians were more inclined to give priority to the microeconomic argument – that is, the impact of higher farm prices on agricultural production.[1] Ultimately, the production argument for prices, favored by the politicians, did triumph; but the victory was tempered by considerations urged by economic bureaucrats – considerations such as the impact of food prices on budget subsidies, inflation, and the poor.

To put the discussion in perspective, the chapter begins with two general profiles. In order to demonstrate the points at which politics can, and does, influence what is ostensibly a technical or economic decision about prices, in the first section I shall describe the policy process, as it was redesigned after the creation of the Agricultural Prices Commission (APC) and the Food Corporation of India (FCI). In the second, I shall deal with the increasing ruralization of political representation in India. Next, I shall move to three key points in the rise of peasant power over the decade. Section 4.3 will discuss the first phase (1971–3) when, faced with the beginning of what turned out to be an unending series of political attacks on technocrats making agricultural policy, the APC began to lose its political innocence. Section 4.4 will discuss how, in the next round, farmers' resistance at the state and ground levels frustrated a policy change decreed from above – namely, nationalization of foodgrains trade in 1973–4. Section 4.5 will, finally, trace the implications of the defeat of Mrs. Gandhi and the victory of the Janata party in 1977. Agrarian ideologues reached the uppermost levels of power between 1977–9. They managed to change several aspects of economic policy; they could not *drastically* alter it.

4.1 THE POLICY PROCESS: INSTITUTIONS, NORMS, AND PRINCIPLES

Established in 1965, the Commission on Agricultural Costs and Prices (CACP), called Agricultural Prices Commission until 1985,[2] is the institutional keystone of the economic bureaucracy dealing with agricultural price policy. It is a technical advisory body that recommends support and/or procurement prices for the major agricultural commodities, including foodgrains, every year.[3] Its recommendations are not mandatory. The political wing of the government – the cabinet – can accept or reject them.

The terms of reference of the CACP require consideration of the following

---

1 As would be expected, the politicians did not speak with one voice. Most of them, however, argued this way. As the decade ended, a consensus on the necessity of "remunerative" agricultural prices had started to emerge.
2 I shall use the two names interchangeably. This section will use CACP; but in the next section, to be consistent with the quotations used, I shall revert to the original name, APC.
3 In addition to wheat and rice, the CACP recommends prices for sorghum, millet, maize, oilseeds, pulses, sugarcane, cotton, and jute.

objectives while recommending food prices:[4] (1) provision of incentives to the producer and maximization of production; (2) the likely effect of the prices recommended on the rest of the economy, particularly on the cost of living, level of wages, industrial cost structure, etc.; (3) balanced growth of the different crops.

The CACP is involved with three sets of prices: support, procurement, and issue prices, respectively. Support prices are the floor below which producer prices are not allowed to fall in the event of abundant supplies, so that higher production does not entail an income loss for farmers. To achieve this, support prices seek to cover the costs of production of the farmer, and the government buys *all* grain offered at this price. Procurement price, on the other hand, is the operative price when supplies are not abundant and market prices tend to rise. It is a price at which the government purchases the quantities required for public distribution and for building up a buffer stock. Issue prices are the prices at which consumers buy grain from the public distribution network. They are determined on the basis of the costs of procurement, storage, and distribution; but more often than not, the level of issue prices has heavily depended upon the ability of the government to bear the subsidy that public distribution entails.

Price recommendations of the CACP are considered by the central ministries of Food and Agriculture, Finance and Planning, and, in the case of export crops, also by the Ministry of Commerce. The Finance Ministry considers the impact of food prices recommended by the CACP on the general price level in the economy and on budgetary subsidies. The Planning Ministry's concern is the general price level, too: on that depends the real value of planned investments. The Food and Agriculture Ministry is concerned with the impact of these prices on food production and procurement. Both how much is procured and how much is produced may be sensitive to the price given to the producers.

Opinions of the chief ministers of state governments are also sought on the CACP recommendations. This is because procurement takes place in the states whose agencies, in addition to the central government's Food Corporation of India (FCI), are involved in buying grains from farmers and traders. The purpose of consultations with the states is to come to an agreement over prices and statewise procurement targets. On the basis of pre-agreed quotas, states contribute to the central pool of foodgrains. The central pool, in turn, feeds the public distribution network, which is operated by the state governments. Through roughly 350,000 retail outlets, the distribution network feeds the entire country, though it started primarily for the urban centers.[5]

---

4 Government of India, 1965, *Report of the Foodgrain Prices Committee*, Delhi: Ministry of Food and Agriculture, pp. 20–1.

5 Deepak Ahluwalia has convincingly demonstrated that there is no "urban bias" in the public distribution network: 56% of wheat, 71% of rice, 64% of sugar, and 59% of edible oil were bought in the rural areas in recent years. See Deepak Ahluwalia, 1993, "Public Distribution of Food in India," in *Food Policy*, February. Also see D. S. Tyagi, 1990, *Managing India's Food Economy*, New Delhi and Newbury Park, CA: Sage Publications, pp. 36–9 and 86–98.

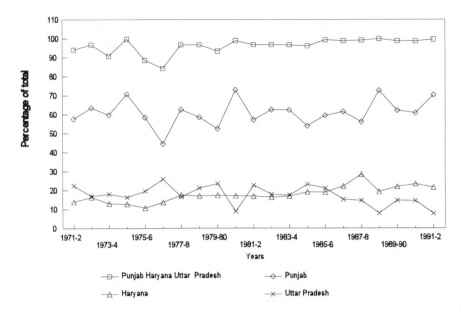

Figure 4.1. States' contribution to central pool (wheat, 1971–2 to 1991–2). *Source:* Ministry of Agriculture, Government of India.

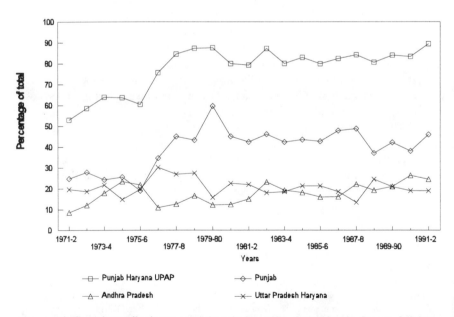

Figure 4.2. States' contribution to central pool (rice, 1971–2 to 1991–2). *Source:* Ministry of Agriculture, Government of India.

The states can be divided into surplus and deficit states. Surplus states are those which contribute more to the central pool than they take from it. Conversely, when offtakes exceed contributions, the situation is one of deficit. The surplus states typically ask for high producer prices: the higher the price, the greater the income of the surplus state. Contrariwise, deficit states in the past pressed for low prices: the lower the producer price, the lower the budgetary burden on a deficit state. Due to increasing agrarian mobilization since the early 1980s, however, even deficit states have started demanding high prices. This change has predictably led to an increasing budgetary burden on state governments, too.

In the main, there have been three wheat surplus states – Punjab, Haryana, and Uttar Pradesh – all located in North India.[6] There have been four rice surplus states, which include the South Indian state of Andhra Pradesh in addition to the above three.[7] Surplus states end up having a large voice in decision making, for on their contribution and cooperation depends the viability of the public distribution network. Figures 4.1 and 4.2 demonstrate the extent to which these four states have dominated the central surplus. Since 1971–2, Punjab, Haryana, and Uttar Pradesh have accounted for more than 90 percent of the total wheat procurement, Punjab itself contributing between 50 to 70 percent every year. In the case of rice, the three North Indian states and Andhra Pradesh contributed between 52 to 60 percent of the total rice procured between the early to mid-seventies. Their proportion has gone up to between 80–90 percent since the late 1970s (mostly due to the rise in Punjab's contribution). Punjab's overwhelming preponderance in the food economy is unmistakably clear.

After the considerations of the central ministries of Finance, Planning, and Food and Agriculture, and the state governments, the CACP may or may not change the price it originally recommended. The final decision is taken by the central cabinet. The cabinet has on several occasions fixed a price higher than the one recommended by the CACP. The price thus fixed *for the entire country* is the price at which the central procurement agency – the FCI – buys grains from the various purchasing centers in the country. State governments can pay a higher price to the producers for their own buying operations so long as they can fund such operations from the state budget. However, they must contribute quantities to the central pool in accordance with a pre-agreed target for which the central government would pay the central price, not the marked-up state price.

4.1.1 Where politics enters the policy process

Politics influences the government's decision making about agricultural prices at three levels. First, whether accepted or rejected, the CACP's recommendations

---

6 Madhya Pradesh is the other state that has sometimes produced a surplus.
7 Some major rice-producing states – Tamil Nadu, West Bengal and Bihar – have not been surplus producers. Their requirements, due to their population size and dietary patterns, have been higher than their production levels. Orissa and Madhya Pradesh, on the other hand, have in some years been rice surplus states.

constitute the benchmark for the final decision of the cabinet. In addition to the chairman, who is an economist, the Commission has 3 to 5 members. It matters whether the predominant view in the Commission is tilted more toward the intersectoral or intrasectoral view of prices: that is, whether most members think of the economywide implications of food prices, or of the implications of farm prices for food production. Who should be appointed to the CACP? What should the CACP's terms of reference be: should farmers' returns or the economywide implications of farm prices be the main concern of the CACP? Political and bureaucratic debate has often raged over these issues.

The Commission works on a cost-plus principle: producer price is equal to the cost of production plus some appropriate margin. The principles of cost determination are, therefore, a second area of political debate and struggle. In a country with regions and states at different levels of technological development, there is bound to be a large variation in costs across regions and, within the same region, across different farm sizes. In Punjab more than 90 percent of the area under foodgrains is irrigated, whereas in West Bengal only 25 percent is.[8] Since irrigation affects yields per acre – therefore, costs per unit of the output produced – one would expect costs to vary according to the extent of irrigated land. Similarly, small landholdings may not be able to achieve economies of scale. Biochemical inputs of the new technology are considered scale-neutral but mechanical inputs are not. Different farm sizes, therefore, would also have varying cost structures. Whose costs – regionwise, sizewise – should be considered while recommending price? Is there a technical way of resolving the problem? Is the technical solution, if any, also politically acceptable? These issues have surfaced repeatedly in political debates.

Third, there is the point at which the "technical" judgment of the CACP gives way to an open political process. The central government declares the final all-India price. It can provide a markup on the price recommended by the CACP. Since their cooperation is essential for a successful procurement of grains, the views of the surplus states must also be accommodated. If dissatisfied with the markup provided by the central government, state governments can, additionally, markup the price for their own purchases from the farmers and traders. Tables 4.1 and 4.2 provide evidence of how pervasive the state markups were until 1977.[9]

Thus, since the mid-1960s the politics of India's food-price policy has essentially taken two broad forms: (1) changing the way the benchmark institution – the CACP – functions by altering its composition and by attacking the guiding

8 Government of India, 1992, *Agricultural Statistics at a Glance*, Delhi: Ministry of Agriculture, p. 102.

9 For state purchases, until 1977–8, food credit was available from the Reserve Bank of India. Since state governments started paying higher producer prices regularly with huge overdrafts, the Reserve Bank canceled this facility. Since then, the incidence of markups by state governments has drastically declined. States now have to finance markups from their own current budgetary resources.

Table 4.1. *Mean excess percentage
of wheat procurement price fixed
by state governments over the price
recommended by the Agricultural
Prices Commission*

Average of eleven years (1966–7 to 1976–7)	
State	
Bihar	7
Gujarat	9
Haryana	9
Madhya Pradesh	4
Punjab	6
Rajasthan	8
Uttar Pradesh	8

Source: Raj Krishna and G. S. Raychowdhry,
1980, "Some Aspects of Wheat and Rice Price
Policy in India," *World Bank Staff Working Paper No. 381,* Washington, D.C., April, pp. 3–4.

Table 4.2. *Mean excess percentage
of rice procurement price fixed
by state governments over the price
recommended by the Agricultural
Prices Commission*

Average of twelve years (1964–5 to 1975–6)	
State	
Andhra Pradesh	3
Assam	8
Bihar	12
Haryana	4
Kerala	7
Madhya Pradesh	5
Maharashtra	3
Orissa	4
Punjab	5
Tamil Nadu	3
Uttar Pradesh	4
West Bengal	8

Source: Same as Table 4.1

principles of its decision making; and (2) over and above the benchmark, adding openly political markups whenever necessary or possible. There has been a tension between the two forms. If the second is pursued too far, it calls into question the very rationale for having an institution specializing in price policy: why should the government have an institution if its recommendations are never acceptable and markups are required on a regular basis? The government needs the technical expertise of an institution like the CACP. Therefore, of the two forms, the main focus of politics has been to change the functioning of the benchmark institution by politically redefining what guiding principles are legitimate, what considerations ought to enter into its decision making, and what its composition should be.

4.2 THE CHANGING FACE OF INDIAN POLITICIANS

State politics in India has always been dominated by rural politicians. The political leadership at the uppermost tiers of the polity, however, was primarily urban to begin with. Over time, the top tiers have also changed their character. Consider the occupational background of the lower house (Lok Sabha) of the Indian parliament since independence.[10] Table 4.3 gives a detailed breakdown of all occupational groups from the first to the eighth Lok Sabha. Figure 4.3 captures the time trend with respect to three key groups – agriculturists, lawyers, and businessmen (traders and industrialists).[11] An unambiguous rise in agrarian representation is evident.[12] It is generally accepted that, except for the primarily urban-based parties such as the Bhartiya Janata Party (BJP), the rise in agrarian representation has affected most political parties. The trend, of course, is more pronounced in the case of parties with an overwhelmingly agrarian base and program, such as the Lok Dal and its successor, the Janata Dal.

The changing social base of the highest echelons of the polity should indicate the emergence of a structural agrarian pressure on the Indian state. The structural pressure in the *polity*, however, did not automatically and instantly translate into

10 I have not considered the Upper House (Rajya Sabha) because of its relative unimportance in the power hierarchy in a parliamentary system.

11 In the figure I have not included the category political and social workers. This category was created in 1962, not at the time of first parliamentary elections in 1952. Because social work cannot provide sufficient income in India, it is generally reasoned that a number of these "social workers" had agricultural, urban rental or business income. More disaggregated data are not available.

12 It might be argued that many of the occupations listed in the table are mere derivatives. A number of lawyers, for example, come from an agricultural background and still derive some income from their agricultural lands. One might therefore say that so long as the total representation of lawyers and farmers remains roughly unchanged, as indeed it has in the Lok Sabha, there is no reason to believe that agrarian representation has increased. In response, it can be argued that the profession of lawyers itself has undergone considerable ruralization since independence. Thus, even if the combined percentage of the agriculturists and lawyers has remained the same, this mix is more rural now than in the 1950s.

Table 4.3. *Occupational backgrounds of the Lok Sabha, 1952–1989 (percent)*

Occupation (prior)	1952	1957	1962	1967	1971	1977	1980	1984	1989
Agriculturists	22.5	29.1	27.4	30.6	33.2	36.0	39.3	38.4	40.4
Social workers	—	—	18.7	22.9	19.0	20.0	17.2	19.0	17.0
Lawyers	35.6	30.5	24.5	17.5	20.5	23.4	22.2	18.0	15.6
Traders & Industrialists	12.0	10.2	10.3	7.5	6.8	3.3	6.3	7.3	4.4
Educationists	9.9	11.3	5.8	6.5	7.1	8.4	6.7	7.6	8.7
Writers & journalists	10.4	10.2	5.8	4.8	6.3	2.1	2.7	1.3	3.7
Doctors & engineers	4.9	3.5	3.9	4.2	2.9	2.8	3.0	5.2	—
Civil & military service	3.7	4.0	0.9	3.2	3.4	1.7	0.9	1.6	—
Ex-princes	1.1	1.4	2.1	1.4	0.4	0.6	0.2	1.1	—

Note: The 1991 break-up has not yet been released.
Source: Lok Sabha Secretariat, New Delhi.

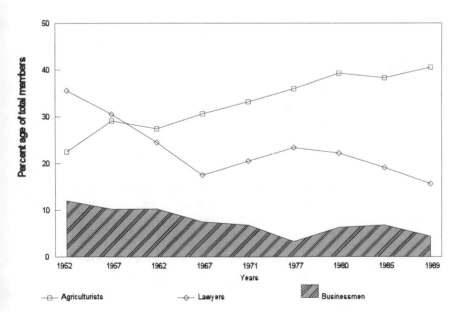

Figure 4.3. Occupational background of Lok Sabha (Lower House of Parliament). *Source:* Lok Sabha Secretariat, New Delhi.

a pressure on *policy*. The policy change came slowly. The three case studies presented below demonstrate the changing trend.

4.3 HOW THE POLITICIZATION OF PRICE POLICY BEGAN (1971–1973)

By 1970–1, India's food economy had emerged from the shadow of the mid-1960s. In the early sixties the average annual production was about 82 million tons, plummeting to 73 million tons during the two drought years of 1965–7. In 1970–1 India's food output stood at 108.4 million tons. Wheat imports from the United States dropped from a high of 10 million tons in 1965–6 to 2 million tons in 1970–1. Domestic procurement in the same period went up from 3.5 million tons to 8.1 million tons.

The government was buoyant. In the early 1970s, Mrs. Gandhi used to argue that the policy emphasis on growth and production had left the poor behind. However, when asked whether the green revolution had benefited only the rich farmers, she remarked: "The green revolution has resulted in increased foodgrain production, correspondingly larger availability of foodgrains for consumption and a certain measure of price stability which has been beneficial to all classes. The High Yielding Variety program is . . . being progressively extended to cover larger areas and a larger number of farmers."[13] Another indication of the new confidence was the government's decision to lift food zones for wheat in 1970–1. The aim of food zones had been to facilitate government procurement by bottling up grain in surplus areas, not allowing it to be transported to deficit areas except on public account. Times of plenty seemed to be in the offing, and no regulative coercion, at least for wheat, appeared necessary. The confidence, as it turned out, was rather premature, but, more important for our purposes here, this period also initiated a recurrent tussle between the politicians and technocrats on two issues: (1) what the appropriate level of producer prices should be; and (2) whether the institution setting the price, the APC, should have farmers' representatives to ensure fairness to the countryside.

For three successive years, 1970–1 to 1972–3, the APC,[14] under the widely respected leadership of Dharm Narain,[15] argued that rising wheat supplies called for a lowering of wheat procurement price. The Commission gave six arguments in favor of a *price reduction*. First, an imbalance was developing between demand and supply. The APC calculations showed that over the previous six years

13 *Lok Sabha Debates*, 4th ser., vol. 38, no. 23, March 25, 1970, p. 111.
14 In this section and the next, for consistency with the quotations from political debates, I shall drop the term CACP and use the original name of the commission, the Agricultural Prices Commission (APC). APC was the term used in debates throughout the decade.
15 Dharm Narain's work on food prices done at Cambridge University, had already become a classic: *The Impact of Price Movements on Areas Under Selected Crops in India, 1900–39*, Cambridge: Cambridge University Press, 1965. By the early seventies, he had firmly established his reputation as an applied agricultural economist.

wheat supply had grown at an annual rate of 14 percent. Demand had lagged far behind and, even under the most relaxed assumptions, it was not likely to grow at more than 5 percent annually. If prices were not lowered, said the APC, food-grain stocks would mount (which could not be exported due to low international prices).[16]

Second, the APC pointed to the emerging distortions in the intercrop balance, arguing that "the country not only needs wheat but also more oilseeds, cotton, sugarcane and pulses."[17] Rice, in particular, called for special attention, for which, the Commission argued, resources financing high wheat prices could be used.

Third, the procurement price was way above the cost of production. Data showed that in Punjab and Haryana in 1970–1 and in Western Uttar Pradesh in 1971–2, the cost of production of wheat was Rs 61.04, 48.1 and 49.7 per quintal, respectively,[18] whereas the procurement price had been kept at Rs 76 since 1968–9. A "moderate reduction," the APC argued, would still put the wheat procurement price above the cost of production.

Fourth, and this the APC found critical, the subsidy implications of keeping the wheat producer prices at the existing level were becoming unreasonable. Wheat was being procured at Rs 76 a quintal and issued out of government stocks at Rs 78. Costs of procuring, distributing, and carrying the stocks of grains were Rs 11, 7, and 8, respectively. The government loss on indigenous wheat was thus Rs 24 per quintal. If 5 million tons of wheat were to be distributed through the public network, the total subsidy, the APC calculated, would be a staggering Rs 120 crores (plus the carrying costs).[19]

The level of subsidy could be reduced if procurement prices were lowered or consumer (issue) prices increased. Issue prices, in the judgment of the APC, did not deserve to be increased: "There is an obvious oddity in the situation in which prices undergo a spurt in the face of increasing production and mounting stocks of the cereal. That the producers have benefitted from the wheat revolution is only as it should have been. But there must come a stage when the benefit starts percolating to the consumers, too."[20]

The APC gave two more arguments in its three-year-long advocacy of reducing wheat price. First, in recent years the trend in international prices of wheat had been downward, whereas in India the trend was just the opposite.[21] Second, since those who depended on the public distribution system were mostly low-

---

16 Government of India, 1972, *Report on Price Policy for Rabi Foodgrains for the 1972–73 Season*, Agricultural Prices Commission, March, p. 3. Hereafter, these reports will be cited giving year, season and page numbers, without other publication information.

17 Ibid.

18 Later reproduced in the *Rabi Report for 1973–74*, p. 2.

19 *Rabi Report for 1972–73*, p. 2.

20 Ibid., p. 3.

21 *Rabi Report for 1970–71*, pp. 9–10.

Table 4.4. *Wheat procurement price:*
The APC versus the government

Year	Price recommended by the APC	Price declared by the government
1969–70	Rs 76	Rs 76
1970–1	Rs 72	Rs 76
1971–2	Rs 74	Rs 76
1972–3	Rs 72	Rs 76

Source: Various APC Reports. I have chosen only two varieties here, which constitute the bulk of production: Mexican and indigenous (common white).

income consumers and those who sold grain to the government were mostly surplus farmers, "within the class of consumers the distribution of the burden of an increase in the issue price would be regressive in nature, whereas within the class of producers the distribution of the incidence of a reduction in procurement price would tend to be progressive."[22] Thus, on the ground of income distribution, reducing the procurement price made sense.

The APC's economic argument ran into serious political difficulties. For three years in a row, the government refused to lower the price. The state chief ministers did not agree with the APC. They, instead, believed that "such reduction would have acted as a disincentive to the farmer and would have adversely affected production in subsequent years."[23] Every year, the central government, in the light of this political reaction, turned down the recommendation of the APC. Table 4.4 shows the consistency with which the APC took its stand, and the equal consistency with which the final price was higher.

More ominous for the APC was the beginning of what became a relentless political attack on the Commission's capability and biases. Did the APC have agriculturist members or not? Raised countless times in the Lok Sabha in the next decade, this question first came up in 1972. A member of Parliament argued: "The Agriculture Minister has admitted in a press conference that there was no agriculturist on the Agricultural Prices Commission. Is this how we are going to provide relief to the farmer – by appointing a Commission which has no agriculturist? It is like appointing a cobbler to perform the function of a dentist."[24] The analogy drawn was not empty rhetoric. It anticipated the political sentiment

22 *Rabi Report for the 1971–72*, p. 8.
23 From the preface to the 1970–1 Rabi report, written by the Agriculture Secretary, Government of India. The same point was repeated in 1971–2 and 1972–3. Quoted again in Parliament, *Lok Sabha Debates*, 5th ser., vol. 13, no. 29, April 17, 1972, p. 31.
24 *Lok Sabha Debates*, 5th ser., vol. 13, no. 29, April 12, 1972, p. 141.

of later years: that agricultural policy could not be left to urban-trained agricultural technocrats. Irked by the insistence of the APC that the procurement price be lowered, and unpersuaded by the economic logic it presented, a demand to change the composition of the APC began to emerge in the upper tiers of the polity.

Two more enduring themes emerged in this period – that of the cost of production, and the relationship between industrial prices and agricultural prices. "Would the Agriculture Minister tell us," asked a member, "whether, while fixing the price, adequate attention is paid to maintaining some kind of parity between agricultural and industrial prices, and to the cost of production?"[25] The answer to the latter question was yes – except that the APC came increasingly to be disbelieved.

Scarcely debated in political circles until the late 1960s, the APC hereafter became a controversial institution. After 1971, food prices were politically debated every year; so was the APC. It is unclear what the Commission could have done to avoid this fate, except to remember that administered prices, once increased, cannot be easily lowered. Being an economic body, it made an appropriate economic argument under the leadership of a chairman with impeccable professional credentials. The economic body, however, was beginning to swim against an emerging political tide.

4.4 NATIONALIZATION OF FOODGRAINS TRADE AND ITS FAILURE (1973–1974)

By the late 1960s and early 1970s, with Mrs. Gandhi's leftward move in politics, the Marxist intellectuals were back in the economic decision making. They believed that industrialization required a transfer of resources from agriculture, that raising agricultural prices would slow down industrial progress, and that the Indian state had the capacity to tame the rural sector for "larger social purposes." In the end, however, the Indian state was tamed, not the peasantry. Nothing reflected this better than the nationalization of foodgrains trade in 1973–4. This major policy initiative was a watershed in the evolution of the state–countryside relationship. When the APC recommendations were rejected between 1971 and 1973, the power of the government was not at stake. The government, after all, had the authority to reject the APC's advice. Nationalization of grain trade was not a policy recommendation of an advisory body; it was a decision taken by the Indian state. Yet nationalization failed miserably, revealing the limits of state power.

Wholesale trade in grains has traditionally been in private hands in India. In February 1973, just before the wheat harvesting season, the central government banned private wholesalers and authorized the Food Corporation of India (FCI)

25 Ibid., April 17, 1972, p. 31.

to act as the sole purchasing agency in the market. Only private retailers were allowed to stay in business. Whether farmers should sell their produce at a fixed price only to public agencies or whether they could divide their sale between the public and private agents was no longer a matter of choice. They were required to sell wheat to the government at the administered price of Rs 76 per quintal. A target of 8.1 million tons was set for procurement.

In the event, the farmers sold only 5.1 million tons of wheat to the government. Within a few months, the government takeover of the wheat trade was lifted, private wholesale trade was restored, and the proposed nationalization of the rice trade was also dropped. Procurement price for rice was increased from Rs 56 per quintal to Rs 70. Subsequently, the procurement price of wheat for the next season was also increased by 40 percent – from Rs 76 to Rs 105 a quintal. This was the largest ever increase in a single year in the procurement price. It also amounted to an acceptance by the government of its defeat at the hands of the surplus producers.

Why was grain trade nationalized? Why did it fail? What lessons were drawn from the failure by the Indian government?

4.4.1 The political and economic context

As explained in the last chapter, there was a temporary eclipse in the power of the left-of-center faction in the Congress party after Nehru's death. With the land-slide victory of Mrs. Gandhi in the 1971 elections (in an alliance with the Communist party of India) on the slogan Abolish Poverty, the ideological and political landscape changed once again. Enjoying a revival, the left faction came to dominate key decision-making posts in the economic bureaucracy. By 1972, D. P. Dhar, with known left inclinations, headed the Planning Commission, and P. N. Haksar, similarly inclined, headed the Prime Minister's Secretariat.

Within a year after Mrs. Gandhi's election victory in March 1971, delibera-tions on the Fifth Five-Year Plan (1974–9) began.[26] Three interventions in the rural sector were envisaged: a renewed commitment to land reforms, renewed proposals for a state takeover in trading in foodgrains, and a substantial govern-ment loan program for small farmers, marginal farmers, agricultural laborers, and artisans.

The main thrust of the poverty alleviation strategy took the form of new credit-based programs for the poor. The plan finally prepared in 1973 calculated that if the desired levels of expenditures on poverty programs were to be made while maintaining a GNP growth rate of 5 percent, investment outlays of Rs 31,400 crores over the plan period would be required. Adding this to the expected current expenses and estimating the likely domestic revenues and foreign aid, the Commission found a resource gap of Rs 6,850 crores, a gap that had to be met or reduced through mobilization of resources.

26 In May 1972, the Planning Commission released its approach paper to the Fifth Plan, titled "Towards Self-Reliance, Approach to the Fifth Five-Year Plan."

Additional taxation seemed to be a solution for the resource gap. By the early seventies, indirect taxes had come to constitute about 80 percent of total tax revenue, with direct taxes accounting for a mere 20 percent. Rural incomes had remained virtually untaxed since independence. Agricultural income accounted for 45 percent of the national income at the end of the Fourth Plan, but direct agricultural taxes contributed a mere 1 percent to the total tax revenue. The K. N. Raj Committee, constituted by the Planning Commission to look into the problem, recommended an agricultural income tax, but no state government accepted the proposal. The planners met with a political defeat. Land reforms were also defeated. The state governments adopted a time-tested strategy: accepting the proposals of the central government but doing little by way of implementation.

The fate of the grain-trade nationalization was, however, still in balance. It was argued that nationalization would eliminate the middleman and bring about price stability. It would also establish public control over agrarian surplus, deemed necessary for industrialization.[27] On these arguments, the Planning Commission could not win the approval of its political masters. It took an emerging economic crisis to swing the scales in its favor.

A return of the monsoon vagaries provided the setting for a potential economic crisis. After consistently climbing for five years and reaching a peak of 26.4 million tons in 1971–2, wheat production declined to 24.7 million tons in 1972–3 (dropping further to 21.7 million tons the next year). Foodgrain output as a whole declined by considerable margin – at 97 million tons, it was down 7 percent from 105.2 million tons in 1971–2. Such agricultural fluctuations were not unusual in India. The steady progress in the late sixties had simply changed the climate of expectations.

Politically speaking, these fluctuations in output were not so disturbing as the impact of lower output on public stocks and food prices. In July 1972, government stocks of grain stood at 9.6 million tons. After a failed *kharif* (monsoon) crop, stocks had dwindled to 3 million tons by January 1973.[28] Lower procurement, higher offtake from the public distribution system (since food prices in the "open market" had increased), and low planned imports[29] accounted for the reduction in stocks.

Moreover, between January 1972 and January 1973, foodgrain prices increased 20 percent.[30] By February 1973, it was becoming clear that a smaller wheat crop would push up the prices even more. (As it turned out, food prices did increase by 29 percent in 1973–4.) Ever faithful to food prices, the wholesale

---

27 Author's interview with Sukhamoy Chakravarty (then Member, Planning Commission), Delhi, August 12, 1984.
28 *Economic and Political Weekly*, January 20, 1973, p. 96.
29 India's agricultural turnaround, India's decision makers thought, had made imports unnecessary. As against 2.05 million tons of grain imports in 1971–2, less than half a million tons was imported in 1972–3. Cf. *Rabi Report for 1975–76*, Table 7, p. 25.
30 Wolf Ladejinsky, "The Rural Scene," in The World Bank, 1974, *The Economic Situation and Prospects of India*, p. 103.

price index for the fiscal year 1972–3 was 13–15 percent higher than in 1971–2, with possibilities of further increases if food prices were not controlled. (The wholesale price index rose by 30 percent in 1973–4.) In a Latin American scenario, this rate of inflation would hardly have been a matter of concern. But in a country of a low-inflation threshold, where the only other example of double-digit inflation over the last decade had been in 1965–6 (15.6 percent), which was a year of acute drought and political turbulence, a repetition of the mid-sixties caused considerable nervousness in government circles.[31]

At this point, the old rivalry between the Planning and Finance ministries, on the one hand, and the Agriculture Ministry, on the other, flared up again. Over the objections of the Agriculture Ministry, Planning and Finance managed to push the proposal about nationalization of grain trade, a proposal contained in the original Fifth Plan approach paper but dormant since then.[32]

4.4.2 The taming of the Indian state

On February 26, 1973, the Food and Agriculture minister announced the government takeover of wholesale trade in wheat. The aim was "to eliminate speculation and the distortions in price," to maintain "assured availability to consumers . . . at reasonable prices," and to bring about "economy in the costs of wholesale trading by elimination of unnecessary intermediaries. . . ."[33] Private agents in retail trade were allowed to operate: first, because the government was not expected to cover all towns, particularly the small ones; and second, because retailers did not have the financial capacity to buy large quantities and affect prices. By virtue of their financial strength and market power, the wholesalers were "the manipulators and creators of runaway prices": they could not be allowed to operate in a situation of scarcity. The state chief ministers, never enthusiastic about a state takeover of the grain trade, had to accept the proposal of the central government. The stamp of the Prime Minister's approval, coupled with their own abject dependence on her, eroded their traditional opposition to grain-trade nationalization.[34] They also accepted the procurement price set at the

---

31 The Finance Ministry's concern was publicly expressed at the time of budget presentation to Parliament on February 28. Y. B. Chavan, the Finance Minister, referred to "the abnormal increase in prices" during 1972–3 as one of the most pressing problems to be given the highest priority. (See *Economic and Political Weekly*, March 10, 1973, p. 539.) In his budget speech a year earlier, Chavan had drawn attention to the increasing food subsidy, too.

32 *Economic and Political Weekly* (March 3, 1973, p. 465) reported that the decision was essentially taken by the Planning Minister, D. P. Dhar, with the support of Mrs. Gandhi. This was confirmed during the course of my interviews. It was also revealed that the APC and its chairman, Dharm Narain, were completely bypassed. Dharm Narain, though against increasing prices, was never in favor of nationalization of trade.

33 Statement in Lok Sabha by Fakhruddin Ali Ahmed, the Minister of Agriculture, *Lok Sabha Debates*, 5th ser., vol. 23, February 26, 1973, p. 250.

34 After the 1972 state assembly elections, Mrs. Gandhi initiated the new practice of *nominating*

level of the preceding year, even though foodgrain prices in the open market had increased substantially. Finally, a procurement target of 8.1 million tons was accepted as against 5.1 million tons procured a year back.[35]

The administrative machinery was tightened. Outlawed wholesalers were raided and many arrested on grounds of illegal trading.[36] Employees of the Food Corporation of India, the procuring institution, were also arrested for indulging in "malpractices," a term used for aiding illegal traders in mopping up the marketed surplus.[37] Despite such tightening, little wheat came to the public agencies. A black market flourished, where a quintal of wheat fetched Rs 120–50 whereas the government was paying only Rs 76. Some coercion was used against farmers but, in response, opposition parties started mobilizing farmers against nationalization. Somewhat rattled by now, the central government and Congress party made it publicly known that nationalization was not against farmers but against traders. The Congress Working Committee, meeting two months after the takeover, passed a resolution castigating wholesale traders for their lack of social and national sensitivity and stating that, by eliminating the middleman and his margin, the takeover in fact was aimed at making a better price available to the farmer.[38]

Wheat arrivals, however, did not pick up. Supplies from the public distribution system had to be reduced because stocks were plummeting. By early May, food riots were reported in the towns of Maharashtra, including cases where mobs "attacked the houses of the local District Congress Committee president and another party notable . . . demanding food mainly."[39] Food riots were also reported in Madhya Pradesh and Gujarat.[40] And political turbulence began in the states of Bihar, Kerala, and West Bengal due to food shortages.[41]

By the middle of June, the central government was so desperate that, instead of applying further coercion, it developed an incentive scheme to increase procurement. According to the scheme, states that fulfilled 25 percent of the target initially set for them would receive a bonus of Rs 4 per quintal; those fulfilling between 25 to 50 percent would get Rs 5 per quintal; those that succeeded in

---

chief ministers of her choice as opposed to having the state-level party organizations elect them, which was the practice under Nehru. Most of the new state chiefs owed their positions to her, not to their own bases in their respective states. With Mrs. Gandhi strongly supporting nationalization, these chief ministers presumably had no choice but to accept the proposal. Thus, a new political trend also produced an economic policy initiative. Nehru also had always wanted to nationalize grain trade, but he was always forced back by the state bosses.

35 The calculation was as follows. A 25 to 30 million ton crop was expected. Assuming that the marketed surplus was 30–35 percent of the output, 8.1 million tons seemed to be in the range of possibility.

36 Agriculture Minister in Parliament. *Lok Sabha Debates*, 5th ser., vol. 29, July 30, 1973, p. 133.

37 Ibid., vol. 23, November 26, 1973, p. 39.

38 *Economic and Political Weekly*, April 28, 1973, p. 781.

39 Ibid., May 5, 1973, p. 815.

40 *Lok Sabha Debates*, 5th ser., vol. 31, August 31, 1973, pp. 222–5.

41 Ibid., vol. 27, July 29, 1974, p. 307.

procuring 50 to 75 percent would receive Rs 7 per quintal; and those fully meeting their quota, Rs 10 per quintal.[42]

In the end, despite using both carrots and sticks, the government could procure only 5.1 millon tons against a target of 8.1 million tons. Possibilities of food aid as well as imports were frantically explored outside the country,[43] but the world supply situation had drastically changed by 1973 and grain prices were very high.

In early July, a decision on rice trade was expected. The Congress Working Committee postponed the decision. Finally, in September, after consultation with the state chief ministers, the idea of nationalizing rice wholesale trade was dropped. States were left "free to adopt a system of procurement best suited to prevailing local conditions."[44] Only three states, Assam, Maharashtra, and Orissa decided to keep the government monopoly intact.[45] Asked why rice trade was not taken over, the Agriculture Ministry stated in Parliament: "when we think of implementing and administering the food economy, naturally, as a responsible government, as a responsible party, as a Ministry which has to administer day to day problems, we have to be practical."[46] As a further measure of pragmatism, the government increased the procurement price for paddy from Rs 56 to Rs 70.

Causes of failure. Why didn't farmers sell enough surplus to the government?[47] As noted, the difference between the government price and the black market price was critical. Procured grain came mostly from those "with no staying power and compelled to sell early in the season."[48] The black market price was one and a half to two times higher than the government price. There was enough room for deals between the surplus producers and the legally nonexistent but actually operating wholesalers. Moreover, such deals were aided and abetted by the official machinery at the ground level. The potential "rents" from allowing illegal trading were large enough to have enticed a number of ground officials to ignore their official duties. To make matters worse, the state- and district-level politicians – some farmers themselves – also appeared to have aided farmers, wholesalers, and defaulting officials.[49] A subterfuge from within the state and a

42 *Economic and Political Weekly*, June 23, 1973, p. 1097.
43 Ibid., June 16, 1973, p. 1050, and June 30, 1987, p. 1137.
44 *Lok Sabha Debates*, 5th ser., vol. 33, November 26, 1973, p. 32.
45 Ibid., pp. 32 and 206.
46 *Lok Sabha Debates*, 5th ser., vol. 32, November 23, 1973, p. 355.
47 I shall not separately discuss the role of traders but essentially concentrate on the role of surplus producers. The power of grain traders in the Indian polity is much smaller than that of the surplus farmers. Viewed as venal profiteers, traders enjoy virtually no legitimacy in the Indian political system, whereas farmers do. As a consequence, no political party except the BJP, with a strong base in the trading community, supports the cause of traders.
48 Ladejinsky, "The Rural Scene," p. 107.
49 "It is freely admitted," reported the *Economic and Political Weekly* (July 14, 1973, p. 1180) "by ruling party leaders that not many Congress rich farmers . . . have sold their crop to the government agencies at the fixed procurement price."

collusion between state officials, surplus producers, and traders defeated nationalization. Wolf Ladejinsky summed up the reasons as follows:

Nationalization necessitated a strong dosage of effective coercion but of this there was little. Farmers sold or did not as suited them; wholesalers didn't sit idle; retailers indulged consumer-hoarders; and smugglers had a field day. Monopoly procurement couldn't help but fall short of the target, and half a success was no success, not when every ton counted. And so it came about that the twin policy of the wheat takeover . . . and immobilization of customary wholesale trade channels caused a large quantity of wheat to disappear underground and find its way into the thriving black market. The consequences were all too obvious: millions who depended on the distribution system for their food had to do with their short rations and not infrequently the fair price shops had no ration to dispense.[50]

4.4.3 Consequences and lessons of failure

The government, predictably, came under a great deal of fire. Political attacks on the government continued throughout 1973–4. Opposition parties saw a unique political opportunity in the government's failure. Two years after Mrs. Gandhi's landslide victory, the government, unable to provide enough food to the fair-price shops and control food-price inflation, was becoming immobilized. By March 1974, when the next wheat procurement season started, food prices had increased by 30 percent within a year, the largest ever increase in food prices after independence.

The Agriculture Ministry faced questions and criticisms throughout 1973–4. Finally, Planning Minister D. P. Dhar, the chief architect of the wheat-trade takeover, was asked to face the Lok Sabha. Dhar, in a major speech, presented development theory as political rhetoric:

If we look at investments which we have made in agriculture, we find that there has been a unidirectional flow of resources into agriculture without our making any savings from agriculture for investment. And the essence of growth is the capacity to save. . . . Isn't it time when we should consider the question of taking such measures which would make resources and savings available for investment from the agricultural sector. . . ?

. . . The investments made in the agriculture sector through rural electrification programs, for energization of wells and other lift irrigation systems are almost all running at a loss. . . . Irrigation rates in most parts of the country are so fantastically low that even today we are paying a total sum of about Rs 170 crores a year as a loss only on the maintenance of irrigation systems. . . .

The agriculture sector is a highly subsidized sector. . . . Some segments of our agrarian population have received enormous benefits from the enormous investments which have been made in this sector and the community as a whole would ask them to part with a part of the debt so that we could invest it for Plan development purposes. . . .

You must not forget the class that has benefitted. We are afraid of touching that class and we must touch that class. I can not understand the logic of leaving 3 percent of agricultural population alone to wallow in opulence at the cost of the community. . . .

Agreeing that a lesson had been learned, he also explained why nationalization had been given up:

50 Ladejinsky, "The Rural Scene," p. 108.

The Government has been accused of surrendering to vested interests. It's a wrong inter-
pretation. The simple point is that the takeover of wholesale trade was not an end in itself.
We believed that it would be a good instrument for supporting the public distribution
system and for building adequate reserves. . . . But the question has to be worked out in
relation to the objectives of food policy. . . . After careful consideration, . . . we feel that
it would be more helpful to rely on the traditional market mechanism for acquiring the
needed quantities of foodgrains. . . .[51]

This was the last *public* speech given by a cabinet minister, or a major political
leader, in India in favor of extracting surpluses from agriculture for financing
development. After Dhar, no politician had the courage to argue that industrialization required a transfer of resources from agriculture. Dhar's was the last
openly political defense of an economic postulate.

The notion that the power of the state could be used to tame the dominant class
in the countryside was set to rest after 1974. In the event, its epitaph was written
by the Prime Minister herself. In May 1974, about the same time as Dhar made
the Lok Sabha speech, the Planning Commission met to discuss mobilization of
resources for the Fifth Plan (1974–9). It recommended agricultural income tax as
the best way to generate resources and finance the plan. Mrs. Gandhi "told the
planners unequivocally that there was no question of taxing agriculture, adding
that none of the experts in the Planning Commission and in the government . . .
seemed to her to have a realistic appreciation of the political factors and constraints applicable to these matters. Agriculture could not be taxed for political
reasons and so alternative ways of financing the plan had to be found."[52]

As for pricing, the wheat procurement price in the 1974–5 season was increased from Rs 76 to Rs 105 per quintal. The APC recommended a procurement
price of Rs 95 per quintal, which the government raised to Rs 105,[53] the largest
increase allowed in a single year in the procurement price up to then. This
decision had implications beyond 1974–5. The base for subsequent procurement
price decisions was raised within a year by 40 percent. The APC, thereafter,
could not go below this base, irrespective of the size of the crop. As it turned out,
the 1974–5 crop was bad but the next two years had good crops. What was a
procurement price of Rs 105 for a bad year became the support price for the
bumper years as well.

Also, throughout 1973–5, the Lok Sabha reverberated with the demand to include
agriculturists on the APC. Mrs. Gandhi complied with the demand in late 1975.
Chowdhry Randhir Singh, a Congress M.P. and an agriculturist, was appointed to the
four-member Commission. He took charge in April 1976. Throughout his tenure, he
disagreed with the professionals in the APC and wrote a note of dissent every year
against the majority recommendation of the Commission, asking a higher price. On
his own admission, he could influence the functioning of the APC, but lacking a

51 *Lok Sabha Debates*, 5th ser., vol. 50, May 10, 1974, excerpted from pp. 386–411.
52 *Economic and Political Weekly*, May 25, 1974.
53 *Lok Sabha Debates*, 5th ser., vol. 38, April 8, 1974, p. 56.

majority, he could not do so nearly as much as he would have liked to.[54] Soon, politicians in Parliament started demanding that the APC be chaired by an agriculturist and also have a majority of farmers, not of professionals. This demand was not met in the 1970s. A critical mass of decision-making elites, whatever their political rhetoric, remained wary of politicizing a technical body to such an extent. However, a stronger political push arrived soon, though in a different form.

4.5 THE RISE AND FALL OF THE JANATA PARTY AND THE TRAJECTORY OF AGRARIAN POWER (1977–1980)

Mrs. Gandhi's defeat in the 1977 parliamentary elections brought the Janata party to power, which formed the first non-Congress government in New Delhi. Although called a party, the Janata was essentially a coalition of several existing parties.[55] Bhartiya Lok Dal (BLD), a party with a powerful following among the peasant castes of North India, was one of the key constituents of Janata. An undisputed leader of the BLD and a powerful peasant leader, Chowdhry Charan Singh became a central figure in the Janata party. Over the next three years, Charan Singh presided over some of the most important ministries: Home, Finance, and, upon the death of the Janata coalition in mid-1979, he became the prime minister of the country, though only for a few months.[56]

With Charan Singh and the BLD in power, a rural voice directly entered the highest strata of decision making. Until then, only the relatively less powerful ministries – for example, Agriculture – had represented rural interests in any direct sense. Whether the issue was preempting agricultural income tax or defeating nationalization of the grain trade, it was rural control over state governments which led to these pro-rural outcomes; for none of these policies could be implemented without the cooperation of state governments.

The Janata, like the Congress party, was an umbrella party whose range extended from the left-of-center socialists to the right-of-center Jan Sangh. Compared to the Congress party, all constituents of Janata had a less heavy-industry, more pro-agriculture ideology. But the extent to which agriculture could be promoted was a matter of some dispute. Thus, despite a consensus on giving greater weight to agriculture in economic policy, differences over the precise contours of agricultural policy emerged: what level of agricultural prices could be considered remunerative; how to restructure the APC; to what extent public resources should be used to subsidize agricultural inputs; which inputs ought

54 Interview, Chowdhry Randhir Singh, Delhi, January 23, 1985.
55 The coalition was hastily put together in response to Mrs. Gandhi's surprising call for elections after a year and a half of emergency during which she had suspended the democratic process and jailed most of the opposition leaders.
56 The electorate returned Mrs. Gandhi to power in 1980. For a description of the squabbles leading to the demise of Janata, see Myron Weiner, 1983, *India at the Polls, 1980*, Washington and London: American Enterprise Institute for Public Policy Research.

to be subsidized, and by how much. Public policy also became heavily entangled in a fierce power struggle between the various constituents and leaders of Janata, each trying to consolidate their hold over the fledgling party and government.

4.5.1 Chowdhry Charan Singh: An agrarian ideologue in power

The ideology of the BLD and the political strategy employed by its leader, Charan Singh, had a significant impact on policy struggles. In order to fortify his own position and that of his party in the Janata coalition, Charan Singh used the method of mobilizing thousands of peasants for rallies to demonstrate his mass support. As a result, agrarian policy moved beyond the cloistered confines of interbureaucratic struggles: it now had to respond to the visibility of rural inter- ests on the streets. Most political parties and the powerful metropolitan media had to begin to come to terms with this new force.

There were two sides to Charan Singh's politics: an ideological side that remained reasonably consistent throughout his public career since 1937, and a strategic side, which changed depending upon the exigencies of the situation. Venerated in rural Uttar Pradesh for his ideological consistency, he was equally disliked in urban North India for his strategic shifts.[57] A combination of the two, however, did make Charan Singh a formidable political force.

Charan Singh's ideology. Charan Singh's ideology was built upon a strong op- position to heavy industry and a stout defense of peasant proprietorship in agri- culture.[58] The heavy-industry bias of Nehru's development model was, accord-

---

57 Charan Singh's political career can be summarized as follows. Born in a Jat (peasant caste) family of Western Uttar Pradesh, he joined the Congress party in the 1930s. Despite disagreeing with the policies of the Congress party, he remained in it for as long as the party was strong (1937–1967). He was a minister in the State of Uttar Pradesh from 1951–67. After the first post-Nehru elections in 1967, when the Congress party failed to win a majority of seats in the state legislative assembly, he left the party. Winning the support of the opposition parties, he became the state chief minister for a brief while. Later, he formed a new party, Bhartiya Kranti Dal (BKD), which became the second largest party in Uttar Pradesh after the 1969 elections. Once again he became the chief minister, but his government fell before long. In 1975, during the emergency, he was jailed with other opposition leaders by Mrs. Gandhi. In 1977, after the emergency, he moved from state politics to national politics.

58 Charan Singh spelled out his views in detail in his various works. The best known are: *Abolition of Zamindari: Two Alternatives*, Allahabad: Kitabistan, 1947; *Joint Farming X-Rayed: The Prob- lem and Its Solutions*, Allahabad: Kitabistan, 1959; *India's Economic Policy: The Gandhian Blueprint*, New Delhi: Vikas Publishing House, 1978; and *The Economic Nightmare of India: Its Cause and Cure*, Delhi: National Publishing House, 1981. A critical survey of his worldview has been provided by Terence Byres, 1988, "Charan Singh (1902–87): An Assessment," *The Journal of Peasant Studies*, vol. 15, no. 2, (January), pp. 139–89. For Charan Singh's struggles within the Congress party in the 1950s and 1960s, see Paul Brass, 1984, "Division in the Congress and the Rise of Agrarian Interests and Issues in Uttar Pradesh, 1952 to 1977," in his *Caste, Faction and Party in Indian Politics*, vol. 1, Delhi: Chanakya Publications.

ing to him, wrong because it was capital-intensive, whereas India's high population density and its consequent need for massive employment required small-scale industry and low-capital intensity. He was against industrialization based on transfer of resources from agriculture; rather, an agricultural revolution was a necessary precondition for sound industrialization. Singh defined "agricultural revolution" as a technological revolution that would increase production per acre in a system based on peasant proprietorship – a system based on family farms having a size between 2.5 and 27.5 acres. Peasant proprietorship was necessary because "a peasant owner has been known to work harder and for longer hours than a tenant or a wage laborer,"[59] something collectivization or farm cooperatives could never achieve. The farm size should be between 2.5 to 27.5 acres, because, according to him, evidence and experience suggested that farms larger than 27.5 acres were inversely related to productivity and those smaller than 2.5 were not viable. By technology that would revolutionize agriculture, he meant "better farming practices in general," in which he did not include large-scale machinery such as tractors, which, like large machinery in industry, were labor-displacing. He was also initially against chemical fertilizers but changed his position in the 1970s.[60]

Charan Singh's main criticism of the Congress model of development was that it neglected villages and was excessively industry- and city-biased. How did this anti-rural model survive in a predominantly agrarian society? "Political power," he argued, "lies in the hands of urbanites to whom urban interests naturally come first."[61] "To the town dweller," he added, "the farmer was a mere grist in the mill of economic progress on whose bones the structure of heavy industry was to be reared."[62] Charan Singh's mission was to put rural India securely on the power map.

Factional struggles in the Janata party and agricultural policy. Charan Singh's party accepted this ideological vision, but so long as the party was important only at the state level, the question of changing the country's economic policy and resource allocation between agriculture and industry did not arise. After 1977, with Charan Singh's party in power in Delhi, an opportunity presented itself. Charan Singh's first victory came when the program of the Janata party was formulated: "The relative neglect of the rural sector has created a dangerous imbalance in the economy. The farmer has been consistently denied reasonable

59 Singh, *Abolition of Zamindari*, p. 132.
60 The hostility to chemical fertilizers expressed in *Joint Farming* is considerably diluted in *India's Economic Policy.*
61 Singh, *The Economic Nightmare*, p. 208. This view is identical to Michael Lipton's famous urban-bias argument. Although the quotation I have cited is from 1981, Charan Singh had been writing about urban bias in Indian development since the mid-1950s, almost a decade before the idea was first developed by Michael Lipton.
62 Singh, *The Economic Nightmare*, p. 205.

and fair prices for what he produces. Allocations for agriculture and related development have been grossly inadequate and the need for improving conditions in the villages has received scarce attention."[63] A new idea about agricultural prices in the Indian context – "parity prices" between agriculture and industry – was also explicitly incorporated in the party manifesto: "The farmer must get remunerative prices based on the principle of parity that balances the prices at which he sells his produce and the price he pays for the goods he buys. If the rural sector is to grow and flourish, it must be accorded favorable terms of trade as a matter of overall national policy."[64]

Whether these two propositions – change in investment patterns in favor of agriculture and paying "parity prices" to farmers – could be realized depended upon how far the other constituents of the Janata party were willing to go with Charan Singh. He believed that his party was the main reason for Janata's rise to power, and therefore he should have a suitably powerful role, both in government and in the affairs of the Janata party. The other main constituents of Janata – the Congress faction, led by Prime Minister Morarji Desai, and the Jan Sangh – were unwilling to concede primacy to the BLD and Charan Singh.[65]

Swings in personal political fortunes were the first expression of this struggle. After a year in government, Charan Singh, India's Home Minister,[66] was sacked by Prime Minister Morarji Desai on the ground of indiscipline. Not so easily tamed, and to demonstrate his strength, Charan Singh organized a landmark peasant rally in December 1978.[67] An estimated one million peasants – mostly from North India but from other parts of the country as well – came to Delhi. A 20-point charter of peasant demands was framed and the Janata government was stridently criticized for its betrayal of farmers. The principal demands included: greater representation of farmers on the APC and on all other government bodies dealing with rural areas; parity prices between agriculture and industry; larger subsidies for fertilizers, irrigation, electricity, and other inputs; and an aggressive governmental search for foreign markets for agricultural exports.[68]

---

63 The Janata party, *Election Manifesto 1977*, Delhi, p. 12.

64 Ibid.

65 Plan investment in the agricultural sector did go up from 22 percent of the total investment in the Fifth Plan under Mrs. Gandhi to 26 percent under Janata, but that was not a big victory for Charan Singh. All constituents of Janata wanted to allocate more resources to agriculture. Even the Congress faction (O), traditionally inclined toward big industry, had shifted its position after it became a constituent of the Janata party.

66 Home is typically considered to be the second or third most powerful ministry, along with Finance and External Affairs.

67 Singh's supporters had organized a similar peasant rally on his birthday a year before, when he held the Home portfolio. However, it was not as massively attended. Now out of government, Singh had to make a stronger point. His political strategy during 1977–80 seems to have been to consolidate his personal position, as well as that of his party, through periodic demonstrations of mass support. No Janata leader could match him in this act.

68 For details, see Marcus Franda, 1980, "An Indian Farm Lobby: The Kisan Sammelan," *American Universities Field Staff Reports*, Washington, D.C.

The massive success of the peasant rally,[69] had a twofold effect. Its first impact was on the metropolitan media and its vast national network. News about the emerging peasant ferment had hitherto been confined to local and regional newspapers, or to insignificant spaces in the national newspapers. The metropolitan media was now face-to-face with a new reality. "Peasant power" made the headlines and entered the editorial rooms. Typical of the urban response was the editorial in the *Hindustan Times*, according to which a peasant organization, "speaking exclusively for the rural areas and articulating a set of comprehensive demands . . . has every chance of becoming a major political force, bringing on the national scene a distinct political culture which may not always be in tune with modernity."[70]

The second effect of the rally was Charan Singh's restoration to power. Within a month of the rally, Singh was brought back into the government, this time with an enhanced status. Called Senior Deputy Prime Minister, he was also given charge of the Finance Ministry. He quickly proceeded to make a budget for the country that "had the breath of the people and the smell of the soil."[71] Singh reduced the various indirect taxes on chemical fertilizers (by as much as 50 percent), mechanical tillers, diesel for electric water pumps; lowered interest rates for rural loans; increased subsidy of minor irrigation; and earmarked funds for rural electrification and grain-storage facilities. Hardly concerned about the outcry in the media that it was a "kulak budget," he had made his political point.

4.5.2 Struggle over parity prices: Technocrats over politicians?

The Janata party had promised "parity prices" in its election manifesto. The notion of parity price requires some explanation. Parity can have two meanings: parity between input and output prices; and parity between the prices of goods sold by the agriculture sector and the prices of those it buys. The second notion is more inclusive. The first notion means that adjustment in output prices would be made in accordance with changes in input prices so as to protect some acceptable level of return from farming. The second notion not only includes inputs but also the goods bought by the rural sector, including consumption goods. It therefore implies that agricultural prices would be fixed according to the costs of rural living, not simply the input costs of farming. The Janata manifesto meant parity in this second sense.

The proposal for parity prices was therefore aimed at converting the *price*

---

69 "For two days, the traffic in and around Delhi was completely disrupted, as rows and rows of tractors, trucks, buses, and bullock carts poured into the city. Most of the Ring Road, the beltway that surrounds New Delhi, was used as a parking lot on the day before and during the rally. The largest open spaces in the city – the Red Fort grounds, the Ferozeshah Kotla grounds – all became kisan grounds for the two days." Franda, ibid., p. 23.

70 *The Hindustan Times*, December 25, 1978. Subsequently, such editorials became a normal fare.

71 Ping Ho Kwon, 1979, "Singh Takes the First Step to Capitalism," *Far Eastern Economic Review*, March 23, p. 76.

policy into an *incomes* policy. Rural incomes would be protected irrespective of what happened to the supply and demand of agricultural products, or to relative technical changes in agriculture and industry. In principle, an excess of supply over demand or cost reduction via technical change should bring prices down. By focusing exclusively on incomes, however, parity prices would prevent this from occurring. A policy like this would have been a great boost to the countryside – in the short and medium run. But it required a change in the terms of reference of the APC. The original terms of the APC defined producer incentives primarily with respect to input costs, not living costs.

The Agriculture Ministry drafted the revised terms aimed at parity but faced opposition from other ministries.[72] In particular, economists in the Planning Commission, as well as the then APC chairman, opposed the proposal on technical grounds.[73] Their argument is worth quoting at length:

The parity approach was perhaps relevant in a chronic surplus situation which prevailed in the United States in the inter-war period. In that situation the main objective was to support the real farm income at some level. In Indian conditions, the main justification for an agricultural price policy is either to stimulate production growth or to induce desirable changes in the crop-mix. The Indian policy is correctly based on the assumption of a continuing long-term excess demand situation (interspersed with short-run surpluses of particular crops). The present . . . policy of covering the full cost . . . in the procurement price is an appropriate one. . . . Such full cost pricing automatically escalates the procurement price when input prices go up. Therefore, the *input price* part of "prices paid by farmers" is already fully covered by the present policy. So far as the other part of "prices paid by farmers," namely, the *cost of consumption goods*, is concerned, there is very poor justification for linking the procurement price to it in Indian conditions. . . . The farmer deserves no more protection than other classes in society. . . . Protection against price increases in consumer prices is deserved the most by the rural and urban poor in the unorganised sectors. But for such protection the right method is not . . . escalation of the procurement price but . . .extension of a rational public distribution system to cover the bulk of the poor – farmers and non-farmers – in the unorganised sectors.[74]

Further, the parity price formula was undesirable because: "if mechanically followed, it would have the effect of freezing price relationships as they obtained in the past and, by disregarding the changing realities of demand and supply, it would have the effect of obstructing the optimal allocation of productive resources."[75]

In short, then, the economists made three generic arguments against a revision

---

72 Bhanu Pratap Singh, then Minister of State for Agriculture and an important member of Charan Singh's party, had drafted the proposal. S. S. Barnala, Agriculture Minister at the time, fully supported it.

73 The late Professor Raj Krishna, then a member of the Planning Commission, along with Dharm Narain, who was still the chairman of the APC, led the counterattack.

74 Memorandum from the Planning Commission to the Ministry of Agriculture, April 23, 1979. I am thankful to the late Raj Krishna for making this memo available to me before his death and for permitting me to quote it. I should add that it was not a confidential memo.

75 From the Summary of Discussion held under the chairmanship of Dr. Raj Krishna, Planning Commission, "On Parity Approach for the Fixation of Agricultural Prices," April 3, 1978.

in the terms of reference of the APC: (1) input–output price ratios were already covered in the existing terms, guaranteeing returns over input costs; (2) in India, price policy could not be used as an incomes policy for which other instruments were more appropriate; and (3) a parity price formula, by freezing price relationships, went against the principle of supply and demand (resources would continue to be invested in sectors where it was profitable to invest them *now*, no matter what happened to the demand for the products of that sector *in future*).[76] Ultimately, the economists' argument did triumph. The terms of reference of the APC remained unchanged during the Janata rule.

In some circles of India's economic bureaucracy, the parity price case has come to be known as one where the technocrats defeated the politicians in the struggle for economic policy. This judgment seems somewhat overstretched. Although it is certainly true that the case against parity prices was forcefully argued by some leading and highly respected government economists, it is unlikely that, left to themselves, the economists would have won the battle. Support came from both Prime Minister Desai and Finance Minister H. M. Patel.[77] Patel had already expressed his view in Parliament: "The term parity means that in any price that [the farmer] gets, account would be taken of the inputs. Whatever price he has to pay for them he should be able to recover when he sells the produce."[78] The vicissitudes of Charan Singh's personal political fortunes also assisted the economists. For the proposal to go through, support of the Prime Minister's office, and/or the consent of Finance and Planning were required. Given the nature of the Janata coalition, Charan Singh's party, or like-minded agrarians, could not dominate all of these ministries.[79]

76 The economists, however, did agree that the terms of trade ought to be reviewed from time to time and, if a sharp fall in agriculture's terms of trade took place, some adjustment ought to be made in the procurement price. Beyond that, the argument for parity was rejected.

77 Both belonged to Congress (O). It is unclear whether their support came because of political reasons – namely, need to contain Charan Singh – or was due to intrinsic economic reasons. From my interviews, it seems it was a mixture of both. Desai and Patel were, among other things, keen on price stability and looked at increases in food prices with concern.

78 *Lok Sabha Debates*, 6th ser., vol. 8, December 9, 1977, p. 355.

79 However, mention should be made of a peculiar discrepancy I have discovered in Charan Singh's position on parity prices. On all public platforms, as well as in his 1981 book, he advocated parity prices. In *India's Economic Nightmare* (1981), he wrote: "According to all canons of justice and fair play, the procurement price of agricultural produce should be based on the principle of parity between agricultural and non-agricultural prices . . ." (p. 201). Further, "fixation of procurement prices of agricultural produce according to the principle of parity is not a novel or chimerical idea. Both communist China and democratic U.S.A. have followed it" (p. 202). Charan Singh took these positions in the peasant rallies too. In his 1979 book, however, he took a very different point of view: "Production of agricultural products in quantities surplus to the needs of the community must necessarily result in a fall in agricultural prices. . . . If, and when, this fall occurs and persists over time, the most obvious course, dictated by elementary principles of economic science and by their own self-interest, is for workers from agricultural pursuits with lower incomes to shift to non-agricultural pursuits, or industries and services with higher in-

4.5.3 Personnel changes

An attempt was also made to alter the functioning of the APC by making personnel changes. In October 1978, A. S. Kahlon was chosen by the government to succeed Dharm Narain, chairman of the APC since 1969–70.[80] This personnel change reflected the ideological proclivities of the agrarian bloc in Janata. Whereas Narain had repeatedly stressed the need to halt the rise in procurement prices, Kahlon was convinced that, if anything, a larger increase in procurement prices was required to "keep the tempo of production going." Whereas Narain's analysis always took note of the impact of food prices on the rest of the economy, Kahlon was primarily concerned with their impact on food production. The two chairmen did not disagree on what needed to be done in the rice economy. Rice production had still not taken off, and since wheat surpluses had started accumulating, even Narain was arguing for reducing price incentives for wheat and diverting the freed-up resources toward increasing incentives for rice production. Kahlon pitched for an increase in both, on the grounds of keeping incentives intact and enlarging public stocks of grain, so that in case of a decline in supply, the country would have enough stocks to fall back upon.

To illustrate the difference between the two approaches and how politicians saw them, consider the arguments made by these two heads of the APC in identical circumstances. By 1977–8 India's food production once again inspired confidence. After two bumper crops, public stocks had a record 20.6 million tons of grain in July 1977. Wheat stocks stood at 14.6 million tons. Rice made up the rest, with coarse grains constituting a negligibly small proportion of stocks.

Another good crop was expected in 1978–9. The APC under Narain argued: "When the need is for a policy of aggressive support purchases to prevent the price of wheat from falling below the level of existing procurement price, there is demand in some quarters for a substantial hike in the procurement price. . . . A step-up in the price in the present situation carries some important implications which . . . cannot be brushed aside."[81]

---

comes. . . . *It is not a calamity but a consummation much to be desired.* . . . Those who cite the example of the U.K., the U.S.A., or other highly developed countries fail to realize that while the problem for these countries is how to make the few persons that there are still left in agriculture stay therein, the problem for India, in fact, for every underdeveloped country is just the contrary, viz., how to ensure that release of workers from agriculture is not impeded" (*India's Economic Policy*, pp. 40–1; emphasis added). In fact, the entire section in the book on farm prices (pp. 35–44) is an argument against a price-support policy, and Singh takes issue with the specific proposal presented by B. P. Singh, then Minister of State of Agriculture, on parity prices (pp. 36–7). Seen in the entirety of his work, Singh's 1979 writing seems to be a thoroughly puzzling outlier.

80 Kahlon was a professor of agricultural economics at the Punjab Agricultural University (PAU). His views on the role of prices in production were very different from Narain's. For details, see A. S. Kahlon and D. S. Tyagi, 1983, *Agricultural Price Policy in India*, New Delhi: Allied Publishers.

81 *Rabi Report for 1978–79*, p. 5.

The APC then outlined what these implications were:[82] (1) a higher procurement price would mean a higher budget subsidy, already at Rs 450 crores, or a higher consumer price, which, according to the APC, did not make sense, as stocks were to be diminished, not further increased; (2) the need was to encourage production of pulses, some of which, mainly gram, competed with wheat for acreage in winter, and therefore required better price incentives as well as diversion of resources from wheat so that the technological base of pulse production could be improved; (3) as wheat costs were up, the point was to reduce them by putting resources into irrigation and improving yields in areas bypassed by the green revolution, instead of keeping wheat margins intact in advanced areas by increasing prices to make up for the rise in costs. The APC therefore recommended that the procurement price of wheat be maintained at the last year's level of Rs 110 per quintal.[83]

With Kahlon at the helm, for the next three years the APC, while accepting that "wheat production has maintained a steady rise,"[84] ignored argument (1) even though food subsidy continued to rise; dismissed (2) on the ground that "in the case of gram, no technological breakthrough is in sight yet," and therefore "no pitching up of administered price can fully compensate for lags in gram technology"; and turned argument (3) around to recommend an increase in procurement price – because costs had gone up, price had to go up as well. Wheat production, it should be emphasized, had increased in both years, which Kahlon did not consider as important as the increase in costs. Kahlon added one more argument in favor of price increase: "rise in the international price of wheat since 1977 . . . calls [for] . . . the developing countries . . . to look more and more towards national self-sufficiency in food production with particular emphasis on wheat which has become costlier in the international market."[85]

Thus, while Narain tried to balance the micro- and macroperspectives on food production, Kahlon was essentially working on the basis of a microperspective, without any consideration of the larger impact of food prices on budgetary subsidies, income distribution, or the general price level in the economy. In the Indian context, a macroperspective, as already explained, typically calls for restraint on food prices, whereas a microperspective uses price incentives as a basic tool for raising production. A far cry from the Nehru era, when a macroperspective on food prices dominated the economic and political landscape, a rise in agrarian power and a microperspective on food prices seemed to mesh.

But the movement toward this marriage had long been in the making, which suggests that structural pressures in the polity favoring the agrarian sector had been building up no matter which party ruled the center. Table 4.5 shows how

---

82 Based on ibid., pp. 5–7.
83 The government did not accept the recommendation and raised it to Rs 112.50.
84 This quote, and the ones below, are from the *Rabi Report for 1979–80*, pp. 2–7.
85 *Rabi Report for 1980–81*, p. 2.

Table 4.5. *Wheat procurement price:*
The APC versus the government

Year	Price recommended by the APC	Price declared by the government
Under Narain		
1970–1	Rs 72	Rs 76
1971–2	Rs 74	Rs 76
1972–3	Rs 72	Rs 76
1973–4	Rs 72	Rs 76
1974–5	Rs 95	Rs 105
1975–6	Rs 105	Rs 105
1976–7	Rs 105	Rs 105
1977–8	Rs 105	Rs 110
1978–9	Rs 110	Rs 112.50
Under Kahlon		
1979–80	Rs 115	Rs 115
1980–1	Rs 117	Rs 117
1981–2	Rs 127	Rs 130
1982–3	Rs 142	Rs 142

Source: Various APC Reports. The two varieties are Mexican and common white indigenous.

often the APC price recommendations under Narain were upwardly revised even by the Congress government. In fact, only in two years during the Congress rule in the decade was the APC recommendation accepted. Janata, by appointing a more politically acceptable chairman, simply preempted a possible source of bureaucratic tension, ensuring that the institution recommending producer prices had the same perspective as the political bosses.

4.5.4 Assessing the significance of Charan Singh and the Janata party

The Janata government did not last beyond mid-1979, nor did Charan Singh remain in government after December 1979. But Singh's significance survived his fall.[86] To be sure, by the end of the decade, agricultural price agitations had started breaking out in parts of India including places where Singh had no political standing. The state of Tamil Nadu, in particular, had witnessed a violent riot in 1978. But these agitations were all regional or local. They became an

---

86 Janata broke up into its constituents in the 1980 elections. Mrs. Gandhi returned to power with a solid majority in the Lok Sabha. Of the former Janata constituents, Charan Singh's Lok Dal did best, emerging as the second largest party in the Lok Sabha; but it finished far behind Mrs. Gandhi's Congress party.

important political force only in the 1980s. It is unlikely that these agitations, and the issues they raised, would have caught the national political attention so quickly if between 1977 and 1980 Charan Singh had not made them into issues of central political concern. Similarly, agrarian representation in Parliament had been rising; but before Charan Singh no leader of stature so completely identified his political career with rural India. Charan Singh did not singlehandedly transform rural India into a national political force, which ideally he would have liked to do, but it would be fair to say that he dramatically represented an emerging political trend and, in doing so, contributed to its strengthening.[87] He forced the urban media, political parties, and the top echelons of government to acknowledge a new force in politics.

A comparison with C. Subramaniam may be useful here. Subramaniam changed the agricultural policy of the country but did not mobilize rural India for political purposes. He was essentially a technocratic politician, not a flaming ideologue or a fiery political mobilizer. Charan Singh's impact was precisely the opposite. He was unable to give a new direction to the country's economic policy, which he would have if the parity price formula had gone through or the resource allocation between industry and agriculture had been durably altered. But, through peasant mobilization and an unrelenting advocacy of the villages, he contributed to the emergence of rural India on the national power map. His politics led to a change in the ideological discourse of Indian politics, an effect Subramaniam was unable to achieve. After Charan Singh, all political parties had to accommodate the new peasant power in their political programs and strategies.

4.6 SUMMARY

As argued earlier, the change in agricultural policy in the mid-1960s had been primarily a state initiative, with remarkably little input from rural India. The decade of the 1970s, however, began to change this relationship. Pressures on the Indian state and on agricultural policy mounted as rural power expressed itself in two forms – one old, the other new. Blocking the implementation of unfavorable policy measures at the state and local levels was the well-known, old form. It continued in the 1970s, as an unwelcome nationalization of grain trade was squarely defeated. However, as the decade ended, rural-based parties made a transition from state politics to national politics, which enabled them to exert direct influence on the policy-making organs of the Indian state.

The economic and policy implications of the change in power structure did not, however, correspond to the best-case scenarios that the new agrarian force was striving to achieve. The new power realities did succeed in preventing the worst-case scenarios from taking place: for example, a fall in prices that would

87 For tributes to Charan Singh made by political leaders, see *Asli Bharat*, December 1990, special issue on Charan Singh's birthday.

have normally accompanied an accumulating grain surplus. The new power configuration also succeeded in substantially changing the composition of the state institution responsible for setting prices so as to ensure favorable policy outcomes. But the best-case scenario – a change of the very principles of price policy in a partisan rural direction – remained unrealized. The economic bureaucrats in the government fought the rural politicians, using standard notions of economic theory as their armor. While they were unable, as one would expect, totally to subdue the politicians, they were not totally subdued either. Given that all spaces in the landscape of power were not occupied by agrarian partisans, the technocrats were able to exploit the divisions in the political wing of the government to restrain the agrarian ideologues. The net result was tilted toward agrarian India, but in the absence of countervailing checks and balances in the system, the tilt would have been considerably steeper.

As the 1980s started, yet another index of agrarian power emerged. Farm-price agitations – robust, stable, and widely supported in the countryside – spread to many parts of the country: Maharashtra, Tamil Nadu, Karnataka, Punjab, Gujarat, Uttar Pradesh. More importantly, the leadership of rural India would no longer be a monopoly of political parties. Previously little-known leaders, heading nonparty political formations, increasingly came to the fore. Political parties redoubled their efforts to wrest the initiative from the nonparty political actors, but nonparty mobilizations maintained their vibrancy. Both in party and nonparty politics, rural pressure thus began to accumulate.

5

Organizing the countryside in the 1980s

Is the peasantry capable of organizing for collective action? Students of peasant behavior have long wrestled with this question. Three images have dominated the literature. The first image – one of collective docility – goes back at least to Marx's statement that peasants are like "potatoes in a sack," isolated from each other and unable to organize. The second image, having its roots in the success of Mao Zedong with peasant mobilization in China but coming to dominate the intellectual landscape during the Vietnam War, suggested the reverse. Peasants were now considered to have the ability to engage in revolutionary collective action.[1] A third image, sketched mainly by James Scott, who earlier had been one of the proponents of the second view, made a forceful entry in the 1980s.[2] Going under the rubric of 'everyday resistance,' the third image is about "the vast and relatively unexplored middle ground . . . (between) passivity and open, collective defiance." As peasant rebellions are rare, this image concentrates on the everyday acts of dissent – "clandestine arson and sabotage, . . . footdragging, dissimulation, false compliance, pilfering, slander, flight, and so forth" – acts that "require little or no coordination or planning" and are routinely used by peasants to express protest.[3]

---

1 The reformulation started with Barrington Moore's *Social Origins of Democracy and Dictatorship: Lord and Peasant in the Making of the Modern World* (Boston: Beacon Press, 1967). Later, three more landmark works were added to the trend: Eric Wolf, *Peasant Wars in the Twentieth Century* (1971), James Scott, *The Moral Economy of the Peasant* (New Haven, CT: Yale University Press, 1976) and Samuel Popkin, *The Rational Peasant* (Berkeley and Los Angeles: University of California Press, 1979).

2 James Scott, *Weapons of the Weak*, New Haven, CT: Yale University Press, 1984. See also the special issue of *The Journal of Peasant Studies* on "Everyday Forms of Peasant Resistance in Southeast Asia," ed. James Scott and Benedict Tria Kerkvliet, vol. 13. no 2 (January 1986). The citations below are from Scott's introduction to the issue.

3 Yet another argument has been added to this vast literature on peasant collective action. It is, however, about village-level social organization, not about intervillage political mobilization. In his study of the management of village commons in the South Indian state of Andhra Pradesh, Robert Wade argues that (1) when the net benefits of collective action are high, and (2) when the

This chapter deals with yet another "unexplored middle ground," which is covered neither by acts of revolution nor by docile silence, or indeed by everyday forms of struggle. Best called "democratic peasant mobilization," it has a history in the developed countries but virtually no track record in the developing world.[4] It holds the conceptual ground between revolutionary fervor and individual non-compliance: it is collective action for protest, not for revolution.

Democratic peasant mobilization marks the Indian rural scene in the 1980s and 1990s. It is primarily sectoral. Its ideology is captured in the image that its leaders have relentlessly propagated: that of a Bharat–India divide, where *Bharat*, the Hindi term for India, notionally subsumes the oppressed rural many, and India, the English name for the country, represents the dominant urban few. It has a primarily reformist objective – namely, to pressure the government for higher agricultural prices, loan waivers, and a better urban–rural balance in the country's resource allocation. At no point has this mobilization threatened the existing class structure in a revolutionary way, but it has been powerful enough to rock the politics of many important and populous states of India: Tamil Nadu and Karnataka in South India; Maharashtra and Gujarat in the west; Punjab and Uttar Pradesh in the north. Since it has emerged in so many states, and with such persistence, it has managed to exercise considerable pressure on national politics too.

A remarkable feature of this mobilization is that it has on the whole been led by nonparty organizations. These organizations have, by and large, kept institutional autonomy from political parties and, in most cases, refrained from contesting elections. Political parties have so far not been able to displace the nonparty organizations from the leadership of these agitations. Rather, political parties have reformulated their political programs to support the demand for remunerative prices and for greater allocation of public resources to the countryside. Some parties have even supported the demand for loan waivers.

The new agrarian mobilization in India raises many analytical puzzles. Consider some of the more striking ones.

1. It is generally believed, particularly by economists but not exclusively by them, that higher food prices benefit the surplus producers at the expense of the rural poor, who are net buyers of foodgrains and who therefore are hurt by higher

---

risks of harm, if collective action is not undertaken, are also high, the customary free-rider problem will disappear and voluntary collective action will result. See Robert Wade, 1988, *Village Republics: Economic Conditions for Collective Action*, Cambridge: Cambridge University Press. Wade himself recognizes that his argument may be applicable only to management of village commons, not to peasant collective action per se.

4   This may be contested as too strong a claim. Movements on land-access issues, after all, have been launched in various parts of the developing world. However, the key distinction is that once land issues become large-scale, they typically cease to be reformist and tend to become revolutionary. On entitlement to land, the only democratic mobilizations have been launched in the two Indian states of Kerala and West Bengal. For an account, see Ronald J. Herring, 1983, *Land to the Tiller*, New Haven, CT: Yale University Press.

food prices, at least in the short run. The truly massive rural participation in the farm-price movements, however, seems to suggest that the rural poor have also supported the demand for higher food prices. Why is a customary economic claim not at the same time a political fact? If the poor buy more food than they sell, then their support is counterintuitive in the short run. If, on the other hand, they believe that higher prices in the long run might lead to higher employment or higher wages, their support still remains counterintuitive. For it is not clear why a possible long-run benefit should be preferred over a definite short-run cost. Are some noneconomic factors at work? Is the new mobilization an attempt by the rich peasantry to consolidate itself politically after gaining economically from the green revolution? If so, how does the rich peasantry win the support of the poor?

2. Why did the leadership of these agitations go to nonparty organizations, not to political parties? Still more puzzling, why is it that more of these organizations, despite attaining wide popularity, did not turn into political parties, and the few that did, failed miserably? Since it might safely be supposed that parties in power would be in a better position to affect government policy, what does the inability of nonparty organizations to become successful parties tell us about the potential and limits of nonparty mobilization to affect a key economic policy of the country?

3. Why should there be farm-price agitations when agricultural policy is based on price incentives? India's food policy, after all, was changed in the mid-1960s. Since then, price incentives and investments in new agricultural technology have been the cornerstones of food policy. Why didn't these agitations emerge earlier when, under Nehru, the country's leaders and planners explicitly stated that food prices had to be kept low and food had to be procured at lower than market prices? Why, in other words, have the farmers been agitating for higher prices since the late seventies? Has the *definition* of agrarian interests been influenced by a change in state policy?

4. And finally, we also have a comparative puzzle. Farmers in most developing world countries are disorganized.[5] Olson's famous theoretical argument about why it is generally hard to organize large and dispersed groups has been used by Robert Bates to explain why farmers have little political power in Africa.[6] The size of the farm group in India is large and farmers are dispersed; still, farmers

5 I shall use the terms "peasants" and "farmers" interchangeably. Eric Wolf's work (*Peasant Wars of the Twentieth Century*, New York: Harper and Row, 1969) emphasizes the distinction between the two on the ground that peasants produce primarily for home consumption and farmers primarily for the market. Increasingly, more and more peasants are becoming part of the market nexus, turning this distinction into one of historical relevance only.

6 Robert Bates, 1981, *Markets and States in Tropical Africa*, Cambridge: Cambridge University Press; and 1983, *Essays in the Political Economy of Rural Africa*, Cambridge: Cambridge University Press; Mancur Olson, 1965, *Logic of Collective Action*, Cambridge, MA: Harvard University Press.

have become organized. What explains the Indian exception? Or is there an exception here?

In the remaining parts of this book, I shall seek to solve these puzzles. This chapter will concentrate on puzzle 1. Puzzles 2–4 will be addressed in the following chapters. My argument will be that, despite its apparent counterintuitiveness, both evidence and logic suggest that rather than having a narrow class base in the surplus-producing rich peasantry, the new agrarian mobilization has the support of all sections of the *landed* peasantry. However, the *landless* agricultural laborers do not relate to these agitations in any single identifiable way. In their case, all conceivable patterns – support, opposition, and apathy – exist, whose causes I shall explore. I shall also examine the impact of these agitations on party politics and governmental policy.

5.1 THE NEW AGRARIAN MOBILIZATION: SCALE AND ISSUES

Although coming of age in the 1980s, the new agrarian mobilization was born in the early seventies. The agitations did not start in the least developed Indian states but in the more developed ones, and in the more prosperous districts – in the Coimbatore district of the southern state of Tamil Nadu in 1970[7] and in the Ludhiana district of the northern state of Punjab in 1972.[8] Unlike many parts of the country having subsistence agriculture, these districts are well endowed with irrigation facilities, and their agriculture by the late sixties had already become heavily market-oriented.[9] Input and grain prices, therefore, had an important role to play in their farm economies. In 1970, Coimbatore farmers successfully agitated against the decision of the state government to increase electricity charges. By 1972, their demands had expanded to include remunerative agricultural prices, input subsidies, and waiving of agricultural loans. In the same year, there was also a protest in Ludhiana, Punjab, against the decision of the central government not to increase the support price for wheat in 1972.

These beginnings were small, but over time they evolved into a movement supported by larger organizations. In 1973, a statewide nonparty organization was formed in Tamil Nadu, called Tamil Nadu Agriculturists Association (TNAA), under the leadership of Narainswamy Naidu. By the late seventies, the

---

7 For the origins of the Tamil Nadu farmers movement, see M. V. Nadkarni, 1987, *Farmers' Movements in India*, Delhi: Allied, pp. 60–69. Also see K. C. Alexander, 1981, *Peasant Organizations in South India*, Delhi: Indian Social Institute, pp. 131–5.

8 S. S. Gill and K. C. Singhal, 1984, "Punjab: Farmers' Agitation," *Economic and Political Weekly*, October 6, pp. 1728–32.

9 For agricultural statistics on Ludhiana, see G. K. Chaddha, 1986, *The State and Rural Economic Transformation, A Study of Punjab*, New Delhi and Beverly Hills, CA: Sage Publications. For Coimbatore, see M. V. Nadkarni, in ibid., pp. 63–4.

TNAA had started organizing large-scale protests. In 1980, it reportedly had a membership of three million farmers.[10]

The Punjab organization, called the Khetbari Zimindara Union (KZU) had also become a state-level nonparty organization by the early eighties.[11] In 1980, the KZU rechristened itself, acquiring its current name, Bharatiya Kisan Union (BKU). Between 1973 and 1980, the KZU organized agitations on power rates for tubewells, rates for water and diesel, support prices for sugarcane, etc. By 1983, the BKU had functioning organizational units in all districts of Punjab except one.

The real turning point for these agitations came in 1980. Between 1977 and 1980, the role of Charan Singh and his party, Lok Dal, in the central government had already sensitized the top echelons of the political structure in Delhi to the emerging agrarian power (see Chapter 4). Singh's exit from power was quickly followed by price agitations in the states of Maharashtra and Karnataka, though the leaders and organizations heading these agitations had little to do with Singh. Sensitization of the power organs above and an unrelated but autonomously increasing agrarian unrest below coincided powerfully, attracting national political attention. The leaders of these agitations showed a capacity to formulate effective political strategies and to articulate powerful slogans for rural mobilization. Sharad Joshi in Maharashtra, in particular, stood out as a strategist and communicator, whose imaginative slogan of the Bharat–India divide became the new idiom of rural mobilization.

With higher agricultural prices as their principal objective, these organizations, over the next few years, led many successful agitations. Their rallies and demonstrations attracted a large mass of farmers – the numbers ranging between one to four hundred thousand on a number of occasions. By 1987, two more agitations of a similar kind emerged in the states of Gujarat and Uttar Pradesh.[12] *The Times of India* editorialized:

The peasants have started to flex the political muscles that their economic betterment has given them. . . . In national terms, [they] cannot claim that [they] have received a raw deal. Witness the manner in which agricultural inputs have been subsidised for the past two decades. . . . But it is precisely because the farmers have been enabled to move beyond subsistence economy that they have acquired the capacity to launch the kind of sustained struggle they have. It is going to be difficult to either contain them or to accommodate them in the current economic arrangement. They cannot be contained

10 Nadkarni, *Farmers' Movements*, p. 67.
11 Gill and Singhal, "Punjab," p. 1729.
12 For details of the Gujarat agitation, see *India Today*, March 15, 1987; for Uttar Pradesh, "Farmer Power," *Front Line*, February 20–March 4, 1988, and "Farmers on the March," *Indian Express* (Sunday Magazine), February 21, 1988. On the U.P. agitations, see two articles by Dipankar Gupta: "Peasant Unionism in Uttar Pradesh: Against the Rural Mentality Thesis," *Journal of Contemporary Asia*, vol. 22, no. 2 (1992); and "Country–Town Nexus and Agrarian Mobilization: Bhartiya Kisan Union as an Instance," *Economic and Political Weekly*, vol. 23, no. 51, December 17, 1988.

because they command the vote banks in the countryside to which every party seeks access. And they cannot be accommodated because there is a limit beyond which the urban population cannot be expected to transfer resources to them. For to allow agricultural prices to rise unduly is to undermine the very basis of economic development, add to the woes of the poor in both urban and rural areas and fuel unrest in urban centers which is already proving difficult to control. . . . A new spectre of peasant power is likely to haunt India in coming years.[13]

For the worldview underlying these agitations, I turn first to Sharad Joshi, the most widely noted new farm leader.[14] I shall then set forth the similarities and differences that other peasant leaders have with Joshi's movement and ideology.

5.1.1 The new agrarianism: Ideology and issues

Joshi outlines three distinguishing features of the new agrarianism.[15] First, unlike the old agrarians ("Tolstoy–Ruskin–Gandhi"), the new agrarians do not celebrate village life for its blissful simplicity and spiritual richness: "it does not glorify the pastoral/agrarian pattern."[16] Rather, new agrarianism has material foundations:

the quality of life of an individual, as also of a community, is to be assessed by the degrees of freedom it enjoys. The three degrees of freedom are: number of occasions available for

---

13 *The Times of India*, February 3, 1988. This editorial was written after an agitation in Western Uttar Pradesh in the winter of 1987–8.

14 Joshi has published widely, spoken eloquently about his worldview, and led scores of agitations under the banner of his organization, the *Shetkari Sanghthana* (Peasant Organization). Holder of a master's degree in statistics from the University of Bombay and a former civil servant who also worked with the United Nations in the 1960s, he turned to dryland farming in the mid-seventies. He speaks three languages fluently: English, Marathi, and Hindi. On the Agrarian Question, he displays considerable knowledge of the writings of Marx, Rosa Luxemberg, Stalin, Lenin, Gandhi, Michael Kalecki, Theodore Schultz, Michael Lipton, and Ashok Mitra. His background in statistics, moreover, has equipped him for questions of sampling design and procedures of statistical inference relevant to the analysis of agricultural cost data. Between 1989 and 1990, holding cabinet rank, he headed a committee set up to reform agricultural policy by the Government of India. Before the recommendations could be put into effect, the government fell. Some changes, however, did come about (see Chapter 6). Only one scholarly account of Joshi's movement exists at present: Cornelia Lenenberg, 1988, "Sharad Joshi and the Farmers: The Middle Peasant Lives!" *Pacific Affairs*, vol. 61, no. 3 (Fall). My account here is based on his writings and many rounds of interviews conducted between 1984 and 1991. His main writings are: Sharad Joshi, *Kisan Sanghthan: Vichar Aur Karyapaddhati* (Peasant organization: Worldview and strategy), Varanasi: Sarva Seva Sangh Prakashan, 1983; *'Bharat' Speaks Out*, Bombay: Build Documentation Center, 1986; and *Samasyayen Bharat Ki* (Problems of rural India), Alibagh: Shetkari Sanghthan, 1988.

15 Based on Joshi, 1986, *'Bharat' Speaks Out*, pp. 65–81. The distinction between the old and new agrarianism, the former being associated with Mahatma Gandhi, has also been pointed out by Lloyd and Susanne Rudolph, 1987, *In Pursuit of Lakshmi*, Chicago: University of Chicago Press, chap. 13.

16 Joshi, *'Bharat'*, p. 74. Mahatma Gandhi's defense of agrarianism, spelled out in his *Hind Swaraj* (Indian self-rule), was based on an antipathy toward the dehumanizing and consumerist impact of big-factory industrialism. He preferred the morally rich and need-based village life, small industries, and handicrafts.

exercising a choice; number of options for the choice; the size of the spectrum of choices. The larger the number and the variety of means at disposal, the higher will tend to be the degrees of freedom and hence material opulence is desirable in itself . . . not for the enjoyment or happiness it brings. . . . Increased production, higher productivity and accumulation of capital form the very core of all social and economic activity.[17]

Second, unlike the peasant movements of the past which pitted tenants against landlords, low castes against high castes, the new peasant movements are "not divisive." The essential conflict, according to Joshi, is not intrarural but between the countryside and the city, between Bharat and India. The misery in the villages is not caused by the "slightly better off farmer in the neighbourhood" but by an "outside exploiter," the urban India: "Transcontinental imperialism," represented by the British, "has been replaced by internal colonialism."[18]

Finally, as "savings in agriculture expropriated through a policy of cheap raw materials and artificially depressed prices"[19] constitute the main technique used by the new exploiters to transfer resources, the third feature of new agrarianism is its "almost exclusive concentration on the question of agricultural prices." [20] Joshi argues that remunerative prices, if given, can eradicate poverty not only in the countryside but in the country as a whole. He explains the reasons underlying that claim:[21]

1. Since farmers "respond rationally to price movements," they will react to price incentives by increasing acreage and investment, and by adopting improved technology.
2. Since farmers' response will increase demand for labor, wage earners will also benefit. Very soon in this process there arrives a point when "the rate of increase in farm wages is higher than the rate of increase of agricultural prices."
3. As a consequence of the additional incomes so received, farmers will undertake non-agricultural activities, creating employment, and spend incremental incomes in a way that can lead to higher industrial growth. Indeed, "some of the more remarkable spurts in industrial activity have come immediately following temporary reprieves in agricultural price conditions."

Thus, according to Joshi, price incentives in agriculture and a "natural" process of capital accumulation driven by agricultural revolution can benefit the entire economy and break the vicious circle of poverty. As opposed to this, an accumulation process driven by an industrial revolution (before an agricultural revolution has taken place) is, in his view, always premised upon a coercive extraction of agricultural surplus.

The primacy of agricultural prices is conceded by the other new peasant leaders but, in their judgment, prices cannot be a "one-point program." Their agendas have been broader. Beyond input and crop pricing, the issues they have raised can be classified into three categories: agricultural, rural, and social.

17 Joshi, *'Bharat'*, p. 74.
18 Ibid., pp. 75–7.
19 Ibid., p. 69.
20 Ibid., p. 76.
21 The quotes below are from ibid., pp. 79–80.

The strictly agricultural demands common to most state agitations have included the waiver of past agricultural loans (on the ground that unfavorable farm prices have yielded incomes grossly insufficient for loan repayment); abolition of land revenue; cessation of taxes on agricultural implements such as tractors, pumpsets, etc.; and provision of crop insurance.

Next, there are issues not strictly agricultural but rural: a larger allocation of public resources for village development (roads, schools, drinking-water facilities) and rural industrialization; in some quarters, a demand for reservations in educational institutions and government employment for farmers' children;[22] and old-age pensions to farmers.

Some social issues have also been raised. These include checks on alcoholism, better status for women, campaign against wife-beating, and abolition of dowry. Most of these are not so much aimed at the government as toward raising the consciousness of the mobilized and widening the support base of these movements by including women.[23]

Some of these issues are specific to only a couple of states; some are exercises in plain rhetoric; and others are simply attempts to widen the support base of the movement. On the whole, prices and loans have been the core of the movement, which is not surprising. With increasing marketization, Indian agriculture has become heavily price- and credit-based. The significance of prices in a market-oriented agriculture is self-evident. The need for credit is linked to the rise in the capital intensity of farming after the green revolution. Adoption of new technology required credit; and the government, for its part, also vastly expanded its credit operations in agriculture in order to facilitate the green revolution.

5.2 THE SOCIAL BASE OF THE FARMERS' MOVEMENT: SECTORAL OR CLASS BASED?

By far the most difficult question about these movements concerns their social base. Do they have a class character, or does new agrarianism represent the interests of the entire countryside? The question is important, because on it have depended political judgments about whether these movements ought to be supported, as well as about whether and how long they might persist. At issue is not only an economic question (who benefits from higher farm prices and loan waivers and why) but also a political question (who participates in these movements and why). If groups which, according to economic reasoning, lose from higher food prices nonetheless participate in the movement, how is that to be

---

22 Not all farm leaders agree with the demand for a quota in educational institutions and employment.

23 Sharad Joshi's interview with Rajni Bakshi, "The Uprising," *The Illustrated Weekly of India*, January 18, 1987, p. 47. First raised in Punjab, these issues were also highlighted in Uttar Pradesh and Maharashtra between 1986 and 1988.

viewed? Is it an example of "false consciousness," of coerced participation; or is the intellectual reasoning itself narrow or wrong?

This conceptual difficulty is compounded by the quality of available evidence. Evidence bearing on the political question (who participates and why) is not entirely unambiguous. Nor is the economic evidence (on who benefits and why) conclusive, once we move beyond the short-run effects of increases in food prices on the poor to consider the long-run effects as well.

In what follows, a resolution of the above difficulty via a *combination of inductive and deductive reasoning* is proposed. This methodological point may need some elaboration in view of the objections to deductive analysis in some circles. As this book is not a study of peasant movements but of economic policy, and as my claim is that peasant mobilization influenced policy, peasant mobilization is an independent variable for this study. Being so, a comprehensive *empirical* investigation of the independent variable – why peasant movements arose, which classes support them and why – cannot be undertaken; only the connections between the independent and dependent variables can be explored. If we do not follow this procedure, we run into an infinite regress. Every independent variable, after all, can be turned into a dependent variable, for it, too, is a result of something. Where one draws a line and what becomes an independent variable therefore depends on the object of investigation – on what is to be explained.

How might we combine induction and deduction to establish the social base of the new peasant movement? Because there is no dispute in the literature about the support of the rich and middle peasantry for higher prices, their support for these movements can be taken as given. As for the rural poor, one can divide them into two categories: the landed poor (small farmers) and the landless laborers. Looking at the field reports about who participates in these movements, I shall argue that, while there is evidence of small-farmer support, the evidence itself may be selective, not randomly drawn. This means that, in and of itself, the existing evidence does not permit general inferences. However, if we can deductively discover the *logic* of why a small farmer may support price agitations, we should be able to (1) explain why we empirically observe such support, despite its counterintuitiveness, and (2) make a generalization about small-farmer support. Although not entirely conclusive, such a generalization will be more admissible than if the mere evidence of uncertain validity is used. The inductive and the deductive may thus be combined to generate reasonably robust conclusions (which can be used until an exhaustive inductive investigation refutes them). The same method will be followed for the landless laborers.

5.2.1 Economic argument I: The distributional case against food price rise

Of those writing on Indian agriculture, Ashok Mitra, M. L. Dantwala, Dharm Narain, Alain de Janvry and K. Subbarao, and John Mellor have been at the fore-

Table 5.1. *Price elasticities for selected items*

	Cereals	Pulses	Sugar
Rural			
For those below the poverty line	−0.73	−0.83	−0.84
For those above the poverty line	−0.30	−0.44	−0.63
Urban			
For those below the poverty line	−0.66	−0.87	−0.91
For those above the poverty line	−0.04	−0.19	−0.33

Note: The minus sign indicates the movement of consumption in the reverse direction: the higher the price, the smaller the consumption.

Source: Planning Commission, Perspective Planning Division, 1977, *Studies on the Structure of the Indian Economy and Planning for Development,* as quoted in Y. K. Alagh, "Notes on Sectoral Price Policies in the Indian Institutional Context," a paper presented at the Institute of Economic Growth Silver Jubilee Seminar, New Delhi, April–May 1984.

front of those arguing that higher food prices hurt the poor in the short run.[24] Higher food prices benefit those who have a surplus to sell in the market. It is typically the rich peasantry, and in some parts of the country the middle peasantry, which can produce a surplus. The small peasant may sell after the harvest, but only to buy greater quantities subsequently in the off-season. He is therefore a net buyer of foodgrains; higher food prices hurt him. The landless peasant is also hurt, as the rise in food prices depresses the real value of his wages.

In comparison to the poor, the food consumption of the rich is relatively unaffected by prices. In 1977, India's Planning Commission estimated the price elasticities of demand for selected items in the urban and rural areas (Table 5.1). A 10 percent increase in the price of cereals (wheat, rice, and coarse grains), it was found, reduces the already low food consumption of those below the poverty

24 Ashok Mitra, *Terms of Trade and Class Relations,* London: Frank Cass, 1977, and Delhi: Rupa, 1979. M. L. Dantwala, 1986,"Technology, Growth and Equity in Agriculture," in John Mellor and Gunwant Desai, eds., *Agricultural Change and Rural Poverty, Variations on a Theme by Dharm Narain,* published for the International Food Policy Research Institute, Baltimore: Johns Hopkins University Press, and Delhi: Oxford University Press; and "Agricultural Policy in India," in C. H. Shah, ed., *Agricultural Development of India,* Delhi: Orient Longman, 1979. Alain de Janvry and K. Subba Rao, 1987, *Agricultural Price Policy and Income Distribution in India,* Delhi: Oxford University Press; K. Subbarao, 1985, "Incentive Policies and India's Agricultural Development: Some Aspects of Regional and Social Equity," *Indian Journal of Agricultural Economics,* vol. 15, no. 4 (October–December). John Mellor, 1986, in Mellor and Desai; and Dhram Narain, *Studies on Indian Agriculture,* ed. K. N. Raj, Amartya Sen, and C. H. Hanumantha Rao, Delhi: Oxford University Press, 1988.

line by 7.3 and 6.6 percent in the rural and urban areas, respectively.[25] The corresponding figures for those above the poverty line were 3% in rural and 0.6% in urban areas.[26]

Left at this level, these considerations lead to a disturbing conclusion. In the early 1980s there were 105 million rural households in India. Of these, 10 million were landless and another 50 million operated marginal (less than 1 hectare) landholdings. It would seem, therefore, that food prices acutely affect the nutritional well-being of nearly 60 percent of rural India.[27] Hence the famous rhetoric of M. L. Dantwala that lowering food prices was equal to "instant socialism."[28] The urban poor, thought to be about one-fourth to one-third of the urban population, are also hurt by higher food prices, though a subsidized public distribution system provides them some cushion.

5.2.2 Economic arguments II: Introducing the long-run considerations

A large body of economists, though by no means all, would agree that the short-run implications of a food-price increase are regressive for the poor.[29] Disagree-

25 Similar estimates are available for other countries, but in India's case, the problem is magnified because of the sheer number of those below the poverty line. For comparative figures, see P. E. R. Pinstrup-Anderson, 1985, "Food Prices and the Poor," *European Review of Agricultural Economics*, vol. 12; also reprinted by the International Food Policy Research Institute, Washington, D.C., 1985.

26 A second type of evidence – on the market dependence of the poor for foodgrains – complements the first. It is widely believed that the rural poor depend on the market for foodgrain consumption much more than do the rich. See Ashok Mitra, *Terms of Trade and Class Relations*, Delhi: Rupa, 1979, and London: Frank Cass, 1977, p. 120.

27 Calculations based on the 1980–1 agricultural census, Government of India. The 1985–6 agricultural census does not significantly alter the percentages.

28 In Mellor and Desai, *Agricultural Change*.

29 Leaving aside the so-called price fundamentalists associated mainly with Theodore Schultz and the Chicago School – economists in whose judgment efficiency gains linked with price signals far outweigh any distributional implications – this agreement would cut across both economists relatively sympathetic to using price policy as an appropriate instrument of agricultural development, such as Raj Krishna, John Mellor, and Peter Timmer, and those who are unsympathetic to using agricultural prices as a tool for raising production but would set food prices primarily to achieve income-distribution objectives, such as Amartya Sen, Paul Streeten, and Lance Taylor. The following writings are representative: Raj Krishna, 1982, "Some Aspects of Agricultural Growth, Price Policy and Equity in Developing Countries," *Food Research Institute Studies*, vol. 18, no. 3; John Mellor, 1987, "Determinants of Rural Poverty: The Dynamics of Production, Technology and Price" in Mellor and Desai, *Agricultural Change*, and 1978, "Food Price Policy and Income Distribution in Low Income Countries," *Economic Development and Cultural Change*, vol. 27, no. 1 (October); Peter Timmer, 1986, *Getting Prices Right: The Scope and Limits of Agricultural Price Policy*, Ithaca and London: Cornell University Press, chap. 5; Paul Streeten, 1987, *What Price Food? Agricultural Price Polices in Developing Countries*, London: Macmillan; Lance Taylor, 1984, *Structural Macroeconomics*, New York: Basic Books. Amartya Sen in fact shows that, given the already low nutritional levels of the poor, such increases could even be catastrophic, making a difference between life and death. See Amartya Sen, 1981, *Poverty and*

ments generally arise when one begins to examine the long-run effects of food-price increase.

A whole series of long-run consequences can be visualized. Three effects – on employment, wages, and agricultural productivity – merit special consideration. Higher food prices may hurt the poor in the short run, but if higher prices, on the supply side, lead to higher production and, on the demand side, to higher demand for the services of the poor (as surplus producers spend their newly acquired incomes), either employment or wages (or both, after a point) should go up. The landless may thus benefit from the employment or wage effect in the long run. As for the small farmers, if higher prices give them an incentive to adopt new technology, then higher productivity may make them self-sufficient in food, and their dependence on the market for consumption may disappear. Moreover, if productivity-increases end up generating a small surplus on their lands, they can gain further from their sales in the market. In sum, the poor – both the landless and the small peasant – may be better off in the long run as a result of higher producer (and, typically, therefore higher consumer) prices for food. Conversely, food prices, if lowered, may lead to a decrease in employment and a consequent increase in poverty.[30]

Do these dynamic effects, posited a priori, overpower the short-run effects? Do we know enough about how these various effects have unfolded in the real world?

Economic models, known as computable general equilibrium (CGE) models, seek to capture the dynamic effects. A discussion of the difficulties that beset these models is beyond the scope of this chapter. Some economists have written critically about both their merits and limits. Taylor and Lysy argue that the distributional results of the CGE models depend crucially on certain assumptions, making it extremely difficult to derive strong empirical judgments.[31] Therefore, it should not be surprising that, using these models, two economic studies which do aim at measuring the dynamic effects of agricultural prices on

---

Famines, London and Delhi: Oxford University Press. Also see Michael Lipton, 1987, "The Limits of Agricultural Price Policy: Which Way at the World Bank," *Development Policy Review*, vol. 5, no. 2 (June).

30 Some, however, argue that this effect is very unlikely. For employment to go down as a result of lower food prices, (1) the employment intensity of food crops has to be higher than that of commercial crops and (2) the elasticity of substitution of food crops for nonfood crops with respect to price must also be high – both of which are unlikely. See essays by John Mellor, Amartya Sen, and Vijay Vyas, in Mellor and Desai, *Agricultural Change.*

31 "There is a fair amount of agreement among economists on most equations in a formal model. . . . Disputes arise over the closure assumptions, yet these may determine the whole character of the results. Both the politics and economics of the rules by which a policy-oriented economist's implicit model is closed bear close scrutiny before he can be taken seriously – he may well be assuming at the beginning of his analysis precisely what he wants to say!" Cf. Lance Taylor and Frank Lysy, 1979, "Vanishing Income Distributions," *Journal of Development Economics*, vol. 6, p. 15.

income distribution in India came to opposite conclusions – one claiming that, on balance, the rural poor benefited,[32] the other arguing that they lost.[33]

Practitioners of price-policy analysis, therefore, contend that enough empirical knowledge about the long-run versus short-run trade-offs does not exist at this point. Peter Timmer explains: "The dynamic effects of food price policy interventions are likely to dominate the static effects, but the main issue is whether they reinforce or cancel each other. Much remains to be learned in this area, and comparative case studies of modern economic history rather than econometric analysis are likely to provide much of that knowledge."[34]

To sum up, the weight of the economic debate converges on the view that food-price increases hurt the poor in the short run. But the long-run and dynamic effects remain unknown. Therefore, *on purely economic grounds*, firm conclusions on whether only the upper peasantry or the entire rural sector benefits from higher food prices cannot be made.

5.2.3 Toward politics: A dialogue between observers and participants

If an argument based on a presumed economic result – the income-distribution effects of higher food or agricultural prices – cannot conclusively be made, can the argument be formulated differently? Political arguments about the class bias can be reconstructed on the following lines:[35]

32 Quizon and Binswanger found that between 1960/1 and 1980/1, rural wages did not keep pace with price increases. As a result, there was an income shift from wages to profits, but, once they factored in employment effects, they concluded that "the rural poor did not suffer excessively from the adverse wage trends because agricultural employment increased somewhat. . . . They also had substantial gains in nonagricultural incomes and, as consumers, they benefited from the decline in agricultural prices during the last five years of the 20-year period." See Jaime Quizon and Hans P. Binswanger, 1985, "The Impact of Agricultural Growth and of Selected Government Policies on the Distribution of Income in India," Report No. A3U21, Agriculture and Rural Development Department, the World Bank, Washington, D.C.

33 "Price-support programmes are, in the short run, highly regressive on the distribution of real income, creating sharp losses in purchasing power for the rural and urban poor. *Even in the longer run*, with output responding to price incentives, the real incomes of the landless and of the urban classes fall." Cf. Alain de Janvry and K. Subbarao, *Economic and Political Weekly*, Review of Agriculture, December 22–9, 1984, p. A-177. For a critique of the model, see D. S. Tyagi, "On the Relevance of Farm Prices," *Economic and Political Weekly*, March 1, 1986. De Janvry and Subbarao, in response, do concede that labor market assumptions in principle critically determine distributional outcomes, but defend their assumptions as realistic. See their "On the Relevance of Economic Modelling for Analysis of Food Price Policy," *Economic and Political Weekly*, June, 1987, pp. 1001–6.

34 C. Peter Timmer, 1986, *Getting Prices Right*, Ithaca and London: Cornell University Press, p. 147.

35 The political arguments below are based on the debates appearing in newspapers and magazines. *Economic and Political Weekly* has over the years consistently published opinions. Also see *The Link* (Delhi), January 26, 1981; *Seminar*, special issue on "Farmer Power," December 1988;

1. *Geographical spread*. Price agitations have mostly emerged in the "better-off" states – states that have a reasonably high degree of irrigation and commercialization, such as Punjab, Tamil Nadu, Gujarat, and the western part of Uttar Pradesh, not in the underdeveloped states, such as Bihar, Orissa, Assam, or the eastern part of Uttar Pradesh. Moreover, even in states whose agriculture is not so well endowed with irrigation, such as Maharashtra and Karnataka,[36] these movements have been stronger in the relatively better-off districts (for example, Shimoga in Karnataka and Nasik in Maharashtra).

2. *Crop spread*. Even though a general goal of price increase of all crops has been articulated, commercial crops have been at the forefront of these agitations – sugarcane, tobacco, and cotton. These are grown mostly by big farmers, not by small farmers who instead concentrate on paddy and coarse grains for household consumption. In Punjab and Western Uttar Pradesh, agitations for food crops have also been launched, but that is because, due to technological development, even food crops are heavily marketed in these states. Big farmers dominate the marketed surplus of these crops. The crops grown mostly by the poor peasantry – coarse grains – have not attracted the attention of agitation leaders.

3. *Loan Waivers*. The main non-price demand, loan waivers, primarily benefits the rich peasantry, because it is widely known that overdue loans are highest in the big-farmer category, whereas the loan repayment record of small amd marginal farmers has been far better.

4. *The Wage Neglect*. Higher crop prices are on the agenda, but not higher minimum wages for landless workers.[37]

These arguments made by political observers are contested by the new peasant leaders. Their responses can be summed up as follows.[38]

Argument 1 is true, but trivially so. It is only natural that price agitations first appear, and are stronger, in the more commercialized regions; for that is where prices matter critically at the current stage of agricultural development. As commercialization proceeds, one would expect the movement to spread to newer areas also.

Argument 2 is untenable because the main slogan of the movement has been agricultural prices in general. At any given moment, however, it may be necessary to concentrate on some crops rather than all. What is tactically necessary should not be considered more important than the principal ideological thrust of the movement. Moreover, to say that small peasants do not produce commercial

---

Lloyd Rudolph and Susanne Rudolph, *In Pursuit of Lakshmi*, chap. 13; and Dipankar Gupta, "Peasant Unionism in Uttar Pradesh," *Journal of Contemporary Asia*, vol. 22, no. 2, 1992.

36 Although industrially developed, these states do not have a well-developed agriculture. They form part of the semi-arid zone of India, dependent mainly on rainfall.

37 There is only one exception. In 1987, Sharad Joshi specifically included an increase in minimum wages on the agenda.

38 Based on author's interviews with Sharad Joshi, as above, and Mahendra Singh Tikait, Delhi, August 12, 1990; supplemented by interviews of other leaders appearing in newspapers.

crops is patently incorrect. Both small and big farmers have an interest in higher prices for sugarcane, all of which is sold in the market. Far from showing a class bias, commercial crops were emphasized first for purposes of developing a mass base.

Argument 3 is fallacious because (*a*) credit is important for all farmers, irrespective of the size, and (*b*) indebtedness afflicts the smaller farmer more than the bigger one, due to the lower financial capacity of the former. The issue of loans, therefore, is a mass issue.

Argument 4 is irrelevant, say the leaders, because wages rise once prices do. The level of wages in commercialized regions, after all, is higher than in backward agriculture.

Finally, these leaders argue that, instead of making these arguments from the outside about who benefits and who does not, it will be more instructive to observe empirically whether the poor actually support these agitations. A quarter- to a half-million peasants that come from a few districts to participate in rallies, says Joshi, cannot possibly all be rich peasants – not even primarily. That, he adds, lies beyond any sensible arithmetic of how the different size categories are distributed in the agrarian population.[39]

How does one evaluate this debate? It would be helpful to divide up the composite category of the "rural poor" into its two constituents: the *landholding* poor – that is, the small and marginal farmers – and the *landless* agricultural laborers.

5.2.4 Support of small and marginal farmers: Evidence and objections

Benefits of higher producer prices to small farmers,[40] if they exist, can be viewed in two ways: across time and across class. The former implies that compared to how they did when prices were low, small farmers benefit from higher prices; the latter means that the small farmers do not benefit as much as the rich and middle peasantry, which produces the bulk of the marketed surplus. In terms of the size of the benefit, class-differentiated results may obtain from higher prices, as they doubtless do. From this, however, it does not follow that the price agitations therefore have a rich-peasant-class character. In order for the latter to be true (even when all classes benefit – some more, others less), one would have to (1)

39 Author's interview with Sharad Joshi, December 1984.

40 Throughout this section, for ease of exposition, I shall not make a sharp distinction between small and marginal farmers. Marginal farmers, in Indian parlance, are a subcategory of small farmers. The rough-and-ready criterion for making the distinction is the size of landholding. Holdings less than 2.5 acres are considered marginal and those between 2.5 and 5 acres are called small. It should be clear that the distinction will break down if irrigation is factored in. In Punjab, where close to 85 percent of the land is irrigated, it is possible now for marginal farmers with up to 1.5 acres of land to produce a surplus for the market. I shall assume that all such farms, for our discussion here, are small. Where special problems concerning marginal farmers arise in the discussion, I shall point them out.

show that an across-class comparison of benefits is superior to an across-time comparison, and then argue that (2) if those benefiting less than others from a given cause nonetheless support the cause, their standards of judgment are flawed. It is not clear why (or whether) the small farmer, even though doing better than before, should (or does) consider himself a net loser just because the bigger farmer is benefiting more than he is from higher prices. It follows that if, compared to a preexisting point of time, small farmers are doing better, that may be reason enough for them to support the movement.

Let us look at the evidence now. Consider the following field report from Punjab: "Since all the farmers, with differences only in degree, have introduced new technology, the green revolution has put the entire peasantry in the market framework. All the farmers have to sell a part (in many cases a major part) of their output to purchase inputs. Therefore, prices of agricultural produce and inputs are a matter of serious concern to all categories of farmers."[41]

Now consider the report from Karnataka:

The movements were of course led by either large or middle farmers not only at the state level but also at the disaggregated levels. But they needed the support of the small farmers to have a mass base. Numbers are important in agitational politics, to organise rallies and protest demonstrations, to block traffic, and court arrest in thousands and make the prisons overflow. . . . A conflict of interest was avoided by centering agitations mostly on commercial crops – a rather dominant instance being sugarcane. . . . No doubt there is disparity among farmers but the bulk of them had a stake in the market in the concerned regions. . . .[42]

Can general conclusions about small farmers' support be drawn from this evidence? Two objections can be raised. First, if there is a clear-cut case in this evidence for a complementarity between the interests of small and big farmers, it is essentially confined to commercial crops (which are, by definition, sold) and does not extend to food crops (of which the small farmers are net buyers). This is damaging, because *the argument about higher prices hurting small farmers concerns food crops, not commercial crops.* Complementarity with regard to food crops must be shown. Second, to the extent that the evidence from Punjab may be taken to mean that such complementarity exists, one will have to reckon with the fact that Punjab, due to its high technological development, is a special case. It is not generalizable.

A response to these objections may be formulated in two steps. First, the turnouts in all states where the farm-price movements have emerged have been large and, typically, all agricultural prices have been on the *movement* agenda, though specific *agitations* may at times be about commercial crops. Short of large-scale coercion or "false consciousness" on the part of small farmers about their interests, such turnouts must indicate widespread support.

No evidence exists for large-scale coercion, nor has a claim to that effect been

41 Gill and Singhal, "Punjab: Farmers' Agitation," p. 1728.
42 M. V. Nadkarni, *Farmers' Movements*, selections from pp. 139–41.

made. The possibility of false consciousness, however, remains, and leads us to the second step of the response. If we inquire at some length into the *logic* of whether the interests of small farmers are served by higher food prices, we may get a better sense of why they would support agitations for prices not only of commercial crops but also of food crops. We shall then have uncovered the "microfoundations" for the rough-and-ready observation of large-scale support. Such microfoundations will also counter the case of a possible "false consciousness."

5.2.5 Why the small farmer supports higher food prices: Microfoundations of a counterintuition

Let us begin with the logic of new technology. Before the advent of the green revolution, key inputs for agriculture could be produced on the farm itself: seeds were traditional and manures organic. Moreover, traditional dug-wells and rainfall used to provide the water required. The green revolution changed the cropping practice. For an increase in yields, it became necessary to make use of High-Yielding Variety (HYV) seeds along with inorganic fertilizers. And since, for best yields, assured water supply at certain key points of the crop cycle was required, reliance on irrigation (and electric power in the case of tubewell irrigation) also became necessary.

All of these inputs – new seeds, chemical fertilizers, power – are purchased inputs. None can be produced on the farm itself. Since input purchases call for cash outlays, it is necessary to sell crops and get as much revenue from that sale as possible. The logic of new technology thus makes all farmers sensitive to prices – both of inputs and outputs. In fact, small farmers can be expected to be *more* sensitive to the immediate postharvest prices than bigger farmers, who can hold on to at least part of their stocks until prices rise after the season, thus making use of a natural interseasonal variation in prices. Lacking the financial capacity of the bigger farmers, smaller farmers do not have such holding power and must sell right after the harvest. Sowing of the next crop must be completed on time, which requires purchased inputs. Since procurement or support prices announced by the government apply mainly to postharvest sales, it follows that small farmers have a clear interest in having them raised. The argument that small farmers are net buyers of foodgrains, and therefore do not benefit from higher prices, fails to take note of this acute short-run *need induced by participation in the input market*. Equivalently, if loans financed the adoption of new technology, repayment of loans is also facilitated by higher prices for the output sold.

It may be contended that, over time, the trade-off between the short-run benefit (higher postharvest income) and the long-run loss (higher financial deficit due to net buying of grains) should become clear to the small farmer, so that his interests would finally lead him to withdraw support from the price agitation.[43] This argument is true statically but not dynamically. It will hold absolutely if yield stays constant. But if more can be produced from the same plot of land, which the new technology makes possible, then, given family size, the food deficit of the small farmer must go down. That should make him less dependent on food purchases in the off-season when prices are high.

Set in motion by increases in yield, this dynamic process means that the off-season buying by the small farmer will disappear altogether. A surplus may even appear, if yield increases are substantial. *The yield effect* of new technology thus tends to counteract the short- versus long-run trade-off, and should enhance the interest of the small farmer in higher grain prices.

Is there evidence that this process, deductively outlined, does actually take place? A time series on marketable surplus according to landholding size is not available. Considerable indications from the green revolution belt are, however, available. In Punjab, for example, farms below 5 acres were unable to produce a wheat surplus in 1962–3; after the green revolution technology was introduced, farms as small as 1.25 to 2.5 acres started producing a surplus of wheat, Punjab's main food crop.[44] Reports from Haryana and Uttar Pradesh confirm a similar trend.[45] If these studies are any guide, then, the yield effect of new technology, leading to small farmers producing a food surplus for the market, is not specific to an area (Punjab or Haryana); it is intrinsic to new technology. It must happen wherever new technology makes headway, though the degree to which it does may differ, depending upon factors such as availability of irrigation and credit, agronomic conditions, etc. In previously underdeveloped regions such as Eastern Uttar Pradesh, which have of late been adopting new technology, a similar process of technological diffusion, and productivity increases, has been in evidence. As a result of the technological spread, the "viability threshold" of farms in the "backward" areas has come down, making smaller farms profitable or at any rate self-sufficient.[46]

A special case: The "pure deficit" farmer. A special class of problems, however, must be noted. A reduced *quantitative* deficit, made possible by higher yields,

---

43 In the case of commercial crops, the long- and short-run distinction need not be so strictly drawn, as the entire output is sold, and the higher its price, the better it is for the farmer.

44 G. K. Chadha, *The State and Rural Economic Transformation*, p. 181.

45 For Haryana, see George Blyn, 1983, "The Green Revolution Revisited," *Economic Development and Cultural Change*, vol. 31, no. 4 (July). For Uttar Pradesh, see Rita Sharma and Thomas T. Poleman, 1993, *The New Economics of India's Green Revolution*, Ithaca and London: Cornell University Press.

46 See the study of Varanasi district in Uttar Pradesh by Gilbert Etienne, 1988, *Food and Poverty: India's Half Won Battle*, New Delhi: Sage Publications. Also G. S. Bhalla and D. S. Tyagi, 1989, *Patterns in Indian Agriculture: A District Level Study*, New Delhi: Institute for Studies in Industrial Development, Indraprastha state. A useful summary of the "narrowing gap" between the Eastern and Western Uttar Pradesh is available in Sharma and Poleman, *The New Economics*, chap. 2.

may or may not mean a smaller *financial* expenditure. With food prices going up, a smaller food deficit today may simply cost more than a bigger deficit yesterday. Since financial expenditure is equal to quantity times price, this may happen if the price increase is not offset by the rise in yields, or if the size of landholding is so small that increased output, despite technical change, does not lead to self-sufficiency for the household. In other words, some farmers may be "pure deficit" farmers.

That this possibility is not simply logical is proven by the fact that even in Punjab, the most technologically advanced agricultural state in India, the onward march of technology has only ensured that those above 1.25 to 2.5 acres, given a family size of five, produce enough to become self-sufficient, not those below that size. It follows that for many in the category of "marginal farmers" (less than 2.5 acres, according to Indian classification) the promise of new technology may be illusory, and if in an attempt to cover the expenses of new inputs demand for higher grain prices is made, the result may simply be deeper debt. For such farmers, demanding lower input prices, which do not increase the financial deficit, would make greater sense than lower input *and* higher output prices, which may increase that deficit. It should not, therefore, be surprising that the immediate cause of several new farm agitations has been an increase by the government in prices of water or electricity, and the agitations so sparked off quickly come to enjoy widespread support (Tamil Nadu, 1971; Punjab, 1973; Uttar Pradesh, 1987, 1993).

Typically, however, even after water or electricity prices are lowered, farm agitations have continued, sometimes with increased fervor. Assuming a marginal farmer will not voluntarily support the demand for higher food prices after he realizes that higher prices only mean bigger debt, might there be other reasons that continue to attract his support?

One reason may still be economic. If price-led higher incomes of the bigger peasants lead to higher employment quickly enough, then it is possible that the new employment opportunities offset the increase in financial deficit. In that case, a marginal farmer household, which is known to supplement the income from land with off-farm work, may also become a net beneficiary of higher prices – and may realize it. Sharma and Poleman, for example, document the remarkable rise in off-farm employment in Western Uttar Pradesh after the green revolution.[47]

A second reason, sociological in nature, may also exist. A landholder, however marginal, may simply choose to identify with the landed classes rather than with the landless. Sociologically embedded notions of status and prestige are supported by being with the landed, not with those lower down in the hierarchy.

A third reason may be political. The choice to have input prices lowered (and loans waived) but at the same time to resist the demand for higher grain prices may not be available in a political movement. A movement tries to aggregate

47 Sharma and Poleman, *The New Economics.*

demands of various sections of the rural population and may not succeed if it concentrates on only one section. Moreover, having a movement may yield other benefits: for example, getting inputs like water and power in time from the huge agricultural bureaucracy, which is known to be corrupt. We do have some evidence of the political rationale for support – namely, a view of organization as a resource to fight corrupt bureaucracy. The following report from Karnataka explains:

When asked about what gains they perceived from the movement, the common farmers said that they received better treatment from government offices and politicians alike and could get their things done without having to resort to bribes and with relatively less trouble and fewer trips than before the movement. . . . Reporting on the aftermath of Malprabha agitation, a press reporter wrote that it 'apparently put the fear of God into the hitherto haughty government officials.'[48]

Similar observations come from Punjab:

The present struggle of the BKU has another dimension. That is [a] fight against corrupt officials who extract money from farmers as a bribe. . . . Two departments have been the targets of BKU, the Punjab State Electricity Board and the police. . . . Of late, the union has also started fighting against the commission agents and food procurement staff against their weighing malpractices. . . .

This has . . . earned the Union prestige and raised it in the eyes of the common public. . . . In the recent past, no union has taken up such cases in Punjab. This has helped the BKU widen its mass base.[49]

Examples from Uttar Pradesh and Maharashtra can also be cited,[50] but the point should be clear. Apart from getting higher prices, the movement also equips farmers to deal with the bureaucracy more effectively. The result is a more reliable power and water supply, without which the potential of new technology cannot be realized. Enjoying a monopoly over supply, the irrigation and electricity boards of the government, in the absence of these pressures, have an unconstrained opportunity to indulge in corruption.

Reduced corruption, one may add, has a larger significance for the small and marginal farmers. The richer farmer, given his connections and status in society, generally has better access to public goods such as water and power. The small farmer, standing alone, is unable to force the bureaucracy to mend its ways. Standing together as a group helps overcome the individual weakness.

Summary. Once the process of technological diffusion gets under way, four scenarios can result from higher food prices for farmers: (1) greater indebtedness

---

48 Nadkarni, *Farmers' Movements*, p. 147.
49 Gill and Singhal, "Punjab," pp. 1729–30.
50 In addition to the obvious issue of prices, a reporter, after surveying the sentiment of the agitating farmers in Western Uttar Pradesh, noted: "Added to this are the ever-present irritants from the U.P. State Power Board maintenance staff. A posting as a power engineer in Meerut division is considered lucrative. The transformers often burn out and the farmers allegedly have to grease the palms of the officials concerned to expedite repairs or replacement. Erratic power and low voltage compound the problems" (*Frontline*, February 20, 1988, p. 7).

if the rise in prices more than offsets the yield-induced reduction in food deficit; (2) smaller food as well as income deficit; (3) food self-sufficiency; and (4) surplus food production. While the desirability of lower input prices is clear in all four scenarios, that of higher grain prices is not evident in the first. Thus, higher foodgrain prices are problematic, but only for a subclass of small farmers, not for all small farmers. The indebtedness of this subclass – alternatively called a class of "pure deficit," or marginal, farmers here – is likely to increase if the movement for higher food prices succeeds only in its price objective. However, some non-price benefits (higher employment, loan waivers), as well as some more general noneconomic benefits and motives (organizational gains from the movement, considerations of status) might counter the direct effect of grain price increases. These benefits illustrate that even the support of marginal farmers may be squarely based on considerations of personal interest, not on a misperception of interests or on coercion.

5.3 THE PLIGHT OF AGRICULTURAL LABORERS

Different categories of farmers view higher wages differently. The big farmers' position is relatively clear-cut: at any given point in time the higher the wages are, the lower will be the profits.[51] The position of small farmers is more complex. If they are entirely dependent on family labor, wages are of little interest to them. If they hire labor, then, like big farmers, higher wages are anathema to them. A third scenario is that of marginal farmers. For an undetermined but large number of marginal farmers, wages are a supplementary, though important, source of income; but, as already explained, prices have also mattered to them since new technology has placed even marginal farmers in the marketplace for input purchases and crop sales.

As for the landless agricultural workers, regardless of the long-run implications of higher agricultural prices for wages, minimum wages in the short run are an important concern. While farmers have pressed for higher prices, laborers have fought for wages. Here is a report from Karnataka:

The Dalits[52] do not accept the view that once prices improve, agricultural wages too will improve. Krishnappa (the President of the Karnataka Dalit Association) pointed out that in Shimoga district itself, both paddy and sugarcane prices have more than doubled in the preceding decade, but wages have remained practically the same. The fact that no agitation, not even a symbolic act of pressuring the government to raise minimum wages, took place has not gone unnoticed by the Dalits. On the other hand, farmers have resisted when the Dalits have asked for implementation of at least the minimum wages. This author witnessed such a case at close quarters in an irrigated village, Kokkampalayan in Coim-

---

51 This, of course, is not to deny that, depending upon productivity, the inverse relationship between wages and profits might weaken, or dissolve, over the medium or long run. However, since it is not clear how long the long run is, the zero-sum short run has a tendency to override what could potentially be a positive-sum long run.

52 The term "Dalits" stands for scheduled caste agricultural laborers.

batore district, in 1979. The farmers were organised and were fighting, on the one hand, against the government for concessions in electricity dues and loan repayments, and, on the other, against the agricultural laborers – mostly scheduled castes – who demanded implementation of minimum wages.[53]

Or, where due to agricultural growth, actual wages have already exceeded the minimum wages, as in Punjab, the struggle has been over higher wages:

The second implication of the BKU [Bhartiya Kisan Union] activity in Punjab is the growing strength of the peasantry via-à-vis agricultural laborers. . . . In 1979, when agricultural workers launched their struggle in Gurudipura village [of Ludhiana] on the wage issue, the BKU president . . . threatened to teach them a lesson in the same way as in Muskbad village [of Ludhiana] where they were forced to take shelter in the sugarcane fields against the farmers' fury.[54]

The demand for loan waivers has also been formulated by the movement leaders in a manner that goes against agricultural laborers. It is well known that institutional loans – from the cooperatives and the commercial banks – go mostly to landed peasants, whereas the loans of the landless come overwhelmingly from the informal credit market dominated by the village moneylender and rich farmer (the two sometimes being the same person). The agitation leaders have asked for a waiver of institutional loans, not all loans; nor have they asked for extension of institutional credit to agricultural laborers, which might enable them to engage in some durable income-enhancing economic activity. Asked why that was so, an activist of the Karnataka Farmers' Association remarked: "if the labourers get monetary or material benefits or loans from the government, they can not repay them since they spend on liquor; or, they would develop their own activities (like livestock rearing) and would not come for agricultural coolie work. Agriculture would then suffer without coolies."[55]

How generalizable are these observations?[56] The evidence cited above suggests the appropriateness of a Marxian understanding of rural class relations. Such an understanding runs counter to the picture of rural India traditionally drawn by anthropologists and sociologists. The latter have often found not class conflicts but a Durkheimian world in the villages – mutually beneficial, personalistic, patron–client linkages between the landlords and their dependents.[57] The services provided by the landlord are both economic and personal: they range from consumption and production loans to providing help in dealings with

53 Nadkarni, *Farmers' Movement*, p. 152.
54 Gill and Singhal, "Punjab," p. 1732.
55 Nadkarni, *Farmers' Movement*, p. 153.
56 There is some evidence that such differences were also evident in Tamil Nadu and Maharashtra. For Tamil Nadu, see R. V. Rajdurai, 1980, "Green Power on the March," *Economic and Political Weekly*, vol. 15, no. 52, pp. 2170–1.
57 The potency of patron–client relationships, always emphasized by liberal sociologists and anthropologists, is now increasingly accepted by Marxist scholars. Two recent examples are Ashok Rudra, "Emerging Class Structure in Indian Agriculture," and Pranab Bardhan, "Agrarian Class Formation in India," both in Pranab Bardhan and T. N. Srinivasan, eds., 1988, *Rural Poverty in South Asia*, New York: Columbia University Press.

the bureaucracy and police, assistance in children's education, in daughters' marriages, funerals, etc.[58] Do the laborers generally oppose the price agitations, or support them because their patrons are among the leaders?

5.3.1 Problems in empirical evidence: The structural position of agricultural workers

By now, it has come to be accepted that both Marxian and Durkheimian scenarios are ideal types. Different parts of rural India show differential proximity to the two scenarios.[59] If a generalization is possible at all, it is that while the normative order of patron–client relationships has been gradually disintegrating, class conflict has not always replaced it.[60] Rather, agricultural laborers have been left in an awkward position.[61] On the one hand, lacking channels of institutional credit, they are dependent upon the richer farmers for consumption and distress loans. On the other hand, their increasing consciousness about their rights, induced in considerable measure by a democratic political order, makes them resentful of the continuing social deprivations and indignities that a hierarchical Hindu social order reserves for them. Agricultural laborers come overwhelmingly from the formerly untouchable scheduled castes, scheduled tribes, or other "low castes," and, for sociological-cum-ritualistic notions of purity and pollution, all upper castes, whatever their internal divisions, share a mixture of condescension, apathy, or outright antipathy toward the lowest castes.

The increasing political awareness of agricultural laborers, however, has not generally translated into organized collective action because (1) unlike the landlords or rich farmers, those who mobilize them – parties or nonparty organizations – are unable to provide credit, insurance, or employment, and (2) over time, even the organizers, including the Communist parties, have been mobilizing on

---

58 A laborer interviewed in Bengal explained why he valued his landlord: "I am a poor man and I do not even have enough to eat every day. I may require urgently some money for a funeral in the family. To whom shall I go?" See Rudra, in Bardhan and Srinivasan, *Rural Poverty*, p. 498.

59 For a balanced treatment of the Marxian and Durkheimian perspectives in the Indian context, see Herring, *Land to the Tiller*, pp. 31–42.

60 André Beteille, 1974, *Studies in Agrarian Social Structure*, Delhi: Oxford University Press.

61 I base the following considerations on a variety of sources dealing with agricultural laborers. Prominent among them are: André Beteille, 1972, "Agrarian Relations in Tanjore District," *Sociological Bulletin*, vol. 21, no. 2; Marshal Bouton, 1985, *Agrarian Radicalism in South India*, Princeton, NJ: Princeton University Press; Jan Breman, 1974, *Patronage and Exploitation: Changing Agrarian Relations in South Gujarat, India*, Berkeley and Los Angeles: University of California Press; Mark Jurgensmeyer, 1979, "Culture of Deprivation: Three Case Studies in Punjab," *Economic and Political Weekly*, Annual Number (February); Joan Mencher, 1978, *Agriculture and Social Structure in Tamil Nadu*, New Delhi: Allied Publishers. Two reviews of the vast literature on the mobilization of the rural poor are: Joan Mencher, 1988, "Peasants and Agricultural Laborers: An Analytical Assessment of Issues Involved in Their Organizing," in Bardhan and Srinivasan, *Rural Poverty*; and Rudolph and Rudolph, 1987, *In Pursuit of Lakshmi*, pp. 376–92.

multiclass lines, not concentrating exclusively on laborers' interests. The landless agricultural laborers constitute at best a mere 20 to 25 percent of the rural electorate, which therefore makes multiclass issues that address the other 75–80 percent electorally much more appealing.[62] Once land reforms ceased to be a big political issue, prices rather than wages began to attract the maximum political attention of political parties. For prices addressed many classes in the countryside; wages, only the laborers.

The agricultural laborers at this point are therefore caught in limbo: the old patron–client order is disintegrating, but the new political parties or organizations that attempt to organize laborers against its injustices are unable to provide the benefits the old order did. Collective weakness coexists with individual resentment and consciousness of rights.

5.3.2 The structural context and strategies of landless laborers

A deep ambivalence thus marks the attitude of agricultural laborers toward the new peasant movement. Independently of whether or not agricultural laborers gain economically from higher prices in the long run, there are two processes operating on them, one pulling them toward the price agitations, the other drawing them away. The economic dependence of laborers on richer farmers – not only for loans but also for employment[63] – tends to generate a pressure toward supporting the higher-caste patrons agitating for higher prices. At the same time, political awareness that organizing can be a means of both fighting social deprivations and striking better wage bargains produces a tendency toward wage struggles and nonparticipation in price agitations. Which way this underlying conflict is resolved in a given situation depends on many factors: what the history of caste relations in a region is; whether agricultural laborers come overwhelmingly from a single scheduled or lower caste;[64] how committed the political parties or nonparty organizations are to the landless; whether other employment opportunities are available, particularly in the neighboring towns; or, equivalently, whether growth in local agriculture has made labor in a previously labor-

---

62 See Atul Kohli, 1987, *The State and Poverty in India: The Politics of Reform*, Cambridge: Cambridge University Press, chap. 3. The Communist party learned this lesson originally in Kerala, where the tenants, having received land under Communist-sponsored land reforms, turned their backs on the party. See Ronald J. Herring, 1988, "Stealing Congress's Thunder: The Rise to Power of a Communist Movement in South India," in Kay Lawson and Peter Merkl, eds., *When Parties Fail: Emerging Alternative Organizations*, Princeton, NJ: Princeton University Press.

63 In a labor-surplus economy, labor contracts can be rotated and somebody else can always be hired to do unskilled work.

64 A classic example of this is the Thanjavur district of Tamil Nadu, which also happens to be one of the most widely studied cases of agricultural labor unrest. In the Old Delta region of the district, where political radicalism has been very strong, 60 to 80 percent of the agricultural laborers come from the scheduled castes, whereas the landlords are predominantly Brahmins. The sociological cohesion of each opposing class has given class conflict an added strength. See Bouton, *Agrarian Radicalism*.

abundant economy scarce. By reducing the dependence on landlords, the last two scenarios tend to increase the bargaining power of the landless.

These factors are so locally specific and indeterminate that it would be meaningless to point to any single typical response on the part of the landless. There are pockets where they have managed to get relatively organized: in Kerala and West Bengal, and in parts of Punjab, Karnataka, Bihar, Andhra, Tamil Nadu, and Maharashtra. Of these, in Kerala, Bihar, and Bengal, price agitations are still not important; in Punjab, Karnataka, and Tamil Nadu, where they are, conflicts between the laborers demanding higher wages and the farmers agitating for higher wages have been reported, but even within these states, there are areas of labor acquiescence.[65] In Maharashtra, the leadership of the price movement has made a special effort to bring the landless together with the upper castes and convince them that higher prices also mean better wages, reducing the possibility of conflict that would emerge from a stronger Dalit organization and repressive upper-caste behavior.[66] All conceivable patterns – opposition, support, apathy – thus coexist.

5.3.3 A recapitulation

The claim that the new peasant agitations are class-driven is weak. Necessary distinctions between the small farmers and landless laborers on the one hand and between input prices, foodgrain prices, and prices for cash crops on the other have not been made.

1. Small farmers. On both logical and empirical grounds, there is reason to believe that the support of small farmers for higher prices for cash and food crops and lower prices for inputs is widespread. Viewed dynamically, powerful economic reasons can be identified for demanding higher prices.

2. Marginal farmers. On economic considerations alone, the subclass of marginal farmers can be expected to support higher prices for cash crops and lower input prices but not higher food prices, unless strong political reasons – organization as a check on the bureaucratic abuse of input delivery – and visible employment effects are simultaneously present.

3. Agricultural laborers. The case of agricultural laborers has deep ambiguities and ambivalences. The political and sociological dilemmas of their existence – organizational difficulties, caste composition – complicate an already

---

65 See a very interesting account of the patterns of landless peasant behavior studied by Mark Jurgensmeyer in three Punjabi villages: one in which the landless are completely unorganized, the other in which there are signs of organization, and a third in which considerable organization has already come about. (Jurgensmeyer, "Culture of Deprivation"). Also see Amrinderpal Singh, "Farm Workers versus Rich Farmers," *Economic and Political Weekly*, October 27, 1979.

66 Joshi's movement in Maharashtra, as already mentioned, is the first new agrarian movement that has finally included higher minimum wages on the movement agenda. For an account of how the Dalits view Joshi's movement, see Gail Omvedt, 1988, "The New Peasant Movement in India," *Bulletin of Concerned Asian Scholars*, vol. 20, no. 2 (April–June).

uncompelling economic argument that higher producer prices lead to higher workers' wages. Patterns of both support and opposition can be detected. Pending further evidence, the scales seem tilted in favor of a view that support when it has existed may be due more to routine compulsions of their dependence upon the rich farmers than to a genuine belief that price rises have a favorable wage effect.

To conclude, while price agitations cannot be considered to be class-driven in the narrow sense of furthering the interests of the rich peasantry, they do not unambiguously serve the interests of the entire sector either. They embrace most of the landed peasantry, but whether the landless also benefit remains questionable. Since up to 20 percent of rural India is landless, a significant section of Bharat, in all probability, does not gain from these agitations. If wages do go up in the long run, a benefit will have accrued; meanwhile, everyday difficulties are likely to overpower any future hope.

5.4 IMPACT ON PARTY POLITICS AND ECONOMIC POLICY

5.4.1 The response of political parties

These agitations became a serious political concern for the parties in the early eighties. Recognition of the issues raised by these movements was hastened by the brief tenure of Charan Singh and his peasant-based Lok Dal in Delhi, but the hold of nonparty leaders over these movements was perhaps of greater concern to political parties.

The first impact of these agitations was ideological. Most party manifestos – which reflect, however imperfectly, the program of a party in India – began to change in the eighties. Of the two main centrist parties, the program of the Janata party has already been discussed in Chapter 4. The Congress party also did not remain unaffected. In the 1971 and 1977 general elections, the Congress manifesto did not contain any references to agricultural prices. The agrarian program of the Congress party in 1977 was "to develop and modernise agriculture" and to "promote the interests of the small and marginal farmers, agricultural workers. . . ."[67] In the 1980 election manifesto, after castigating the Janata government (1977–80) for not protecting the interests of the agriculturists, "despite its loud professions," the Congress conceded that "the working of the Agricultural Prices Commission and the Food Corporation of India needs vast improvement" and promised that "greater attention [will be] paid to the farmer's cost structure" and "input cost indexation of support prices will be instituted so as to safeguard the farmer's income from inflationary trends."[68] Even in the 1984 elections after Mrs. Gandhi's death, when young urban professionals, seemingly unconcerned

67 Congress Party Manifesto (CPM), 1977, reproduced in Weiner, *India at the Polls 1977*, p. 125.
68 *Election Manifesto 1980*, Indian National Congress (I), p. 22.

with rural India, took over the Congress party under Rajiv Gandhi, the party promised "remunerative prices to the kisans [peasants]."[69] The trend continued in the 1989 and 1991 elections.[70]

The transformation of the parties of the left and right is even more indicative of the current trends. Until the mid-1970s, the Communist parties used to believe that the consequences of higher food prices were highly inegalitarian.[71] In the early eighties, the Communist Party Marxist (CPM) reformulated its position. Harkishan Singh Surjeet, a top-ranking party theoretician, wrote in 1981: "Every section of the peasantry, including the poorest of them, is forced to sell a part of his produce . . . to purchase foodgrains for his family's consumption . . . and is therefore interested in such a level of prices as would meet the cost of production."[72] The position of the second main Communist party, the CPI, goes a step further. Indradip Sinha, Surjeet's counterpart in the CPI, not only claimed that all sections of the peasantry now sold (and bought) in the market; he even argued that "payment of remunerative prices to peasants will facilitate the payment of minimum wages to agricultural laborers as well."[73]

On the right, the Bhartiya Janata party (BJP), traditionally an urban party with a strong base in North India, was barely concerned with farm prices in the seventies. The BJP currently advocates remunerative grain prices.[74] Moreover, in order to ensure that the urban consumer prices do not go up substantially as a result of higher producer prices, the party would increase input subsidies and/or consumer food subsidy. Asked why an urban party should support higher agricultural prices, Atal Behari Vajpayee, a leading member of the party and its president between 1981 and 1986, commented that no party in India could possibly have a significant political future on the basis of the urban vote alone, but for broadening into the countryside, a pro-price position was essential in the political circumstances of the 1980s.[75]

69 *Election Manifesto 1984*, Indian National Congress (I), p. 12.
70 *Election Manifesto*, General Election 1991, p. 34.
71 See Mitra, *Terms of Trade and Class Relations*, p. 120. Mitra, before he resigned as Finance Minister of West Bengal in 1986, was one of the chief spokesmen of the CPM. Mitra's own intellectual positions have not changed, but those of the CPM have. On being asked why it changed its position, Mitra was characteristically candid: "In our kind of polity, populism can affect all parties. If you are in the market for votes, even leftist parties will not go against the rich peasantry." Author's interview with Mitra, Calcutta, December 25, 1984.
72 In "Upsurge," *Seminar*, no. 267, November 1981, p. 16. A similar statement is Surjeet's party pamphlet *For a Fair Deal to Cotton Growers*, New Delhi: All India Kisan Sabha, n.d.
73 Indradip Sinha, 1984, "Why Remunerative Prices for Agricultural Produce?" in Y. V. Krishna Rao, G. Parthasarthy, Rajeshwar Rao, M. Yadava Reddy, and Waheeduddin Khan, eds., *Peasant Farming and Growth of Capitalism in Indian Agriculture*, Vijaywada: Visalandhra Publishing House, p. 395.
74 *Mid-Term Poll to Lok Sabha, May 1991: Our Commitments*, p. 12.
75 Author's telephone interview with Atal Behari Vajpayee, Boston, June 22, 1987. Vajpayee also added that whereas land reform, the political slogan of yesteryear, benefited only the small man, higher prices benefit everybody in the countryside – *bade ko bhi fayda, chhote ko bhi.*

5.4.2 Response of the state governments

Since the central government is at a remove from state capitals and towns where most of the agitations have been launched, it is the state governments that have had directly to face the farmers so far. Essentially, they can be said to be caught between the contrary pulls of populism and fiscal realism.

Until the recent economic reforms, the state governments were generally conciliatory on input and crop prices. On a number of occasions, an increase in power or water tariffs was the immediate cause of these agitations. The state governments would argue that such an increase was essential to cover the costs of producing and distributing power, or to reduce the deficits of the state-run electricity and irrigation boards. If agitations broke out as a result – as they did in Tamil Nadu (1970, 1972, and 1977), Punjab (1975 and 1985), and Uttar Pradesh (1986–7, 1988–9) – then, more often than not, electricity and water tariffs, which lie within the purview of state governments, would be reduced. Similarly, markups on the central government's procurement/support prices have also been given. However, since state governments now have to provide for these markups from their own budgets,[76] their strategy has been twofold: (1) pressuring the central government for higher prices so that the budgetary burden on the state is minimized;[77] (2) providing markups only for crops grown in areas where the agitation is the strongest, not across the board for all crops.

As for the demand for a waiver of overdue loans, the state governments were unaccommodating to begin with. They typically argued that a blanket loan waiver was unacceptable to India's central bank, the Reserve Bank of India, and would result only in reducing the future flow of credit to farmers.

Because of the way the Indian credit system is structured, there is substantial truth in this argument. Until 1989–90, roughly 60 percent of the institutional credit in agriculture used to come from the cooperative sector, the rest mostly being supplied by the nationalized commercial banking sector.[78] A blanket loan waiver by a state government essentially means that the government will have to step in to finance the write-offs falling in the cooperative sector, unless of course the commercial banking sector does that. Commercial banks are, however, gov-

---

76 Sensing the political abuse of wide-ranging markups and their increasing occurrence, the Reserve Bank of India discontinued credit for markups in the late seventies, asking states to use their own budgetary funds if they wished to increase the support or procurement price.

77 Based on interviews with politicians. Gundu Rao, the late chief minister of Karnataka during the year 1979–81, was candid in his response: "how else does one deal with the increasing farm pressures at the state level – you give them a high enough producer price or if the state budget does not permit that, you pressure Delhi to increase the price so that the central government finances the increase." Author's interview with Rao in Delhi, January 21, 1987.

78 For figures since 1985–6, see the Government of India, 1993, *Economic Survey 1992–93*, Delhi: Ministry of Finance, Economic Division, p. 165. For a comprehensive review of earlier years, see Suresh Tendulkar, 1983, "Rural Institutional Credit and Rural Development: A Review Article," *Indian Economic Review*, vol. 28, no. 1 (January–June), pp. 102–37.

erned by central rules, not by state rules. Hence, short of the willingness of the central government or the Reserve Bank of India to bear the write-offs, the burden of the waiver falls on the state budget. Since the taxation system in India is heavily tilted in favor of the central government and most of the tax revenue falls in the central bag, the ramshackle budgetary house of most states impedes the generosity of waivers.

In the judgment of two state governments, however, these difficulties were not insurmountable. Political benefits of a selective, if not a blanket, waiver seemed to outweigh its economic costs. In 1980, the Tamil Nadu government decided to waive overdue loans of small farmers only, arguing that (1) small farmers deserved a waiver and (2) that a blanket waiver, by eventually reducing the flow of government credit, would only make the small farmers dependent on the big landlords for credit, thereby reviving the traditional ties of dependence. The Tamil Nadu government thus actually succeeded in weakening the peasant movement in the state in the 1980s, though the financial costs of even the selective waiver must have been quite high. More spectacularly, Devi Lal, chief minister of the state of Haryana between 1987–9 promised to write off cooperative loans (of up to Rs 20,000) in his massively successful state election campaign in 1987. The promise of a waiver was an important reason for Devi Lal's electoral success.[79]

These two cases were unrepresentative. With its lion's share of the total governmental revenue in India and control over the central bank, only the central government, theoretically, has the capacity to grant loan waivers. Large-scale loan waivers are never easy, as they can damage the viability of any financial system.

However, the unlikely did happen. In the 1989 elections, the Janata Dal (party) defeated the Congress and came to power in Delhi. An important Janata leader, Devi Lal moved from the state of Haryana to the center, becoming India's Deputy Prime Minister in the two short-lived Janata governments between 1989 and 1991. Taking a leaf from Devi Lal's success at the state level and seeking to cultivate a rural constituency, the Janata party, in its 1991 election manifesto, had committed itself to loan waivers. The following section, inter alia, deals with how the promise of waivers was kept, and with what financial costs.

5.4.3 The response of the central government

On the whole, the central government has made three kinds of concessions since the early 1980s. Two of these have affected the functioning of the Agricultural Prices Commission (APC) – one relating to its principles of functioning, and the other to its personnel structure. A third type of decision concerns the waiving of loans.

---

79 *India Today*, June 30, 1987.

Changing the terms of reference of the APC was one of the first things done by Mrs. Gandhi's government upon her return to power in 1980. The APC was asked to include the agriculture–industry terms of trade while determining agricultural prices, thus enlarging a key principle of earlier years, according to which increases in the prices of *agricultural inputs* were the prime determinant of support prices, not increases in the prices of all goods, including *consumption goods*, that the agriculture sector buys.[80]

In 1987, two more changes were made – one symbolic, the other more concrete. Meeting the frequent criticism made by some of the movement leaders, particularly Sharad Joshi, the Rajiv Gandhi government gave a new name – Commission of Agricultural Costs and Prices (CACP) – to the APC.[81] A more concrete decision, however, was to change the personnel policy of the Commission. Instead of having just one agriculturist on the APC surrounded by three agricultural experts (agricultural economists, agronomists, or administrators specializing in agriculture), the newly christened CACP would have three agriculturists and three experts, with one more member – a technocrat – in the chair. The decision was implemented in 1988 when price agitations flared up in Gujarat, Maharashtra, and Uttar Pradesh in quick succession. A policy-recommending body, which in its original dispensation in 1965 consisted of technocrats alone, had thus changed its collective face twice: first in 1975, when an agriculturist was appointed to the Commission, and second in 1988, when the Commission was split into two halves, technical and political, though the former half still retained its edge via a technocratic chairman.

In October 1989, barely a month before the upcoming parliamentary elections, the government added two new principles, both favorable to farmers, to the methodology of cost determination on the basis of which the CACP recommends agricultural prices. The matter was considered important enough for the announcement to be made by Prime Minister Rajiv Gandhi, not by his Agriculture minister: "First, we shall determine the wage costs on the basis of the statutory minimum wages for agricultural labor . . . or the actual wages paid, *whichever is higher*. Second, we shall include in the cost of production the labor input of the *kisan* [farmer] at a higher wage reflecting the managerial and entrepreneurial role of the kisan" (emphasis added).[82]

---

80 This was already under way before Mrs. Gandhi returned to power in 1980. She simply stole the march over Janata by quickly implementing the principle that was getting lost in the factional bickering of the Janata party.

81 Joshi had been claiming that the main function of the Commission was to collect cost data and to base price recommendations thereupon, rather than go into issues such as impact of agricultural prices on the rest of the economy, industrial costs, and inflation levels. The Commission, in Joshi's view, simply did not have the competence to estimate such complex economywide implications of agricultural prices. Their inclusion in the criteria of price determination, argued Joshi, only lowered the price level that might be permitted if costs were the only criterion, as, he thought, they should be. Sharad Joshi, "Scrap the APC," in *'Bharat' Speaks Out.*

82 *Lok Sabha Debates*, 8th ser., vol. 53, October 12, 1989, pp. 34–5.

The first principle meant that the labor component of the agricultural costs would be higher than before. Earlier, only the market wage rates were treated as labor costs, even if they were lower than the statutory minimum wage rates (possible in the less advanced agricultural regions). Now, whichever of the two was higher would be taken as the acceptable data. The second criterion essentially implied a markup on the existing paid-out costs. Entrepreneurship is typically not a cost item; the entrepreneur assesses the market and sometimes *reduces costs* to create a niche in the market or to establish dominance for his product. The new government announcement inverted this logic. It made entrepreneurship an addition to costs, not a means to reduce costs.

Rajiv Gandhi himself could not implement the new policy, for his party was voted out in the November 1989 elections. However, the successor Janata government was more than willing to put the new additions through. An important campaign claim of the Janata, after all, was that the Rajiv Gandhi government was a pro-urban, "yuppie" government, oblivious to the needs of the countryside. In April 1990, the Janata government issued a directive to the CACP, asking it to include the new cost principles in its price considerations. It required that, for entrepreneurship, "the total cost computed . . . be raised by 10 percent."[83]

The more dramatic move by the Janata government was made on loan waivers. Earlier, under Rajiv Gandhi, even at the height of the peasant agitation close to Delhi and its environs in 1987–8, and despite a much publicized political decision of a rival party to write off loans in the state of Haryana, the central government (1) agreed only to write off interest if it exceeded the principal amount *in areas hit by drought for three consecutive years*, not in other areas, and (2) promised that recovery of the principal amount would be rescheduled in these areas.[84]

With the Janata in power, the wall of resistance was finally broken down. Devi Lal was also one of the chief architects of the electoral coalition between most non-Congress parties. In the election manifesto, as already indicated, the Janata had promised a waiver of loans. Rewarded for his political services, Devi Lal was made Deputy Prime Minister as well as Agriculture minister. For his support of the Janata against Rajiv Gandhi, Sharad Joshi was made adviser to the Agriculture Ministry and given a cabinet rank.

The Janata government waived all agricultural loans under central jurisdiction up to Rs 10,000 – that is, loans extended by the commercial banks and regional

---

83 A new term – Cost C3 – was introduced for the new cost so computed, on which a profit margin would be given to the farmer. Soon after coming to office, the Janata government set up three committees to look into agricultural policy issues. These committees were headed, respectively, by Hanumantha Rao, a leading agricultural economist; Bhanu Pratap Singh, a rural politician and former minister; and Sharad Joshi, a nonparty peasant leader. The most vigorous proponent of the new cost methodology was Sharad Joshi. The experts under Hanumantha Rao also went along partly.

84 Rajiv Gandhi's statement, *The Times of India*, February 16, 1988.

rural banks; loans from cooperative banks and societies are under state governments. The Janata financed the state governments for half the expenses of cooperative loan waivers with a grant. It also instructed the Reserve Bank of India, India's central bank, to give a one-year loan to state governments so that they could finance the remaining half of the write-off. It was emphasized that the waiver was a one-time affair, not to be repeated. The waiver, according to the government, was aimed at compensating farmers for a deterioration in their terms of trade.[85]

Several technocrats had objected to the scheme. So had some of the political colleagues of Devi Lal. At an earlier time in the country's history, the finance minister would have almost certainly opposed the move.[86] Madhu Dandavate, the Janata's finance minister, simply argued that commitments to the electorate must be kept; moreover, corners could be cut elsewhere.[87] The waiver, he said, was financially affordable.

The cost of the waiver to the exchequer has been variously estimated. The World Bank believes that in 1990 alone the cost was Rs 28.4 billion (roughly $1.5 billion), and the eventual cost would be Rs 80 billion.[88] Ironically, any electoral rewards that the Janata may have reaped were drowned in the factional squabbles in the government, in which Devi Lal identified with rural India and castigated the rest for their urban biases. Eventually, the BJP's mass mobilization for building a temple at Ayodhya restructured the political agenda of the country, pushing the urban–rural issues to the background. Devi Lal's truncated Janata lost the elections badly.

The Congress government, elected to power in June 1991, inherited some of the consequences of the loan waiver, including a fiscal mess, which a program of structural adjustment since July 1991 has been seeking to address. Reporting that "right now, there is a mad scramble for getting the loans waived," the new agriculture minister, Balram Jakhar, viewed as a peasant leader himself and known in his career for pro-agriculture views, explained some of the consequences to Parliament: "People have become bank defaulters and Banks are not advancing any loans to them. It sets a bad precedent. People taking loans later demand that their loans should also be waived. . . . I want to give farmers self respect. I want to protect their honor, but in some other way."[89] So unmanageable

85 Finance Minister Madhu Dandavate in *Lok Sabha Debates*, 9th ser., September 7, 1990, pp. 23–4. Also see a subsequent rationale for loan waivers given by Prime Minister V. P. Singh after his fall from power in *Lok Sabha Debates*, 10th ser., September 3, 1991, pp. 392–8. The loan waiver scheme was officially called the Agricultural and Rural Debt Scheme, 1990.

86 As did Rajiv Gandhi's Finance Minister, S. B. Chavan, *Lok Sabha Debates*, 8th ser., vol. 51, August 16, 1989, pp. 171–80. Also, *Lok Sabha Debates*, August 4, 1989, pp. 23–4.

87 Author's interview with Madhu Dandavate, Finance Minister (1989–90), Delhi, January 10, 1990.

88 The World Bank, 1991, *India: 1991 Country Economic Memorandum*, Washington, D.C., p. 31.

89 *Lok Sabha Debates*, 10th ser., September 3, 1991, pp. 484–5.

did the scheme become, continued Jakhar, that "now the scheme has been withdrawn." Enough fiscal damage, however, had already been done, as the World Bank figures cited above illustrate.

Despite these fiscally profligate attempts to win over the countryside, the Janata's inability to return to power in the 1991 elections and the success of the Bharatiya Janata party (BJP) in placing religious issues on the agenda, relegating the urban–rural issues to the sidelines, raise serious conceptual issues about how far rural power can go. Why are openly pro-rural parties unable to come to power, even though more than 50 percent of India is still rural? Moreover, why are nonparty organizations, despite their popularity, unable to convert themselves into successful political parties? Given a conflict between religious and caste issues on the one hand and economic interests on the other, how do farmers themselves make political and electoral choices? So far we have dealt with the rise of rural power; these questions point to the factors impeding a further rise. Chapter 6 discusses them in detail.

5.5 CONCLUSION

In terms of the rural–urban divide, the decade of the 1980s reinforced a trend that the 1970s had initiated. The rise of Charan Singh and his peasant-based party in national politics had put rural India on the power map. Charan Singh's fall from power at the end of the 1970s coincided with the spread of nonparty agitations that concentrated on higher agricultural prices, loan waivers, and a better allocation of public resources for the countryside. Defying intellectual predictions about representing only the bigger farmers, the agitation leaders developed a substantial mass base that included all classes of landed peasants and, in some cases, even the landless agricultural laborers. They also compelled political parties to incorporate remunerative agricultural prices and even loan waivers into their programs. With the political parties unable to tame the political rise of new leaders and the national media acknowledging the strength of the new peasant leaders, rural India in the 1980s came to enjoy a political visibility that was only partially foreshadowed by Charan Singh's brief tenure in power.

As a result of the rising rural pressure in the polity, several significant changes in policy institutions and norms were made by the policy makers. The personnel policy of the principal state institution involved with agricultural price policy, the Commission for Agricultural Costs and Prices (CACP) has been altered. Instead of being a purely technocratic body, the Commission is almost half political now. Similarly, for determining the level of farm prices, the Commission is not only supposed to look into costs but also, inter alia, the agriculture–industry terms of trade, plus provide a markup based on "entrepreneurial costs." Finally, as the decade closed, loan waivers, at substantial cost to the public exchequer, were also granted to farmers.

Still, farmers continue to claim that India dominates Bharat. Is that true?

6

Has rural India lost out?

Is the rising power of a group or class reflected in changes in the economic behavior of the state? If so, how precisely does that happen? The argument so far has dealt with these questions at two levels. In order to proceed to the central task of this chapter – namely, assessing the impact of group power on economic policy outcomes – let me first recapitulate the argument developed thus far.

First, both in party and nonparty politics, an unambiguous rise in agrarian power has taken place, which, in turn, has led to an ideological reformulation of politics on the agrarian question. All political parties support the demand for higher agricultural prices and subsidies, and call for a better deal for the countryside in economic development.

Has the ideological reformulation of party politics influenced economic policy? The second level of the argument has dealt with changes in policy norms. India's agricultural policy was changed in the mid-1960s. Abandoning the principles of low agricultural prices and labor-intensive agricultural development, the post-Nehru government made farm-price incentives and investments in new technology the key norms of agricultural policy. This change took place long before pressures for higher prices emerged in the polity, indicating that a change in policy principles actually led to a new definition of agrarian interests, not vice versa. However, once the new definition of agrarian interests acquired political momentum, the government reworked the principle of price incentives in a manner more favorable to the countryside. The original definition of incentives was based on a cost-plus formula, where farm costs were taken to mean input costs, over which a margin of profit was given. By 1980, agriculture–industry terms of trade were added to the cost criterion, thereby including not simply the changes in the costs of *farm inputs* but also rural *consumption goods*. Even if the terms of trade went against agriculture due to a reduction of agricultural costs (which would tend to depress agricultural prices), such cost reduction would not be transmitted to the entire economy. Rather, the terms of trade would be adjusted in favor of agriculture politically. In 1990–1, two more modifications were made, both favorable to the countryside. In cost calculations, labor expended on the farm would now be priced at the market level or at the statutory minimum level, *whichever was higher*; earlier, labor had been priced at the market rates only. The second modification concerned "entrepreneurial costs." After agricultural costs were calculated, a 10 percent markup would be added to the costs as a reward for farmers' entrepreneurial function. Thus, even though the cost-plus formula continues to determine prices, how the costs are to be calculated has been changed in favor of the countryside.

The structure of state institutions responsible for agricultural policy has also been transformed. Since the mid-sixties, the Commission on Agricultural Costs and Prices (CACP) has been the institutional centerpiece of agricultural policy. Initially envisioned as a purely technical body consisting of economists, statisticians, and agricultural administrators, the government in the mid-1970s gave the CACP a "farmers' representative" appointed from among the politicians. Going further in 1987, the government split the Commission into three technical members and three farmers representatives.

In short, *rural power* has gone up in the polity, *policy norms* have become more favorable to the countryside, and the *institutional* centerpiece stands transformed. Have the *outcomes* changed for the countryside? Put another way, have farm incomes gone up as a result?

My argument proceeds in three steps.

1. First, the received arguments are critically examined and their inadequacies highlighted (Sections 6.1 and 6.2).
2. The next section develops a simple measure for farm returns and applies it to wheat and rice. Farm returns have depended on what crop one grows and where, a mixed outcome that has come about despite a rise in agrarian power in the political system and despite the policy changes in favor of the countryside (Section 6.3). There does not appear to be a one-to-one correspondence between political power and economic outcomes. Why should that be so?
3. The disjunction between (*a*) the rural power and pro-rural policy changes, on the one hand, and (*b*) mixed economic outcomes, on the other, is caused by three factors that check rural power in the short and medium run: technical change, fiscal realities, and income distribution in society (Section 6.4). Chapter 7 will take a step further and ask whether these constraints are in some sense binding or are they politically manipulable.

6.1 POLICY OUTCOMES FOR FARM GROUPS: TERMS OF THE EXISTING DEBATE

Have the farmers lost out? The existing answers depend on where one looks. The politicians argue that farm incomes have declined, but a raging controversy marks the intellectual debate. The views fall into two categories, class and sectoral. The class-based view is that the rich peasantry has benefited at the cost of the rural and urban poor. The sectoral view is that India's advances in agricultural production, particularly in food, have mainly benefited urban India, much to the detriment of rural incomes.

Four kinds of indicators have been used for supporting these positions: (1)

agriculture–industry terms of trade, assuming that a decline in agriculture's terms of trade represents a loss in rural incomes (and vice versa); (2) comparing *government* prices with *free-market* prices, assuming that if the latter are higher, the government purchases can be said to discriminate against the countryside; (3) comparing *price* trends with *supply* trends, assuming that if the relative supply of a given crop goes up, its price must fall (and vice versa), and if it does not, the producers of that crop are the beneficiaries; and (4) comparing *price* trends with *cost* trends, assuming that if the input costs for a crop go up faster than output prices, incomes or returns from that crop must decline. I shall call these: the terms-of-trade argument, the price-differential argument, the relative-supply argument, and the cost-escalation argument, respectively.[1]

6.1.1 Agriculture–industry terms of trade: Making sense of an article of faith

A remarkable shift has taken place in the course of the past decade in the terms of trade between agriculture and industry in India. . . . The weighted terms of trade between agriculture and industry have over the period [1961/2–1973/4] . . . moved by close to 50 percent in favour of the former. . . . The movement in the terms of trade, we may maintain, does not represent any particular bias in policy, but is the consequence of divergent rates of growth in the two sectors. Is this hypothesis borne out by facts? During the quinquennium 1965–66 to 1970–71 . . . the index of farm production . . . rose by roughly 25 percent; the rise in the index of industrial output . . . over these years was actually less, namely, around 20 percent: even so, the terms of trade moved in favor not of industry but of agriculture, and to the extent of around 25 percent.

Thus wrote Ashok Mitra in a landmark political economy treatise over a decade and a half back,[2] starting a long debate in India over the political meaning of terms of trade. Arguing that an economic explanation for the terms of trade moving in favor of agriculture did not exist, he put forward a political thesis that supported the classic Marxist formulation on the nature of the ruling-class coalition in Indian polity:

This shift in terms of trade can be viewed as mirroring a political arrangement entered into by the urban bourgeoisie with the rural oligarchy. Given the frame of parliamentary democracy based on adult suffrage, urban industrialists, to maintain their control over political institutions, need to enlist the support from among the rural electorate. The task is immensely facilitated by an understanding they reach with surplus-raising farmers and their trading partners, who are in a position to ensure the votes of major sections of small peasants and landless laborers.[3]

---

1 A fifth argument, called the border-price argument and based on a comparison between international and domestic prices, has also recently emerged. Since it is confined entirely to academic economics and has not yet penetrated the policy process, I shall not deal with it separately. See, however, the Appendix.

2 *Terms of Trade and Class Relations*, London: Frank Cass, 1977, and Delhi: Rupa and Co., 1979. All citations from this book are from the Indian edition. The quote above is from p. 108.

3 Mitra, *Terms of Trade*, p. 141. The classic "bourgeois–landlord coalition" argument of Indian

Thus, according to Mitra, a democratic political system imposes the terms of trade price on the bourgeoisie.

The non-Marxist response to Mitra was to argue the opposite: that the terms of trade had in fact shifted in favor of industry.[4] With agricultural price agitations on the rise in the 1980s, the idea of terms of trade acquired a political life of its own, used not only in scholarly treatises but also in bureaucratic and political discourses. In the early 1980s, in an attempt to calm clamoring politicians, the central government added terms of trade to the two principal criteria already existing for the determination of farm prices – costs of production and the potential impact of agricultural, particularly food, prices on inflation.

Does the widespread use of the concept of terms of trade withstand close intellectual scrutiny? What conclusions can one draw from intersectoral terms of trade?

The pitfalls inherent in equating the increases and declines in agricultural incomes with the rise and fall of agriculture's terms of trade can be demonstrated in two ways. First, one can examine the form in which the argument is normally presented and ask whether the form supports the conclusions drawn. One can also go a step further, and inquire whether the argument would be acceptable were its form to change and be made more rigorous.

6.1.2 Terms of trade: An empirical picture

The judgment on the direction in intersectoral terms of trade may differ depending on (1) whether two *endpoints*, the base and the terminus, of a period are chosen for analysis, or (2) the entire *time series* pertaining to that period is examined. Those identifying a strong trend against or in favor of a sector have typically followed the first method. In contrast, plotting the entire series does not show any significant time trends.

The first method has taken two forms: (*a*) using individual years as the base and terminus; and (*b*) taking three-year averages clustered around the base and terminus. The implausibility of method (*a*) should be obvious. Given the dependence of agriculture on weather and the consequent fluctuations in agricultural

---

Marxists has been expanded to include the public bureaucracy. For a threefold dominant coalition, see Pranab Bardhan, 1984, *The Political Economy of Development in India*, New York: Basil Blackwell.

4 The strongest attack came from D. S. Tyagi, 1979, "Farm Prices and Class Bias in India", *Economic and Political Weekly* (hereafter *EPW*), Review of Agriculture, September. Tyagi argued that the official series on wholesale prices, on which Mitra's conclusion was based, overstated agricultural and understated industrial prices, spuriously tilting the terms of trade in favor of agriculture. This notion was further developed in A. S. Kahlon and D. S. Tyagi, 1980, "Inter-Sectoral Terms of Trade," *EPW*, Review of Agriculture, December 27. Also see Nalini Vittal, 1988, "Intersectoral Terms of Trade in India: Reality and Hype," *EPW*, vol. 23, no. 39, Review of Agriculture, September; and B. L. Mungrekar, 1993, "Intersectoral Terms of Trade: Issues of Concept and Method," *EPW*, Review of Agriculture, September.

Table 6.1. *Agriculture-industry terms of trade*
(Base: 1970–1 = 100)

Year	Prices of agricultural products as percentage of prices of manufactured products
1971–2	91.7
1972–3	90.5
1973–4	99.8
1974–5	100.7
1975–6	91.9
1976–7	90.5
1977–8	97.5
1978–9	95.8
1979–80	87.6
1980–1	81.8
1981–2	87.6
1982–3	91.5
1983–4	95.6
1984–5	94.9
1985–6	90.7
1986–7	91.8
1987–8	96.7
1988–9	96.9

Source: Government of India, 1993, *Economic Survey 1992–93*, Delhi: Ministry of Finance, p. S-70.

prices, single years taken as the base and terminus can strongly bias the results. The objective of method (*b*) is precisely to reduce the arbitrariness that may result from single years.

How the two methods – taking two endpoints (three-year averages) or, alternatively, the time series – yield different results can best be illustrated with the help of the latest terms-of-trade time series starting from 1970/1 (Table 6.1).[5] Using moving averages, the APC, for example, deciphered a trend against agriculture in 1980: "Taking the triennium ending 1971–72 as the base, it is observed

---

5 To maintain statistical consistency, the starting point of the analysis is 1970–1, or the early 1970s generally. If one wants to expand the time frame by merging the current cost series, called the Comprehensive Scheme, with the earlier series, called Farm Management Studies, bold but unsupportable assumptions will have to be made. The principles of cost collection and the definition of costs were different earlier. A longer empirical view can thus be obtained, but it will be substantially inaccurate. As will become clear later, the 1970–1 series is sufficient for the purposes of deriving robust arguments about trends in farm incomes.

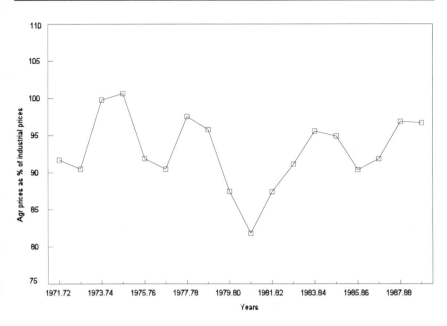

Figure 6.1. Agriculture–industry terms of trade (base: 1970–1 = 100). *Source:* Government of India, 1993, *Economic Survey 1992–93,* Delhi: Ministry of Finance, p. S-70.

that the index of prices paid by agricultural sector has risen at a faster rate than that of prices received by it."[6]

Let us now plot the entire time series contained in Table 6.1 (see Figure 6.1). No trend in either direction is visible for the entire period: it is a random walk. Upward and downward trajectories are essentially short-run. Other exercises carried out for a longer period show similar results: absence of a long-run trend but upward or downward trends for short periods of time.[7]

If politics were the sole, or even primary, reason for the shifting terms of trade, one would have to suppose corresponding shifts in the power of groups or

6 *Report on Price Policy for Wheat for the 1980–81 Crop,* August 1980, p. 13. Consider briefly the method of single years. If 1971–2 is chosen as the base year and 1984–5 as the terminal year from Table 6.1, agriculture's terms of trade improved from 91.7 to 94.9. Contrariwise, if one chooses other combinations – for example, 1971–2 and 1980–1 – we shall get declining terms of trade. Single years thus become completely arbitrary.

7 See, for example, two papers by R. Thamarajakshi: "Intersectoral Terms of Trade and the Marketed Surplus, 1951–52 to 1965–66," *EPW,* Review of Agriculture, June 26, 1969; and "Role of Price Incentives in Stimulating Agricultural Production in a Developing Economy," in Douglas Ensminger, ed., 1977, *Food Enough or Starvation for Millions,* Rome: FAO (Food and Agriculture Organizaiton).

classes. It is unclear how such short-run swings in the power of dominant groups in the industrial or agricultural sector could be established. It seems more plausible to argue that while politics may be one of the sources of shifting terms of trade, there are other variables at work, too.[8]

6.1.3 Do declining terms of trade mean deteriorating incomes?

Returns to farming, or incomes from farming, and agriculture's *terms of trade* are two very different concepts. Returns to farming can go up even while farm sector's terms of trade decline.[9] Stated another way, while agriculture's *barter* terms of trade may deteriorate, its so-called *income* terms of trade may well improve. Why should the dominant class in a given sector care if declining terms of trade do not in fact entail eroding incomes and may even coexist with increasing incomes?

Terms of trade can go against agriculture for both political and economic reasons. In an effort to transfer resources from agriculture to industrialization, governments may wish to turn the terms of trade against agriculture by fixing low prices for agricultural products, particularly food and export crops, and high prices for industrial goods. The classic case of such political twisting is, of course, the Soviet Union during the First Five-Year Plan (1928–32) (discussed in Chapter 2). Such policies ultimately sow the seeds of their own destruction. A "scissors effect" typically avenges big price twists, canceling out the political manipulation. As the government drastically shifts the terms of trade against agriculture, peasants may simply respond by producing less. A declining agricultural output may, in turn, lead to an increase in agricultural prices, frustrating the government design of keeping agricultural prices low. If selling at prices higher than the state-mandated prices is outlawed, the grain may simply be

8 It should be added that even after the problem of *base years* is tackled by constructing a time series, the problem of *commodity weights* remains. There is no uniquely acceptable or easy solution of the problem. Tyagi points to the inaccurate commodity weights used in the official wholesale price-index series on which are typically based most terms of trade comparisons, including Mitra's, APC's, as well as the one attempted in Figure 6.1: "In contrast to the homogeneity of products in the case of agricultural commodities, the products of the group – manufactured articles – are very heterogeneous. For example, rice is not only the same whether grown by farmer X or farmer Y, but it always remains, to a very large extent, the same over the years. Compared with this, poplin (shirting) made by mill X would not be the same as that made by mill Y, and furthermore, the poplin made in 1972 by mill X may not be the same as that it manufactured in 1960. . . . [D]ue to the greater heterogeneity in the products even when many items from many companies are included, the coverage . . . remains partial, and as time passes, [the] coverage tends to become more and more partial due to additions of new items. Furthermore, since the prices of new items are mostly fixed at levels higher than those they replace, the official index tends to underrepresent the changes in prices" (Tyagi, "Farm Prices and Class Bias," p. A-114).

9 In other words, even if, transcending the difficulties stated above, we figure out the terms of trade in a methodologically appropriate way, or even if a clear trend is evident, this problem still remains.

pushed into the black market.[10] In such a situation, the state can, of course, use another instrument: cheap food imports can keep food prices down. But an extended use of this method may lead to a stagnation in domestic food production, leading to an even greater need for food imports, requiring scarce foreign exchange and creating a vicious circle. A number of governments have by now realized the self-defeating nature of such policies.

Terms of trade can also go against agriculture for purely economic reasons, raising some interesting possibilities: (1) new technology and skills may reduce the unit costs of agricultural production (costs per acre divided by yield per acre), while industrial costs remain unchanged; (2) contrariwise, compared to the farm sector, increases in import costs may affect the non-farm sector more; and (3) rising incomes in the society may lead to a larger expansion in the demand for nonagricultural goods than for agricultural goods.[11] It is in the third case that, given costs, declining terms of trade also mean declining returns from farming. Case 1, on the other hand, is a classic example of how a decline in agriculture's terms of trade can actually coexist with increases in returns from farming. As new skills and technology reduce unit costs and increase production, a decline in agricultural prices may reduce the rate of return *per unit* of output (that is, per quintal) but higher yields (quintals per acre) may lead to higher returns *per acre*, ensuring a rise in farm incomes.[12]

Looking at the issue this way, one may add, is not simply a logical exercise. Japanese rice agriculture is the best-researched historical example of agricultural growth despite a stagnation in terms of trade: between 1880 and 1960, for a period of eighty years, the real price of rice remained stable while rice output increased. Hayami shows how, in an attempt to keep industrial wages low (so that the labor-intensive industrialization could proceed), the Japanese government

---

10 Although the Soviet case is the most widely known, similar processes have been in operation in Africa: "It should be stressed that government attempts to control the market for food crops have failed. By contrast with the market for export crops, the market for food crops is extremely difficult to control. Many export crops can be grown only in highly specialized areas, but food crops can be grown virtually by all farm families. And whereas export crops must be moved through a few special locations – ports, for example – food crops can be moved in many ways. . . . As a consequence, food crops can more readily be diverted from official marketing channels." Robert Bates, 1981, *Markets and States in Tropical Africa*, Berkeley and Los Angeles: University of California Press, p. 40.

11 Michael Lipton, 1977, *Why Poor People Stay Poor: Urban Bias in World Development*, Cambridge, MA: Harvard University Press, chap. 13, esp. p. 288.

12 Raj Krishna provided a simple mathematical proof of this. Symbolically, if Q and F are total output and total input, and Po and Pi are output and input prices, then return-to-cost ratio (r) can be written as PoQ/PiF. Let the terms of trade be defined as $p* = Po/Pi$, and total factor productivity as $t* = Q/F$. In growth rates, then, $r\hat{} = p*\hat{} + t*\hat{}$. Thus, profitability can be raised by improving terms of trade ($p*\hat{}$) without technical innovation ($t*\hat{} = O$), or by improving productivity ($t*\hat{}$) at unchanged prices ($P*\hat{} = O$), or by improving both. See Raj Krishna, 1982, "Some Aspects of Agricultural Growth, Price Policy and Equity in Developing Countries," *Food Research Institute Studies*, vol. 18, no. 3, p. 238.

during this period essentially resorted to non-price interventions in agriculture –
for instance, investments in yield-increasing technology – while keeping food
prices in check.[13]

For India, after correcting for many of the commodity-weight problems in the
official series, Tyagi argued that, factoring technology in, the movement of
intersectoral terms of trade can be periodized as follows: Period One (1952/3–
1963/4), when a stagnant technology coexisted with adverse terms of trade for
agriculture; Period Two (1963/4–1975/6), when favorable terms of trade for
agriculture were accompanied by introduction of new technology in agriculture;
and Period Three (1975/6–1983/4), when technological development spread to
newer areas and crops but terms of trade shifted against agriculture. In Period
One, private investment made by farmers in agriculture (machinery and other
equipment), an indicator of how farmers were perceiving income-earning opportunities, stagnated. In Period Two, such investments went up. And in Period
Three, the most interesting case for our purposes, investments continued to go up
despite a shift in terms of trade against agriculture.[14]

To sum up, a deterioration in the terms of trade necessarily means declining
incomes only in a *static* framework – when agriculture is experiencing no technical change. That is the context in which the Soviet debate took place. The
obverse is true in a *dynamic* setting: if new technologies are introduced, agriculture can grow and farm incomes can go up even as agriculture's terms of trade
decline.

6.2 THE OTHER INDICATORS

What about the three other economic views used in the debate: the relative-
supply argument, the price-differential argument, and the cost-escalation argument? Not confined to economics, politicians have repeatedly used them in
pressing their cases. The political power of the economic arguments has depended on who made them and when. The economists' arguments are reviewed
below. How they emerged in the political process is discussed next.

6.2.1 The economic arguments

The relative-supply argument. Being an aggregate measure, intersectoral terms of
trade tend to mask interregional and intercrop differences. It is perfectly possible
for the agriculture sector to do poorly as a whole, while some states and some
crops do well – or vice versa. If, for example, the two principal food crops of the

13 Yujiro Hayami, 1972, "Rice Price Policy in Japan's Economic Development," *American Journal
   of Agricultural Economics*, August.
14 D. S. Tyagi, 1987, "Domestic Terms of Trade and Their Effect on Supply and Demand of
   Agricultural Sector," *EPW*, Review of Agriculture, March 28. The introduction of technology
   significantly qualifies Tyagi's earlier focus on terms of trade as a determinant of rural incomes
   and an indicator of policy bias.

country go through contrasting experiences, one prospering, the other stagnating, a crop-level disaggregation can give more meaningful insights into the regions or classes gaining or losing than any aggregate measures.

Considerations such as these have led analysts to focus attention on intercrop pricing, or what may be called *intrasectoral* terms of trade. Wheat and rice have attracted maximum attention for two reasons. First, their prices affect the incomes and welfare of a large majority of the rural (and urban) population. A second reason is, however, avowedly political. In some intellectual and political circles, allegations have been made that the country's price policy is biased in favor of wheat and against rice. If the economic laws of supply and demand were any guide, argued Mitra and several politicians in the late 1970s, rice prices should have risen faster than those for wheat. That the eastern and southern parts of the country are predominantly rice-growing (and rice-eating) whereas the North is overwhelmingly wheat-growing (and wheat-consuming) is cited to be the source of the regional bias.[15] Moroever, the average size of landholdings in the wheat-growing North is considerably larger than that in the rice-growing East and South. Rice is thus primarily a crop of small farmers; wheat, of big farmers. This distinction is alleged to be the basis of the class bias of farm policy.[16]

This argument died a natural death with a change in agrarian practices. In the

---

15 Ashok Mitra, *Terms of Trade*, p. 127. In political circles, the regional argument became fashionable during the Janata years in Delhi (1977–9). Heated debates took place in Parliament: "the wheat price has been raised on many occasions. . . . the price of paddy was not at all raised for the past many years in spite of the constant and continuous demand by the government of Tamil Nadu . . . and the southern rice-growing states . . ." (*Lok Sabha Debates*, 6th ser., vol. 13, April 19, 1978, p. 286). And: "there is a powerful wheat lobby operating in Delhi and that is the reason that paddy growers are at a disadvantage" (*Lok Sabha Debates*, 6th ser., vol. 19, December 12, 1978, p. 308). It is interesting to note that the regional angle disappeared from Parliament debates over agricultural prices after Mrs. Gandhi's return to power in 1980. Whether or not economics was one of the reasons for the regional argument, politics certainly was. 1977–80 was the first period in Indian politics when the ruling party at the center, the Janata, was almost entirely North-based, whereas the main opposition party, Mrs. Gandhi's Congress, was primarily South-based. The Agriculture minister during this period, S. S. Barnala, was from Punjab, his deputy, B. P. Singh, the state minister for agriculture, from Uttar Pradesh, and the peasant-based Lok Dal, a key component of the Janata coalition and its leader, Charan Singh, had no base in the South. The Congress party's return to power in 1980 restored the earlier pattern – that of a ruling party based both in the North and the South. The regional accusation thereafter disappeared from political debates.

16 Mitra, *Terms of Trade*, pp. 130–1. Others who share the belief that the price policy has a regional or rich peasant bias include Terry Byres, 1981, "The New Technology, Class Formation and Class Action," *The Journal of Peasant Studies*, vol. 8, no. 4, July; M. L. Dantwala, 1979, "Agricultural Policy in India," in C. H. Shah, ed., *Agricultural Development of India*, Delhi: Orient Longman; Prem Shankar Jha, numerous writings in *The Times of India*, especially "Crackpot Economics: Who Is Subsidizing Whom? *The Times of India*, May 23, 1983; K. Subbarao, 1985, "State Policies and Regional Disparity in Indian Agriculture," *Development and Change*, vol. 16, no. 4, and "Incentive Policies and India's Agricultural Development: Some Aspects of Regional and Social Equity," *Indian Journal of Agricultural Economics*, vol. 15, no. 4, October–December 1985.

1980s, Punjab and Haryana in the North took to rice cultivation in a big way and rice ceased to be a crop confined only to eastern and southern India. Moreover, even as rising wheat and paddy output by the 1980s led to accumulating surpluses in the public stocks, the government, against the normal expectation that a rising surplus would lead to a lowering of price, continued to increase producer prices.

The price-differential argument

This argument was popular in the 1960s and 1970s. To support their "urban-bias" arguments about India, Theodore Schultz and Michael Lipton relied heavily on the gap between the government procurement price and the free-market price for food crops. The argument was twofold: (1) for wheat and rice, government procurement prices were anywhere between 10 to 25 percent lower than the free market prices in the 1960s and 1970s; and (2) since the government procured roughly 25–30 percent of the marketed surplus of wheat and rice, government procurement prices depressed farm prices and reduced farm incomes.[17]

The first part of the argument was an incontestable fact until the mid-seventies, but the conclusion drawn was questionable. By withdrawing a certain quantity from the market, procurement was bound to push up the open-market prices. Therefore, the weighted average of the procurement and market prices was the issue, not the differential between the procurement and open-market price.[18]

Starting with the late seventies, developments in the food economy destroyed this argument, as accumulating surpluses made the concept of a *procurement* price, fixed lower than the market price, redundant. Instead, the government price became the *support* price, below which prices of wheat and rice would not be allowed to crash. Farmers would simply be supported at this floor. Indeed, there are regions now – Punjab, Haryana, Western Uttar Pradesh, Andhra Pradesh –

17 "Around 1967–8, about a quarter of Indian cereal marketings were publicly procured, at prices about 25 percent lower than were obtainable in the market. . . . In the 1970s, compulsory procurement of wheat, while not fully enforceable, has been used by the government . . . to hold farm-gate prices. . . . Government procurement, at low prices . . . has been substantial enough to depress farm prices" (Michael Lipton, 1976, *Why Poor People Stay Poor*, New Delhi: Heritage Publishers, p. 295 [Indian edition]). Schultz's views are contained in *Distortion of Agricultural Incentives*, Bloomington: Indiana University Press, 1978.

18 John Mellor, 1968, "Functions of Agricultural Prices in Economic Development," *Indian Journal of Agricultural Economics*, vol. 23, no. 1, January–March. Others who make a similar argument include Yujiro Hayami, K. Subbarao, and K. Otsuka, 1982, "Efficiency and Equity in the Producer Levy of India," *American Journal of Agricultural Economics*, November. Also, all of these writers typically use the concept of elasticity to further reinforce their case. Mellor argued that "levy takes a significant portion of the supply and in effect gives it disproportionately to the lower income consumers with the more elastic demand. The free market is then left to those persons with higher incomes with highly inelastic demand" (p. 34), leading to a disproportionate increase in the open-market prices.

where the government is the main buyer of grains, as prices in the open market are typically lower than the government price.[19] And in states where open market prices are higher, government buying is a relatively minor operation.[20]

The cost-escalation argument

Declining price–cost ratios have also been an important basis for judgments. Costs of production, it is argued, have moved much faster than the prices received by farmers, indicating falling farm incomes and calling for an upward thrust in farm prices.[21] At this point, economists working in the vast network of India's agricultural universities constitute the bulk of the group making this argument. Gunwant Desai, summarizing *fifty-eight* papers presented on "farm price structure" in the 1986 annual meeting of the Indian Association of Agricultural Economics, noted: "papers on input–output prices are nearly unanimous in pointing out that despite increases in farm output and its prices, the farmers' net income has not increased because of increases in the prices of inputs."[22] Over the last decade and a half, the cost-escalation argument has become the main argument of those arguing for an increase in producer prices.

6.2.2 Political reflections of economic arguments

In the *economic* realm, the debate may have remained unsettled, with economists divided on either side. In the *political* realm, however, the scales are heavily weighted in favor of the thesis about falling rural incomes. Politicians in Parliament, or nonparty political leaders outside Parliament, have used the cost-escalation or price-differential arguments to demand higher prices.

The political struggle over agricultural prices has been fought in three arenas: on the streets where peasants have been mobilized; in the halls of Parliament; and, in contrast to the public nature of these two struggles, inside the secluded walls of government bureaucracies. The intrabureaucratic struggle, further, has been of two types: (1) the struggle *within* the CACP; and (2) the struggle *between* the CACP and the Agriculture Ministry, on the one hand, and other wings of the government, particularly the Finance Ministry, on the other.

One would expect the nonparty mobilization to be sectional, for that is the

---

19 Some farmers nonetheless sell grain to private traders, because with the growth of government purchases have come the bureaucratic problems of late payments, long queues, and malpractices.

20 Since the mid-seventies, Punjab, Haryana, and Uttar Pradesh have typically accounted for over 90 percent of the procured wheat. Over 80 percent of the government rice stock has also come from these three states, plus Andhra Pradesh.

21 Price-fertilizer cost ratios formed part of Lipton's argument too, but by now the argument has been generalized to include all costs, not simply fertilizers. Lipton's use of the fertilizer-cost data was prompted by the fact that fertilizer costs are typically the largest expense of farmers.

22 Gunwant Desai, 1986, "Rapporteur's Report on Farm Price Structure," *Indian Journal of Agricultural Economics*, vol. 41, no. 4, October–December 1986, p. 433.

nature of interest-group activity. Since the late 1970s, for all practical purposes, India's parliament, too, has become a sectional institution on the agrarian question. Because all parties support the demand for higher agricultural prices and subsidies, the interparty parliamentary battle can be characterized as competitive agrarianism. Irrespective of which party is running the government, the government is attacked by the opposition parties for ignoring the needs of the farmers. The government typically defends itself by arguing that it has done more for the farmers than the previous government: however, since it is responsible to the entire country, not just to the farmers, it says, some compromises with the needs of the entire economy must be made. Members of the ruling party show ambivalence in debates. Agreeing with their party's government that it is doing more than the previous government, they nevertheless emphasize the need to do much more. And instead of attacking the government per se, which the opposition parties do, they simply single out the nonelected part of the government, particularly the CACP, for being anti-farmer, pleading with the political wing of the government to curtail the biases of the bureaucrats. Both the treasury and opposition benches, thus, have been exerting political pressure on the government.

The parliamentary battles and struggles within the CACP are reviewed below. After Mrs. Gandhi appointed a farmers' representative, Chowdhry Randhir Singh, to the CACP, where he was to participate in decision making with three other "technical" members, the CACP became internally politicized.

6.2.3 Economics as political rhetoric: The politicians' arguments

The politicians have made three arguments about rural impoverishment. Paralleling Sharad Joshi's argument about the Bharat–India divide, the first argument has rested on the visual metaphor of two Indias:

If a foreigner comes to India today, he will come across two Indias. On one side is that part of our country which resides in villages, where there is poverty and malnourishment. There are 118 thousand villages where, even after 30 years of independence, people don't have drinking water . . . where people don't have houses to live, where there are no arrangements for medicines. On the other side are the Oberoi Hotel, Ashoka Hotel, Hilton Hotel, from which it will seem that India is country as rich as America, England and Japan.[23]

The speech should not be dismissed as a maudlin excess, for it is genuinely believed in many political quarters. The trouble with the "two Indias" metaphor, however, is that it is both true and false. Poverty, malnourishment, and lack of housing, though concentrated in villages, are not confined to them. To the glittering world of intercontinental hotels, one may wish to add the Dickensian realities of shanty towns. Moreover, it matters whether one compares Punjab's villages with Punjabi cities or Bihar's countryside with Delhi and Bombay.

---

23 Lok Sabha speech by Kanwar Lal Gupta – member, incidentally, of an urban-based party, Jan Sangh. *Lok Sabha Debates*, 7th ser., vol. 8, December 12, 1977, p. 307.

The latter comparison may support the existence of two Indias, but the former would merely indicate two points on the same continuum, not two different Indias.[24]

Politicians and the price-differential argument

The economic demise of the price-differential argument has entailed its gradual political decay too. Since the mid-1970s, whenever MPs in the Lok Sabha and the farmers' representative in the CACP, Chowdhry Randhir Singh, made this argument, they encountered difficulties. Singh, for example, argued that whereas the government paid Rs 110 and Rs 112.50 for a quintal of wheat in 1977–8 and 1978–9: "the farmers of *Madhya Pradesh* sold their wheat in Indore market for Rs 148 and 135 per quintal . . . *Gujarat* state farmers . . . in Dhandkua market. . . at Rs 130 and 135 per quintal . . . *Maharashtra* state farmers in Amravati market at Rs 139 and Rs 150 . . . *Rajasthan* farmers . . . in Ajmer market at Rs 142 and Rs 140 . . . *Karnataka* state farmers . . . in Bangalore market at Rs 195 and Rs 185 . . ." (emphasis added).[25]

An economist will quickly notice a glaring bias in this list. All the states mentioned – Madhya Pradesh, Gujarat, Maharashtra, Rajasthan, and Karnataka – are deficit states where free-market price has been the relevant price for most farmers, not the government procurement price. The government wheat operations there have been minuscule. Since the mid-seventies, the all-India price has been the operational price primarily in the surplus areas where the government concentrates its buying operations. Farmers are free to sell to private traders. Interstate restrictions on movement of grains, typical of the earlier era, have also been lifted, on the whole.

Unsurprisingly, with respect to surplus-producing Punjab, Haryana, and Western Uttar Pradesh, Singh was nonplussed to find that the free-market prices were the same as the government prices, and were even lower in some markets of Uttar Pradesh.[26] The CACP quietly heard him and published his position as a note of dissent.[27]

24 Besides, even in Bihar there are affluent landlords who enjoy both rural and urban luxuries.
25 APC, *Report on Price Policy for Wheat for the 1979–80 Season*, November 1978, pp. 16–17.
26 Ibid.
27 Chowdhry Randhir Singh continued writing notes of dissent each year and asking for a price higher than that recommended by the APC. In Parliament, many MPs undertook an exercise similar to Singh's at various times. The Agriculture ministers continued to remind them that forced procurement was a thing of the past and that procurement had actually become a support operation. Procurement price in the deficit states was simply not the issue anymore. In surplus states, it was: "Can you imagine a situation where the Food Corporation of India does not enter the market in Punjab? . . . Last year we were late by five days in announcing the paddy prices and so it came down to Rs. 90. . . . If we stop the procurement of wheat and paddy in Punjab, you can't imagine to what level the price would go." Rao Birendra Singh, Food and Agriculture minister (1980–6), *Lok Sabha Debates*, 8th ser., vol. 28, April 19, 1982, pp. 447–8.

Politicians and the cost-escalation argument

The cost-escalation argument has become hegemonic in politics since the late 1970s. Increases in the prices of fertilizers and diesel consequent upon the oil price shocks of the 1970s did indeed lead to a cost inflation in the agricultural economy. Politicians therefore constantly attacked the CACP for failing to increase support prices to a compensating degree.

Cost data are collected in India by the vast network of agricultural universities, most of them manned by professionals with rural backgrounds. Using this data, the CACP determines support prices that would give incentives to producers by allowing a margin over costs. Further along in the process, the central cabinet acts upon the CACP recommendations and typically gives a markup over the CACP recommendation while setting the final support price. Presumably therefore, the price recommended should provide enough incentives to farmers. Members of the opposition and some from the treasury benches claim it does not. The following excerpt from a Parliament debate between the Agriculture minister and opposition members is illustrative:

Rao Birendra Singh (Agriculture Minister): . . . APC gives its recommendations on the basis of data collected through various agencies. It has its own system of data assessment – it gets information on costs of production which is collected by the universities. But after that the government sometimes takes a political decision.
Madhu Dandavate (an Opposition MP): Political decision?
Singh: Yes, when we find that the farmer needs more incentive.
Dandavate: Is that a political decision?
Singh: Well, whatever you may say, it is not scientific. . . . Sometimes we find that even though their data might be correct, the farmers should get more to improve their living conditions. . . .[28]

The Agriculture minister's statement was not simply an act of political salesmanship; it had a ring of truth.

Because the CACP's data are the same as that of agricultural universities whose economists make a case for prices higher than those set by the government, the CACP becomes a target of political attacks. Charges of technocratic insensitivity, urban bias, or plain incompetence have been regularly leveled at the CACP in Parliament and by nonparty leaders: "Your APC knows agriculture only on paper. Have they ever seen villages? Have they ever seen farmers? . . . Those who know villages know the difficulties of farmers. . . . Farmers should have greater representation on the APC."[29]

---

28 *Lok Sabha Debates*, 7th ser., vol. 48, August 13, 1984, pp. 420–1. Professor Dandavate went on to become Finance minister under the V. P. Singh government (1989–90).
29 Ibid., vol. 9, November 24, 1980, p. 297. Incessantly criticized, Rao Birendra Singh, the Food and Agriculture minister (1980–6), once responded candidly: "I am not very sure that putting too many farmers in the APC would improve matters because we have had experience already. They might vie with each other in giving higher recommendation . . . we have to take [a] balanced view" (ibid., vol. 47, August 13, 1984).

In sum, the politicians in Parliament want the CACP to have more farmers' representatives (a goal which they have already partially attained); the nonparty politicians want it either scrapped or its guidelines substantially reformed;[30] and for the intellectuals on the left, the composition of the CACP and its norms of functioning can at best marginally change the economic outcome so long as the nature and class bias of the Indian state do not change.[31] Of the economic bureaucracies of the Indian government, the CACP has thus become a prime object of political attention, mired in attacks from several sides. The CACP now has provision for three farmers' representatives and three technical members, though the chairmanship still remains with technocrats. Given the political trends, the prospects of a politician presiding over a CACP that has more political than technocratic members cannot be ruled out at some time in the future. That will unquestionably shift the power inside the CACP toward farmer politicians.

6.3 RESOLVING THE DEBATE: TOWARD A RETURN INDEX AND ITS RESULTS

Of the four arguments made to judge the direction of rural incomes, the implausibility of the first three has already been demonstrated. What about the cost-escalation argument?

The cost-escalation argument also contains a non sequitur. It draws conclusions about farm *incomes* from price–cost *ratios*. Both cost and price data are about unit costs (costs per quintal) and unit prices (prices per quintal). One increasing faster than the other simply indicates the price–cost ratios *per quintal*, not returns *per acre*. The latter would also depend on yields – that is, how many quintals are produced on a given hectare/acre of land. It is perfectly possible for unit costs to increase faster than unit prices, but if productivity (yields per acre) goes up by a compensating (or higher) proportion, the returns can still be the same (or higher).

Let us observe the logic of the above proposition. Defining returns as a function of price–cost ratios multiplied by yield, we can write the relationship as,

$$R = f(P/C)Y \qquad (1)$$

where R represents farm returns/incomes, P and C represent price per quintal and costs per quintal, and Y yield per acre. Price–cost ratio (P/C) will show us what is happening to the rate of return (*per quintal*). Multiplied by yield Y (quintals per

30 Sharad Joshi, 1986, "Scrap APC – Demand Farmers," in his *Bharat Speaks Out*, Bombay: Build Documentation Center, pp. 32–7.
31 For example, BM, "Agricultural Policy Dictated by Rich Farmer," *EPW*, May 28, 1988, pp. 1107–8. BM (a pseudonym) has regularly written such reports for the *EPW* since 1973. See also Ashok Mitra, *Terms of Trade*.

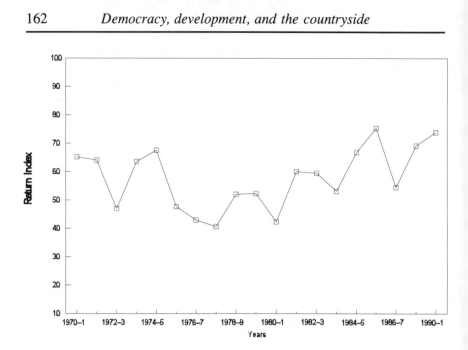

Figure 6.2. Returns over operational costs, Punjab (wheat, 1970–1 to 1990–1). *Source:* CACP, price policy for Rabi crops, various years.

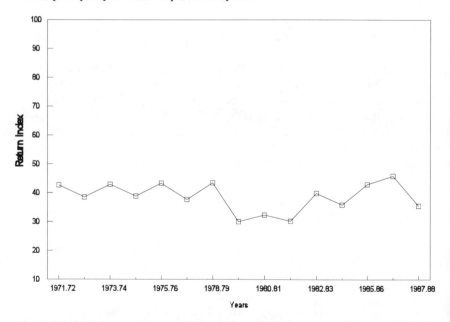

Figure 6.3. Returns over operational costs, Uttar Pradesh (wheat, 1971–2 to 1987–8). *Source:* CACP, price policy for Rabi crops, various years.

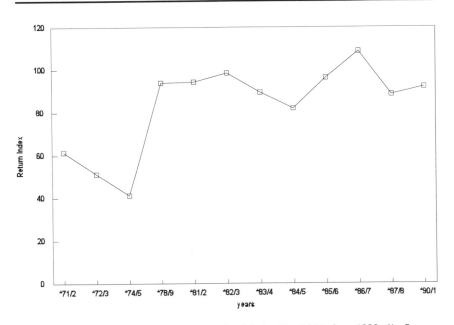

Figure 6.4. Returns over operational cost, Punjab (paddy, 1971–2 to 1990–1). *Source:* CACP, price policy for Kharif crops, various years.

acre), we get a measure for returns *per acre*. We thus get a return index that should give us a better sense of returns from farming.[32]

Let us see the results of the procedure specified above. Consider wheat returns first. Figures 6.2 and 6.3 present results from two major wheat states, Punjab and Uttar Pradesh. Figure 6.2 shows no trend at all in either direction; it is a random walk. A straight line, if drawn, would do violence to the empirical zigzag. Figure

32 It should be emphasized that the formula developed above does not give us exact returns. Rather, it yields a return index. Exact returns, using the same symbols, can be written as

$$R = (P - C)Y \tag{2}$$

The problem with Formula (2) is that it gives us *nominal* returns, not *real* returns. For (2) to give us real returns, we need a price deflator, which is a monumental difficulty in that no uniquely acceptable deflators for measuring farm incomes exist. Because of the way weights are assigned to different commodities, the applicability of both the wholesale price index and consumer price index has been seriously questioned for calculating real farm incomes from nominal figures (cf. note 8 above). Formula (1) surmounts this difficulty: it divides prices, a nominal measure, by costs, another nominal measure, instead of subtracting one nominal measure from the other, which would in the end still leave us with a nominal magnitude. Formula (1) thus yields a proxy for exact returns, *a second-best* measure that overcomes the inherent difficulties of the ideal solution and suffices for the purposes of judging the directionality of farm incomes (whether they have gone down or up over time).

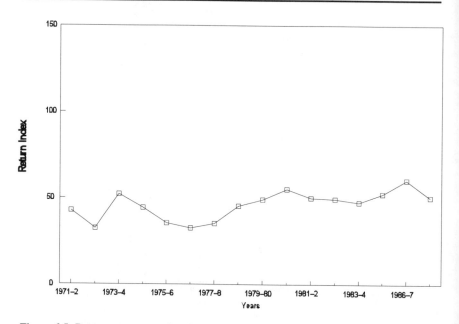

Figure 6.5. Returns over operational costs, Andhra Pradesh (paddy, 1971–2 to 1986–7). *Source:* CACP, price policy for Kharif crops, various years.

6.3 shows either no trend for the entire period, or, if broken up in two parts, mildly declining returns until the early 1980s, and no trend since then.

Take paddy returns now. Figure 6.4, which plots paddy returns in Punjab since the early seventies, shows an unmistakable upward trend after the mid-seventies. Figure 6.5 presents paddy returns from another technologically advanced state, Andhra Pradesh. Once again, roughly since 1976–7, there is evidence of a mild upward trend, though between 1971/2 and 1976/7, we do not see a trend.

A cropwise and statewise disaggregation thus yields a diverse array of results: returns going up, down, or showing no trend at all. We have the makings of a paradox here: while the political power of farm groups, as argued before, has been unambiguously rising over time, incomes from farming have risen or declined depending on what crop one grows, when, and where. If political power were neatly to translate into economic outcomes, returns from both crops should have increased. Farmers have pressed for price increases for all crops; these crops constitute the main source of income for a large fraction of the farming community; and the crop prices are determined by the government. Why has a disjunction between the political and the economic emerged? The disjunction would not exist if politics were entirely determinative. Clearly, we have to go beyond a model driven purely by political determination.

6.4 THE DISJUNCTION BETWEEN THE POLITICAL AND THE ECONOMIC

The role of technology

The first resolution of the paradox can be found in the role played by technical change. Figure 6.6 shows how wheat and rice yields have changed over time in Punjab, indicating faster technical change in rice as compared to wheat, at least since the mid-seventies. Recall Figures 6.2 and 6.4, the former depicting stagnating wheat returns in Punjab, the latter showing rising paddy returns. The role of technical change in determining farm returns should thus be clear. Wheat drove the first wave of the green revolution. By the mid-seventies, however, as the rate of increase in wheat yields decelerated in technologically advanced states, rice varieties initiated the second round of green revolution in these states.

Differential rhythms of technical change thus constitute a factor countervailing (or augmenting) the political power of farm groups. These results should also disconfirm the regional and class explanations given for wheat–rice divergence: that wheat farmers, generally bigger-sized than the mass of rice farmers in the country, or the wheat-growing northern Indian states like Punjab and Uttar Pradesh, wield greater power on the Indian state than the mainly rice-growing South India. Differential technical change rather than regional or class power seems to be determining the result.

The general implications of technical change are worth considering briefly. Given that (1) prices of outputs, costs of inputs, and yields differ according to crops and (2) different states have different crop specializations or cost structure, farm returns would differ cropwise and statewise. Examining other crops, beyond the scope of this study, should empirically confirm this understanding on a larger scale. The role of technical change in determining returns seems intuitively plausible.

A technology-based resolution of the divergence between politics and economics, however, does not answer a different kind of question: why couldn't the government neutralize the income effect of the deceleration of technical change? Recall the return measure from equation (1). Technical change leads to increases in yield: thus, other things remaining the same, technical change, by increasing the value of Y, would lead to higher returns. But the other things do not have to remain unchanged. Apart from yield (Y), returns are also determined by the price–cost ratio (P/C). Wheat returns (or, returns from any crop experiencing a technological deceleration), could be restored, if the government increased support prices (thus pushing up the value of P), or decreased the price of major cost items (thus lowering C), or both. The central government, after all, sets P and significantly affects C by setting, inter alia, the price of fertilizer, which typically accounts for the largest farming expense under new technology.

That the rural political power met with a counteracting force in technical

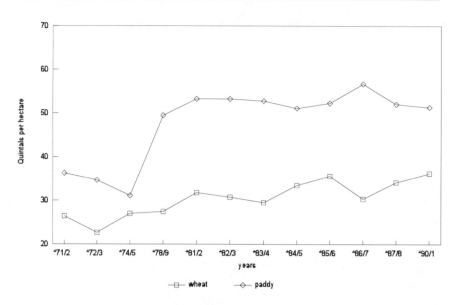

Figure 6.6. Yields, Punjab (paddy and wheat, 1971–2 to 1990–1). *Source:* CACP, price policy for Rabi and Kharif crops, various years.

change can thus be a proximate explanation for the disjunction between the political and the economic, necessary but not sufficient. It is still to be explained why the government did not, or could not, increase wheat prices or reduce fertilizer and other input prices *to an extent* that would offset the results of technical deceleration and restore returns, despite mounting political pressures in favor of such an increase in party and nonparty politics as well as within the CACP.

The demand constraint: How the poor affect the income of surplus farmers

A lack of purchasing power in the economy provides the first answer to the question raised above. A "basket case" in the 1960s, perpetually dependent on American wheat, India has been running a food surplus since the late 1970s. The government has on the whole been procuring 12–18 million tons of foodgrain but distributing between 8 to 10 million tons through the public distribution system. Government foodgrain stocks have thus been accumulating. Table 6.2 gives an indication of stocks in the 1980s. Climbing further, the closing stocks had accumulated to nearly 29 million tons, one-fifth of the total food output in the country, when droughts of 1987 and 1988 brought the stocks down to 11 million tons. In the 1990s, the stocks have been climbing once again.

Table 6.2. *Closing stocks of foodgrains*
(central and state governments, in million tons)

As of	Rice	Wheat	Coarse grains	Totals
1.7.1981	5.84	7.73	0.10	13.67
1.7.1982	5.12	10.18	0.20	15.50
1.7.1983	3.78	13.01	0.17	16.96
1.7.1984	4.62	17.81	0.05	22.48
1.7.1985	7.76	20.74	0.17	28.67
1.7.1986	9.26	18.90	0.13	28.28
1.7.1987	8.35	14.86	0.06	23.27
1.7.1988	4.16	7.55	0.19	11.90
1.7.1989	3.60	9.43	0.02	13.05
1.7.1990	6.94	13.20	0.17	20.31
1.1.1991	9.52	9.42	0.14	19.08

Source: Ministry of Agriculture, *Agricultural Statistics at a Glance,* 1992, p. 82.

India's food surplus, however, is a "pseudo-surplus," for large masses of people remain half-fed. Those who need food do not have the incomes to buy the accumulating government surpluses at the price at which they are offered. This simple economic fact means that the producer price for wheat, if the government had not intervened, would have fallen irrespective of what the cost of wheat production was (a process continuing until such time as enough farmers moved out of wheat farming to restore equilibrium in demand and supply).[33] It also means that if the government had tried to increase producer prices by a still higher margin, it would have ended up with larger public food stocks, which, even with the existing producer and consumer price structure, have tended to exceed storage capacity in the country. Thus, since the rise of food surpluses the demand constraint has caught all governments in a bind, governments increasing producer prices and/or subsidies to pacify farmers and to encourage food production only to realize that, beyond a point, (producer and consumer) prices cannot be increased, while the existing increases are found inadequate by farmers.

A rising surplus can present all manner of problems. Apart from the resources getting locked up in higher stocks, even managerial problems like storage can

33 The government often belabored this economic point in its clash with the opposition: "If the government does not move into the market, if there is no intervention with support prices, you know what will happen, how the market will be exploited by traders. . . . If the government does not purchase in the market, prices (will) fall" (Agriculture Minister Rao Birendra Singh, *Lok Sabha Debates*, 7th ser., vol. 36, April 8, 1983, p. 490).

be formidable. In the 1980s, stocks tended to exceed the storage capacity in the country: "(E)xcess food stocks reflect misallocation of our scarce resources and also increase risks of loss through spoilage."[34] This was also the nearest the government came to admitting a truly bizarre situation: considerable quantities of grain rotting in a poor country where the specter of hunger still haunts millions.[35]

Violation of standard economic principles was one of the first casualties of the demand constraint. For good reasons, economic theory maintains a distinction between the *procurement* price (whose function is to procure food at lower than market prices for public stocks and which therefore is typically relevant in times of relative scarcity) and *support* price (whose function is to keep intact a floor below which grain prices will not be allowed to crash, a price at which the entire crop output will be bought by the government, and which therefore is the price applicable in times of plenty). The central government had normally followed this principle until the mid-1970s. With surpluses emerging by 1976–7, the lower support price should have been the operational price. However, "In the case of major foodgrains," emphasized the Janata government, "support is [now] provided at the level of procurement prices which are higher than the national support prices" because "this has been found to serve the cultivators' interests better."[36] Once a trend was set, the subsequent governments did not reactivate the distinction either.

Exporting grain is, in principle, a solution to the domestic-demand constraint. However, the government "found it impossible to export wheat for the international prices were often lower."[37] Moreover, "an adequate level of food stocks provides an important hedge against both uncertain weather and inflation."[38] Only small quantities could be exported whenever border prices went above the domestic prices.[39] With the economic reform initiated in 1991, the government

---

34 Ministry of Finance, 1985, *Long Term Fiscal Policy*, December, p. 18.
35 No accurate estimates of how much grain rots every year are available. Nor, given the political sensitivity of such an issue, can it be easily known. It is widely believed, however, that anywhere between 2 to 4 million tons of grain are lost this way.
36 Mr. S. S. Barnala, Agriculture minister in the Janata government, *Lok Sabha Debates*, VI ser., vol. 2, December 12, 1977, p. 123. Brackets added.
37 Interview, Rao Birendra Singh, Agriculture minister (1980–6), Delhi, September 18, 1986.
38 *Long Term Fiscal Policy*, p. 18.
39 One may still argue that, given the scarcity of foreign exchange, what India would lose by exporting at a price lower than domestic prices it might gain by earning foreign exchange that has high scarcity value. While the plausibility of such considerations requires detailed statistical exercises, it is equally possible that the foreign exchange earned now by drawing down surpluses would be more than lost at a future date when, faced with weather failures, large-scale purchases from the world market would not only necessitate foreign exchange but would inevitably drive international prices up. Large countries like India and China have a peculiar structural relationship with the international grain markets. If they unload large supplies on the world market, they bring down prices, just as their entry as large buyers always pushes up international prices. Thus, in their case, only small interactions with the international market *in a commodity like food* seem

has begun to accept farm exports as a possible source of foreign exchange in a much more systematic way. Whether farm exports will go up sufficiently is, however, still to be seen.

To sum up, apart from technical change, income distribution, or a demand constraint, has also been a countervailing force to the power of the peasantry. Higher incomes for the poor might have increased the incomes of the surplus producers.

The rising fiscal burden

An emphasis on the demand constraint leaves yet another issue unresolved. In principle, the government can lower the consumer price to draw down the surplus and simultaneously increase the producer price (or lower the price of inputs) to satisfy farmers. Subsidization of the difference between producer and consumer prices is all that is required. Did the government choose this path?

The government has provided a substantial subsidy to farmers, but even high levels of subsidy have not been adequate from the farmers' viewpoint. As Figure 6.7 illustrates, since the early seventies until the economic reforms were initiated in 1991, subsidies in the Indian economy rose consistently. The rising curve of the central government subsidy was largely, though not entirely, due to food and fertilizer subsidies. Figure 6.8 shows that after the oil price hike led to a sharp increase in fertilizer prices in 1972/3, requiring a subsidy to maintain fertilizer consumption and agricultural growth rate, food and fertilizer subsidies have constituted a large proportion of total central subsidies, with the curve only declining with the onset of the recent economic reforms.[40]

Farmers' rising surpluses have thus entailed a high and increasing fiscal burden on the exchequer. In a way, Indian agriculture is thus becoming a victim of its own success. The government is clear about the source of the problem:

In part, the problem reflects the success of our farmers and our agricultural strategy in raising food production to record levels. The problem has been aggravated by high levels of procurement without a corresponding increase in the off-take from the public distribu-

---

practical, making domestic food security an important imperative. Stocks that may rot for lack of storage can obviously be exported, if for some reason they cannot be distributed to the poor, which is undoubtedly their best use.

40 In India's case, food subsidies of the last ten years or so cannot be called consumer subsidies. Given the demand constraint, if the market had been allowed to rule, prices would have come down, both for consumers and producers. The food subsidy increased because the floor at which producers were supported was too high for poor consumers. *A food subsidy is a consumer subsidy in situations of shortage but a producer subsidy in the context of surpluses.* The fertilizer subsidy, however, may not entirely benefit farmers. Domestic costs of fertilizer production in India are high and, given the cost-plus-pricing principle, even inefficient fertilizer producers get protection. In other words, *for a portion of fertilizer supplies* (excluding international imports, which are still substantial, and the relatively efficient fertilizer producers at home), the fertilizer subsidy in India is a subsidy to fertilizer producers, not to farmers.

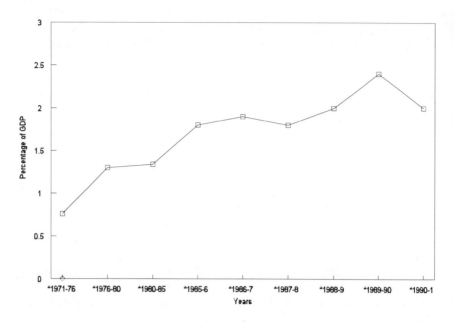

Figure 6.7. Subsidies as percentage of GDP, 1971–2 to 1991–2. *Source:* Ministry of Finance, *Economic Survey 1992–93.*

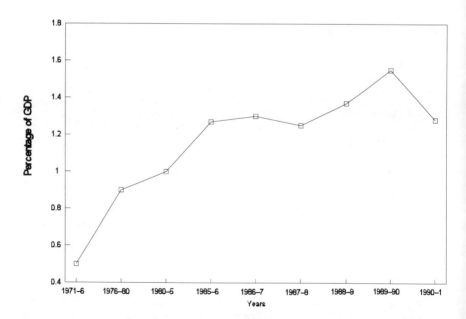

Figure 6.8. Food and fertilizer subsidies (central government). *Source:* As in figure 6.7.

tion system. . . . [T]here has also been a rapid increase in the volume of fertiliser consumption in the country. This, along with the rise in the cost of fertiliser imports and domestic production, has resulted in the growth of fertiliser subsidy from Rs 600 crores to over Rs 2000 crores in the current year.[41]

The subsidy burden has also contributed to the center-state budgetary politics. The central government has at times suggested that state governments should finance their own markups if the central government price is not considered adequate: "There would be no objection if the states want to pay additional amounts out of its own funds."[42]

Two structural factors, however, go against the states. Their share of the total tax revenue in the country is small and the Reserve Bank of India, suspecting political abuse, disallowed the use of credit to finance markups in support prices beyond the level set by New Delhi in the late seventies. The state governments must provide for any such markups from their own budgetary resources. However, because of the central dominance of tax revenue, they lack a solid tax base. Typically, the state governments try to pressure the central government for a higher price before the support price is announced formally.

The fiscal health of state governments has deteriorated for other reasons as well. Subsidized irrigation and electricity for villages are major fiscal items in all state budgets.[43] For irrigation, revenues as a proportion of recurrent expenditures are estimated to have fallen from 22 percent in 1980/1 to only 7.5 percent in 1988/9.[44] Some of the losses are simply the result of the inefficiencies of the irrigation bureaucracy, but a large part is also due to the underpricing of water. In fact, on many occasions, agitations have been launched when the state governments have tried to meet part of the budgetary weight by proposing increases in electricity charges, as in Uttar Pradesh, and by charging betterment levies on irrigation facilities, as in Karnataka.

Agricultural consumers, it is estimated, account for approximately 25 percent of total electricity consumption by now and are responsible for the bulk of the power sector's financial losses.[45] For 1990–1, combined losses of state electricity boards (before subsidies) were about Rs 43.5 billion, of which 41 billion were estimated to be losses on power supplies to the agriculture sector. Frustrated that the Rajiv Gandhi government was repeatedly criticized in the Lok Sabha for not being pro-agriculture, the Agriculture minister argued: "Do we realize that in the

---

41 *Long Term Fiscal Policy*, p. 18.
42 Rao Birendra Singh, Food and Agriculture Minister (1980–6), *Lok Sabha Debates*, 7th ser., vol. 7, July 29, 1980, p. 269.
43 In India, power plants and major canals are typically built with central government allocations, but the operating expenses are borne by the states.
44 Figures supplied by the World Bank. Also see Ashok Gulati, 1989, "Input Subsidies in Indian Agriculture: A Statewise Analysis," *EPW*, June 24.
45 Figures cited in this paragraph come from the World Bank and India's Planning Commission. Due to the sensitivity of these documents, the sources cannot be cited.

case of electricity, the cost of generation, without the cost of transmission, comes to 80 paise (Rs 0.80 per unit)? What is the charge that we recover from the cultivator as a whole in our country? It comes to 17 paise per unit. We are not getting even 1/4th of the cost of generation and the cost of transmission is to be added."[46]

Subsidies notwithstanding, many agricultural consumers simply do not pay the electricity bills. In Uttar Pradesh alone, according to the World Bank, the unpaid electricity bills by 1991 added up to three years' worth. The districts that fall under the influence of peasant leader M. S. Tikait have especially been noted for not paying electricity bills; but the problem is not confined to them.

The 1991 economic reform has begun to reduce the fiscal deficit at the central and state governments. Despite large subsidies, however, farm returns, as already seen, have not kept a sustained upward trend, raising serious questions about the advisability of using prices and subsidies as a method of providing agricultural incentives in India today. Are there other ways of structuring agricultural incentives? Chapter 8 will deal with this question.

Summary. To conclude, an amalgam of forces, not simply rural power, has determined farm incomes in India. The rising political power of the countryside has run up against three countervailing factors: differential rhythms of technical change, income distribution in society, and the mounting fiscal burden of agricultural subsidies. As a result, the best-case scenarios – continual increases in farm returns irrespective of the rhythms of technical change – are not what agricultural groups have been able to achieve. The worst-case scenarios – a fall in producer prices as a result of accumulating surpluses – are what they have been able to prevent.

A METHODOLOGICAL NOTE ON FIGURES IN CHAPTER 6

1. All graphs on farm returns are based on Formula (1).

2. Unless otherwise stated, the source for these graphs is the "Comprehensive Scheme for the Study of Cost of Cultivation of Principal Crops in India." The data are published annually in the CACP reports on the Rabi and Kharif price policy.

3. The producer price (P) used in these graphs is the government procurement/support price. The implications of using this measure are as follows.

(*a*) Government price is relevant only to the "surplus" states (Punjab, Haryana, Uttar Pradesh, Andhra Pradesh). Since the mid-1970s in these states, the government price has been a support price – that is, the price producers have received. Government purchases have been concentrated in these states.

(*b*) For deficit states, the government price is virtually immaterial, as over

---

46 *Lok Sabha Debates*, 8th ser., August 16, 1989, p. 178.

the last fifteen years these states have contributed minuscule amounts of grain to the government stocks. Free-market prices are the prices producers have received. Because there is no good series on farm-harvest prices, statistically sound results on returns in deficit states cannot be provided.

(*c*) Even with respect to the surplus states covered in the graphs, some qualifications need to be made. Support price has been the relevant producer price since 1975–6. In the period 1970/1–1974/5, producers received a weighted average of the free-market price and government price, the former being somewhat higher. Once again, in the absence of a series on farm-harvest prices, statistically exact results cannot be presented. Nevertheless, some reasonable inferences can be made. The shape of the graphs will change, as most will have a higher base; but a higher base will not change the basic conceptual point emerging from these graphs.

(1) In Figure 6.2, a higher base will not change the random walk.

(2) In Figure 6.3, a higher base will simply make the decline in returns amply clear.

(3) In Figure 6.4, the base will not be higher because nearly all paddy in Punjab has always been sold to the government, whereas in wheat the government has traditionally competed with private traders.

(4) In Figure 6.5, a higher base will only make the rise in returns after the mid-1970s more pronounced.

The final result that returns have depended on which crops one grows and where, thus, will not be affected by these qualifications. Moreover, multiplying the number of cases will not change the result, as just four cases are enough to give us the entire array of results: returns going up, down, or showing no trends at all. Inclusion of deficit states, even if a reliable series on farm-harvest prices can be created, in strictly theoretical terms is not required, though they can surely provide additional descriptive materials.

4. The cost (*C*) data are aggregated at the state level.[47] This is a second-best method. Breaking down *C* into *c* of various size categories would have been ideal. It would have, inter alia, shown which classes were losing or winning in a given state, if at all – that is, if costs on all farm sizes were not moving in the same direction. The available data do not permit such disaggregation. They only give us a state-level picture. However, that is better than figuring out the cost index of the country's entire farm sector and deriving results about whether farmers have lost out from intersectoral *P* and *C*. Two levels of disaggregation permit what an intersectoral *P*/*C* times yield would have masked: a crop-specific and state-specific scenario. A class-disaggregated scenario, if it could be generated, would further add to these results. Similar considerations apply to the third variable in the equation, yields, which is aggregated at the state level.

---

47 For how costs are calculated, see the Ministry of Agriculture, 1990, *Expert Committee for a Review of the Methodology of Cost of Production,* Delhi: Government of India, 1990.

7

The paradoxes of power and the intricacies of economic policy

The last chapter emphasized three constraints on rural power: technical change, income distribution, and fiscal compulsions. This chapter asks whether these constraints are in some sense binding or are they politically changeable. For if they are politically manipulable, another set of questions needs to be addressed. Couldn't something be done about reversing the deceleration of technical change in agriculture? Couldn't the purchasing power of the poor be increased? Couldn't a higher fiscal burden be borne?

These questions have an unmistakably political dimension. The pricing and subsidy decisions, after all, emerge within the state. If all political parties are for higher prices, if farmers are also putting pressure on the government, if the Commission on Agricultural Costs and Prices (CACP) is becoming increasingly ruralized, if its terms of reference have been changed in favor of the countryside, then where is the counterpressure born? Obstructing the political power of the peasantry, which institutions and groups represent these abstract forces – technical change, income distribution, and fiscal constraint – in the political system? How are they able to impose their will on institutions and groups that might represent the farmers?

Stated differently, an explanation in terms of technical change, income distribution, and fiscal compulsions can only be a *proximate* explanation for the constraints on rural power. An *underlying* explanation should also deal with the mechanisms, institutions, and groups through which these abstract forces express themselves. The underlying explanation developed in this chapter proceeds as follows.

1. Constructing a counterfactual, it will first be demonstrated that the three constraints identified in Chapter 6 are indeed politically alterable in favor of the countryside.
2. If so, why is rural pressure, though increasing in the polity, unable to overcome the forces that obstruct it? The answer comes in two parts: (*a*) that rural power may have made remarkable gains *outside* the state institutions, but that *within* the state the institutions penetrated by rural ideologues are much less powerful than the ones opposed to a partisan rural view; and (*b*) that the rising rural power is also *self-limiting*. The intrastate

or interbureaucratic balance of forces within the state quietly counters the power and visibility of rural groups in party and nonparty politics. The interbureaucratic balance remains unchanged because the cross-cutting nature of rural identities and interests prevents agrarian pressure from realizing its full potential. Although farm agitations express economic demands and meet the eye, rural votes represent several other interests/identities that counter the economic definition of rural interests, thus limiting the rural pressure that can be exercised on the economic functioning of the state.

7.1 ARE ECONOMIC CONSTRAINTS TECHNICALLY BINDING OR POLITICALLY MANIPULABLE?

The first constraint, technical change, has two sides, one relating to the technologically advanced areas and the other to the technologically backward areas. The seed–water–fertilizer triad of the new technology has varying meanings in the two scenarios. The technologically lagging areas of eastern India (Bihar, West Bengal, etc.) require dissemination of the existing technology. The current variety of seeds will work if water and fertilizer availability is increased or regularized, a process that already seems to be taking place in Eastern Uttar Pradesh and Bihar over the past few years. In the advanced areas such as Punjab, however, improvements in water and fertilizer delivery systems may make only a marginal difference to (wheat) yields since the irrigation ratio (irrigated area : cropped area) is already very high and, compared to eastern India, fertilizer supply has few bottlenecks. A new generation of wheat seeds may be required in the advanced areas. The same may happen eventually in rice once the rice yields from the current variety of seeds reach a plateau.

Thus, higher outlays of public funds committed in response to political pressures may help disseminate technology in backward areas, but such outlays alone may not be able to deliver the goods in Punjab, Haryana, or Western Uttar Pradesh. For a new variety of seeds not only depends on higher fiscal allocations but also on the state of the biochemical sciences. A new seed suitable for India's agronomic conditions cannot be fiscally willed into existence by the political bosses.

For the technologically advanced areas, technical change thus may be a serious constraint, not easily politically manipulable. For technically lagging areas, the constraint can be overcome through a greater provision of irrigation, fertilizers, and seeds. This, among other things, means that Punjab and, subsequently, other advanced areas may have to move out of the wheat–rice crop cycle, leaving it to the less advanced areas to grow these crops, while they themselves switch to higher-value-added crops. Over time, the currently backward areas may themselves experience a similar deceleration in technical change, in which case one can expect corresponding political pressures to emerge there. Thus, at any given moment there will be states that have the potential for price agitations as technical change slows down the rise in farm incomes. However, these are precisely the states where technical change cannot be easily influenced politically, even if the government increases fiscal allocations.

Similarly, income distribution, the second proximate constraint, is not easily manipulable. Since blocked demand for food will emerge from the underfed poor, dissolving the second constraint means an income distribution aimed at the lowest deciles of the population. A redistribution of incomes toward the poor typically requires land reforms, transfer programs, or food-for-work schemes. Three decades of research have shown that land reforms are easy to legislate but monumentally hard to implement. Sizable food-for-work programs that run down the surplus in the short and medium run, or rural development schemes that create a sustained increase in the incomes of the poor, can be run only if the state is prepared to bear the consequent fiscal burden.

All roads, therefore, lead to the fiscal constraint. Whether the issue is dissemination of the existing technology or creation of a new one, whether the solution is running large-scale food-for-work programs or designing other transfer programs, whether the way out is increasing producer prices and/or lowering input prices – in all cases, the fiscal burden on the state will increase.

Three kinds of fiscal activities are potentially involved: *larger* investment in agriculture (through allocations for seed research, irrigation, extension); *greater* expenditures on rural development (income-generating schemes for the poor, or even food-for-work programs); and *higher* subsidies (required if producer prices must be increased or input prices lowered). Of these, the third is the most critical politically. Investments in technology typically lead to returns over the medium and long run. While, arguably, such investments may be a better way of ensuring the continued dynamism of Indian agriculture than routine subsidies, political pressures are not pushing the state in that direction: the farmers' movement is not primarily aimed at the long-run benefit but at immediate gains. Similarly, food-for-work programs or poverty-alleviation schemes, which can indirectly benefit farmers by increasing the incomes of the poor, are also not on the political agenda of farmers, and the direct beneficiaries – the rural poor – are not organized enough to pressure the government to allocate more. Affecting farmers here and now, higher producer prices and lower input prices are the main bone of contention between the state and farmers. Farmers want more than the state is prepared to give.

7.2 CAN THE STATE PAY MORE? A COUNTERFACTUAL CONSTRUCTION OF FISCAL POSSIBILITIES

In principle, higher farm subsidies can be provided if the government does one or more of the following: (1) increase consumer prices to reduce the burden on the exchequer; (2) increase government revenue to finance higher subsidies; (3) increase budget deficits if raising more revenues is difficult; (4) cut government expenditure elsewhere if increasing deficits is ruled out for some reason. The impracticability of the first option in the light of a demand constraint has already been demonstrated.

What about the other three options? Why haven't these logical possibilities become empirical realities? The question leads us into the political economy of public finance, a complex and underresearched subject.[1] Some of its salient outlines, relevant for our purposes, are sketched below. It will be first demonstrated that the state can pay more to the farmers; then an attempt will be made to answer why it does not.[2]

Taxes have been the main source of government revenue in India.[3] Since the late seventies, tax receipts have ranged between 15 to 17 percent of GNP. Since the proportion of indirect taxes has risen from 63 percent of the total tax intake in 1950–1 to nearly 85 percent by now, it is generally agreed that increasing tax revenue essentially involves raising the proportion of direct taxes in the total receipts.[4] Further, since increasing the tax rate for existing taxpayers beyond the salaried class has led only to widespread tax evasion, it is also generally believed that lowering the tax rate but widening the tax base – that is, increasing the number of taxable people – is the most practical solution for collecting higher tax revenue, even though it may not be equitable.[5] In principle, several ways to implement this solution can be devised. It will suffice to note a generally proposed solution: that short of having an agricultural income tax, a sizable increase in tax revenues cannot be easily achieved in India.[6]

1 One of the few political economy works on public finance is John Toye, 1981, *Public Expenditures and Indian Development Policy, 1960–70*, Cambridge: Cambridge University Press. Ending with 1970, Toye's work does not deal with the period marked by farm subsidy issues.

2 A methodological note is in order here. The discussion below is positive, not normative. Whether or not the state *should* pay more is not an issue I discuss here. For every argument made to show that fiscal priorities can be changed, a normative case demonstrating the adverse implications of the proposal for the economy can indeed be made. But that is quite beside the point here. Why that normative case holds politically is the main issue. To put it bluntly: if the state *can* pay more, why doesn't it?

3 The other, smaller source being mainly the savings of the public-sector firms in the oil and natural gas sector. Public firms in other sectors have generally been net dissavers.

4 A good overview is Shankar Acharya, 1988, "India's Fiscal Policy," in Gustav Papanek and Robert Lucas, 1988, *The Indian Economy: Recent Developments and Future Prospects*, Boulder, CO: Westview Press.

5 Tax evasion has often been identified as the culprit that has driven a gap between the expected and actual revenue collection. It should be pointed out that, despite evasions, a tax-GDP ratio of 17–18 percent is quite impressive for a country at India's GDP. It can nonetheless be shown that, even at the given level of income, tax receipts can go up.

6 The most widely known case for an agricultural income tax is the *Report of the Committee on Taxation of Agricultural Wealth and Income* (also known as the K. N. Raj Committee), New Delhi: Ministry of Finance, 1972. The Raj committee was constituted at a time when the left dominated India's economic policy making under Mrs. Gandhi and the talk of taxing the new agricultural rich was widely prevalent. The left was not the only advocate of taxing the beneficiaries of the green revolution. In 1983, the World Bank also favored taxation of agricultural incomes as a way to raise resources, arguing that "The agricultural sector currently generates about 35 percent of national

Agricultural incomes have remained virtually untaxed since independence. Land revenue and agricultural income tax (typically on plantation income) used to constitute 6–7 percent of the total tax revenue of central and state governments in the early 1960s; today, they don't add up to more than 1 percent of the total revenue intake.[7] If agricultural incomes were taxed to finance higher agricultural subsidies, it would not be a solution for the farmers. What one hand gave would be taken away by the other. Moreover, an agricultural income tax entails some formidable administrative and political difficulties. It has often been recommended by economists but always rejected by politicians. In the political circumstances since the late 1970s, when rural groups have already put considerable pressure on the government for higher incomes through increased prices, taxing agricultural incomes would be an act of extraordinary political courage. It is no wonder that policy documents bemoaning the lack of higher revenue in recent years at the same time dismiss the idea of an agricultural income tax: "It has often been stated that exclusion of agricultural income . . . constitutes an important explanation for the weak revenue-raising capacity of the personal income tax. Taxing agricultural income presents many conceptual and administrative problems. . . . The Centre has no intention of seeking any change. . . ."[8]

The difficulties of an agricultural income tax may be formidable, but the fact remains that "the total number of tax payers has remained at about 4 million or so for many years."[9] Assuming a family size of six and only one earning member per taxed family – a reasonable assumption in Indian settings – 4 million taxpayers would translate into 24 million people. Since urban India has nearly 250 to 300 million city dwellers, it would seem that barely 10 percent of the urban population pays an income tax. A potential for higher tax revenues in the urban sector to pay for greater agricultural subsidization does exist.

What of the other two options – increasing budget deficits to finance agricultural subsidies and, if that is not possible, cutting government expenses elsewhere? No theoretical unanimity exists in the economics profession over the respective values of budget deficits and balanced budgets. In the circumstances (and, presumably, even otherwise), the perception of the government would more critically decide whether budget deficits could be raised and, if not, whether other expenses could be cut. A typical government statement is as follows: "if subsidies continue to grow at the present rate, they will either be at the expense of developmental expenditures or they will lead to higher budget deficits which, in

income but only 11 percent of direct tax revenues . . . (The World Bank, *Economic Situation and Prospects of India*, 1983, p. 98).

7 Centre for Monitoring Indian Economy, 1992, *Basic Statistics Relating to the Indian Economy*, vol. 1, Bombay: All India, Table 12.12.

8 Government of India, 1985, *Long Term Fiscal Policy*, New Delhi: Ministry of Finance, December, p. 35.

9 Ibid., p. 23.

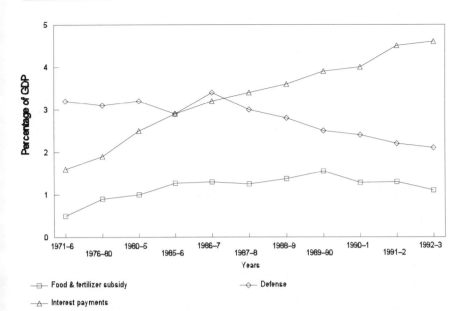

Figure 7.1. Main items of expenditure in central budget. *Source:* Ministry of Finance, *Economic Survey 1992–93,* pp. 22–3; and Centre for Monitoring Indian Economy, *Basic Statistics Relating to the Indian Economy,* vol. 1, All India, 1992, Table 12.13.

turn, will affect cost and prices, thereby increasing demand for further subsidies."[10]

In an acrimonious debate in 1981, occasioned by the increasing popularity of Sharad Joshi's agricultural price movement, the then Finance minister was less theoretical and more direct in stating a direct and positive relationship between farm subsidies and budget deficits: "Your argument is very simple and sitting there you can say 'subsidise it.' I will like you to . . . remember that . . . in the budget, if the Finance Minister, accepting your proposal, comes forward with a heavy dose of deficit financing to give more subsidies, what will be the honorable member's reaction?"[11]

How valid is the claim that if farm subsidies increase, it will either lead to higher budget deficits or, if budget deficits stay at the same level, higher subsidies will be at the cost of development expenditure?

First, for the sake of argument, let us accept that deficits cannot be increased. Is a trade-off between subsidies and development inevitable in that case? Can the so-called *nondevelopment expenditure* of the government not be reduced?

Let us now look at the major expenses in the government budget. Figure 7.1

10 Ibid., p. 19.
11 *Lok Sabha Debates,* 7th ser., vol. 21, December 1, 1981, p. 272.

presents the results. The main triad of government's budgetary expenses – defense, interest payments, and farm subsidies – comes more fully into light. Of the three, interest payments have increased most sharply since the early 1970s.

Why have interest payments risen? Can something be done about them? That the government has borrowed to fund public investment, to meet deficits of the public sector, and even to finance current government expenses are the main reasons. The government has often conceded that to redress budgetary problems "the bulk of the effort . . . will have to come from improvements in the functioning of public enterprises,"[12] which, instead of generating their own surpluses, continually need financial replenishments. The government has also admitted that further budgetary resources can be saved "if a firm check is kept on the growth of Government staff, proliferation of government agencies and unproductive expenditure of all types."[13] Clearly, just as there is room for higher tax revenues, so resources can also be generated if the public sector dissaves *less*, and a check on government expenditures is exercised.

Moreover, before the economic reform of 1991, fiscal deficits were also on the rise, increasing from 4.1 percent of GDP in 1975–6 to 6.3 percent on average between 1980/1 to 1984/5, going up further to 8.2 percent in the second half of the 1980s.[14] It should be clear that rising interest payments contributed more to the increasing fiscal deficits than farm subsidies, and defense also consumed between 2 to 3 percent of GDP in the 1980s. The argument that fiscal deficits must increase as farm subsidies go up can hold, *if and only if* other budgetary heads that have also contributed to higher deficits cannot be cut.

In sum, whether or not farm subsidies can increase is an issue that can be reduced to the following choices. Can more than 4 million urbanites be taxed? Can fiscal deficits be increased if tax revenues cannot be raised further? Can defense outlays, the current expenses of the government, and the deficits of the public sector be reduced if deficits cannot be increased? The answer to each question is yes, for these are political decisions. In the 1980s, the government continually expressed a deep concern over fiscal deficits, yet it *chose* to increase them. There is nothing technically sacrosanct about defense expenditure staying at 2–3 percent of GDP, or increasing to over 4 percent; the outlay for defense depends on what the state *perceives* to be desirable for the country. Public undertakings are certainly required in many sectors; their ineptitude, however, is not a technical necessity but a burden which, if the state *elects* to impose stronger discipline on those undertakings, can be cut. Finally, administrative expenses can be reduced. There is a range of choices available to the state. In the end, the government has been more *willing*, or has found it easier, to bear some increases in the fiscal burden but not others.

12 *Long Term Fiscal Policy*, p. 19.
13 Ibid.
14 Ministry of Finance, *Economic Survey 1992–93*, Delhi: Government of India, p. 20.

7.3 WHY THE STATE DOES NOT PAY MORE: FROM FISCAL POSSIBILITIES TO POLITICAL REALITIES

Why has the government, despite rising rural protest and power, chosen to bear burdens that cut into the resources potentially available to the rural sector? Can the situation change?

Two answers can be given. First, it is necessary to disaggregate the state. The rising rural power in Parliament, in the party system, and in nonparty street politics becomes substantially dissipated inside the state organs. From the viewpoint of decision making, the state institutions substantially penetrated by rural politicians – for example, the CACP – are less powerful than institutions such as the Finance, and Defence ministries, which, for a variety of reasons, do not subscribe to the views of rural politicians. The Finance Ministry in particular stands out in its influence over the conduct of economic policy. Second, rural identities and interests also need to be disaggregated. That the farmers are on the rise about prices and subsidies is what springs to view. Hidden beneath are the multiple identities that clash with the economic interests of farmers. The rise of the peasantry must be juxtaposed with the enormous fact that governments so far have not risen and fallen on prices and subsidies, nor have peasant-based parties come to power, despite the reality that rural India constitutes an overwhelming majority in the country. The reason simply is that rural voting has expressed a variety of concerns that seem as real as economic ones. The cross-cutting nature of rural identities and interests limits the pressure that rural India can potentially exercise on the state.

7.3.1 The towering Finance Ministry

As described at some length in Chapter 3 and argued on many occasions later, three ministries are directly involved in agricultural policy – Agriculture, Planning, and Finance. These bureaucracies are driven partly by their institutional concerns, not purely by political considerations.

To recapitulate briefly, the Agriculture Ministry is normally driven by a micro view of agriculture. Its task is to increase agricultural production, and if price incentives and input subsidies are deemed necessary to achieve that, as is likely to be true in the short run, a case for higher prices and subsidies will be made. The first pressure may emerge from the Food Ministry itself (or from the Food Department, if it is placed within the Agriculture Ministry). The Food minister is concerned with feeding people, the Agriculture minister with production. In a third world country, the former means lowering prices, the latter may mean giving price incentives to producers.

The Planning Ministry also resists higher food prices. Given the large weight they have in the various price indices, food prices affect the general price level in the economy and, by extension, the real value of plan investments. Planners may wish to raise production, but they are also concerned with the economywide implications of agricultural, especially food, prices.

The most powerful representative of the macro-, intersectoral view is, however, the Finance Ministry. The power of Finance lies squarely in the fact that it holds the governmental purse, a power superseded only by that of the Prime Minister. The Finance Ministry is intimately concerned with the general price level in the economy and with the macrobalances (budget, trade, and foreign exchange). Farm subsidies can affect the budget balance, and the fertilizer intensity of green revolution inevitably influences the trade and foreign exchange balance as well.

Normally hidden behind the principle of governmental secrecy, some of the key interbureaucratic dimensions of the problem came out in the open in the 1980s. With prices and subsidies becoming issues not only in bureaucratic politics but also in party, nonparty, and Parliamentary politics, Agriculture ministers were repeatedly pushed to explain why producer prices could not be raised further. Some candidly stated the intersectoral nature of food prices:

I have many responsibilities that are equally important. Agriculture Ministry is my responsibility – my task there is to raise production. Food Ministry is also my responsibility – my task there is to feed people. I have to look at both. . . . The ultimate decision lies with the Cabinet. . . . One has to see how much cloth there is for the coat. . . . The views of the Planning Commission, Finance and Civil Supplies have to be obtained.[15]

The demand constraint and rising surpluses of the 1980s gave the inter-bureaucratic struggle a distinct flavor. They lent ideological legitimacy to the customary power of the Finance Ministry over economic policy. In the 1960s, with food supply lagging, the Finance Ministry was concerned about the impact of higher food prices on inflation. But Subramaniam, as Agriculture minister, could make a forceful argument that without price incentives and input subsidies, food production would not rise either (Chap. 3). With surpluses emerging in the 1980s, the production argument began to lose its bureaucratic vigor, even as it acquired ever-increasing political strength in party and nonparty politics.

If the farmers are not getting remunerative prices, how is it that they are producing surpluses? If they sell more to the government because they cannot sell in the market, but the government cannot sell it to the consumers in turn, how is that to be financed? Concerns such as these typically mark the response of the Finance Ministry. When they also become the arguments of the Agriculture Ministry, the bureaucratic differences between Agriculture and Finance blur, strengthening the latter. The following statement by the Agriculture minister in the early 1980s could well have been made by the Finance Ministry:

How can [the] increase in production be possible if there were no remunerative prices? This is a very . . . simple thing to understand. . . . [T]he farmers' standard should rise. . . . But we cannot compare our conditions with the conditions in other advanced countries. . . . Japan and U.S.A. being prosperous countries, the contribution of their farm

15 Rao Birendra Singh, *Lok Sabha Debates*, 7th ser., vol. 7, July 29, 1980, pp. 251–2.

sector to the gross national income is only 6 to 7 percent. . . . [T]hose countries are able to provide huge subsidies to sustain their farm production. Why? This is because only a very small percentage of their population is employed on agriculture. In Japan . . . [t]hey procure . . . rice for instance by paying several times the international price. But can we afford to do that in India? If we go to the same level of procurement, by raising the procurement price without raising the issue price, according to the estimates of my Ministry, we have to pay subsidy to the extent of 300 crores per year. Can we take upon ourselves that burden? Do you want this country to develop in every field, or do you want this country to spend all its resources on the development of farming and thus all the time remain a poor country?[16]

This was not a lonely lament or a forced defense by the Agriculture minister amid a frenzied political attack. Consider a *policy statement* made by the Agriculture Ministry in the 1980s:

Since the support/procurement prices are to a certain extent cost based, input subsidies help in holding down the procurement/support prices to a reasonable level to subserve the interests of the consumers. Viewed in this framework, both fertilizer subsidies and price support programmes are needed as complementary instruments of the twin policy of promoting productivity and holding the price line.[17]

If the statement had ended here, it would have been virtually indistinguishable from the policy proposals of the ministry in the 1960s and 1970s. But the Agriculture Ministry went on to add:

At the same time, if subsidies continue to grow at the present rate, they will be either at the expense of development expenditure; or they may lead to higher budget deficits, which, in turn, will affect costs and prices, thereby increasing demands for further subsidies. They may also result in inefficient use of inputs. There is, therefore, a need to contain subsidies within a reasonable limit and the farmer has to be prepared to pay a realistic price for inputs like fertilizer, irrigation and electricity.[18]

The latter statement comes close to the Finance Ministry's view – indeed repeats it verbatim.

It has already been demonstrated that the plausibility of these contentions (impact of farm subsidies on budget deficits and on development expenditure) depends on a simple but politically changeable assumption – namely, that the other items of the budget are more important, while the farm subsidies somehow have an upper boundary. That the Agriculture Ministry began to accept this claim and could not point to the range of fiscal possibilities that would cut other subsidies while increasing farm subsidies should indicate the ideological hegemony enjoyed by the Finance Ministry since the rise of food surpluses.

Two conclusions emerge. First, as farm pressures in party and nonparty politics have increased in the 1980s to the extent that there are virtually no dissenting voices left in *party politics* arguing against the farmers' demands, the *interbureaucratic politics* of the state institutions have actually gone in the other

16 Ibid., vol. 10, December 11, 1980, p. 422.
17 Ministry of Agriculture, 1986, *Agricultural Price Policy: A Long Term Perspective*, New Delhi: Government of India, November, pp. 15–16.
18 Ibid., p. 16.

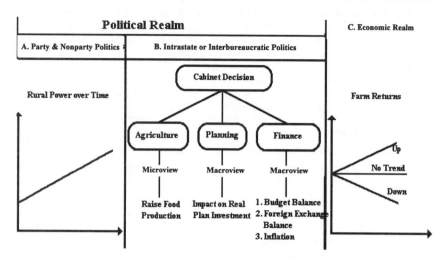

Figure 7.2. The policy process.

direction. In the end, the noisy parliamentary uproars and the agitational politics of nonparty organizations have been dispersed, if not neutralized, by the quiet power of the Finance Ministry. Second, by concentrating on the character of the CACP, the rural politicians have been attacking a wrong target. The idea that more rural politicians and fewer urban-trained technocrats in the CACP would redress the grievances of farmers is fundamentally flawed. By having politicians as members, the CACP is certainly more visible than before, but it remains a relatively less powerful player in the state structure. It has a recommendatory status only. The final decision is taken by the cabinet. The CACP can raise clamors for higher prices, but if it cannot even carry the Agriculture minister with it, it will at best make a marginal difference to the decision. The pressure exercised through the CACP can work if marginal changes make a difference; for crops experiencing a technical deceleration, and for situations requiring larger resources, the CACP may not be enough. The more powerful institutions of the state must be penetrated, or forced to change.

Figure 7.2 schematically represents the refractory process. The analytical space is divided into two parts, political and economic. The political realm, in turn, has two parts. Realm A represents the trends in party and nonparty politics, showing an unmistakable rise in rural power. This is the segment most visible to the eye. Realm B depicts the intrastate, or interbureaucratic realm, where the power of Finance, or its ideological hegemony, bends the trajectory of Realm A to produce the economic outcomes in Realm C, outcomes that do not correspond to the trajectory in Realm C. Without Segment B, or without technical change being a variable, the trajectories of Realms A and C could have been similar. The celebrated works on agrarian political economy have so far not taken the entire analytical space into account. Michael Lipton concentrated on Realm C, inferring the shape of Realm A therefrom; Ashok Mitra also focused on Realm C, without taking technical change into consideration and the fiscal politics it creates in Realm B; and the political observers commenting on the power structure have correctly read the trends in Realm A, assuming incorrectly, however, that outcomes in Realm C must reproduce the trends in Realm A.

The point about a partial mapping of the problem, generally speaking, holds good beyond India, too. For example, in his political economic work on Africa, Bates has dealt with Realms A and C.[19] Arguing that a downward trend in Realm C is a result of trends in Realm A, the puzzle for him was why, despite the countryside constituting a majority in the population, there was no upward trend in Realm A. Why was African peasantry so powerless? Bates gave a compelling resolution of the problem. That even an upward trend in Realm A may not directly determine results in Realm C, however, was not his concern. Rising rural power was not part of his empirical universe, hence missing in his analytical space. The state remained undisaggregated, the Finance Ministry did not enter the scene, and the possibility of disjunctions did not appear.

What can alter the situation for the farmers? Two scenarios can be envisaged: an autonomous change above and a push from below. The former can happen in two ways. Presumably, the Finance Ministry can change its view of the economic priorities if an agrarian ideologue takes charge of it (Charan Singh did in 1979, but only for a brief while) and carries the cabinet with him (Charan Singh could not). Alternatively, if a peasant-based party captures power in Delhi, politics can also be in command. However, since both possibilities in good measure depend on electoral power (of the agrarian ideologue or of the peasant-based party), in the final analysis the issue boils down to whether or not a peasant-based party can come to power – individually or as an overwhelmingly dominant partner in a coalition. Can a peasant-based political party capture power?

7.3.2 The multiple selves of farmers and their political implications

All parties ideologically support the farmers' cause. But only one significant party so far – the late Charan Singh's peasant-based Lok Dal and its ideological successor, the Janata Dal faction headed by Devi Lal – has been willing to run a campaign on the rural–urban divide. However, even agrarian ideologues have had to contend with the fact that a rural-based economic program is not sufficient for an electoral majority. To run governments in Delhi, they have had to enter into alliances with other parties, in which case compromises on policy had to be made, or alternatively, they have had to settle for the status of yet another opposition party. This denouement illustrates a classic distinction: that pressure

19 Bates, *Markets and States in Tropical Africa* (Cambridge: Cambridge University Press, 1981).

groups may concentrate on sectional interests, whereas parties, if they are serious about seeking state power, must coalesce a given sectional cause with those of other groups in society. They must choose inclusionary as opposed to exclusionary strategies of mobilization.

This explanation, however, leaves a deeper paradox unresolved. In a parliamentary system, a majority of total *votes* is not required to gain a majority of representative *seats*; a plurality of votes is enough. Since 70 percent of the country's population is rural, the support of a majority in the countryside should, in principle, suffice for capturing power. A sectional strategy based on an urban–rural divide should therefore be adequate to gain a plurality of total votes in a predominantly rural country.[20] Why, then, does a sectional rural strategy fail?

How farmers vote, how they define their identities and interests at the time of voting, may have little to do with prices and loans. The array of choices may be as follows. Shall I vote for a party that represents my caste or a party that represents my religious community? Or one that expresses my region's interest? Or a national party that advocates the country's unity above everything else? Or for a party that best represents my occupational interests? A farmer may well vote on the basis of caste, religious, or regional considerations. Worse, even those who have participated in price agitations between elections may vote on non-economic grounds during elections. Besides, half a million may show up for agitations between elections, making political news, but more farmers may stay home, distrusting the caste of the leaders of the agitation or the social composition of the leaders' main support base, and so on. Those who stay away do not form part of the agitational news, but they do vote. In other words, a single issue, or a set of economic issues, may clash with other considerations that determine how farmers define their political interests and vote.

Consider two kinds of evidence – direct and indirect – for these claims. In the 1980 parliamentary elections, the Janata party comprising, among others, Charan Singh's peasant-based Lok Dal party had broken up. Each party of the erstwhile Janata coalition was contesting separately, and Mrs. Gandhi's party, Congress (I), was bidding for a return to power. In Uttar Pradesh:

On the face of it, the election seemed to turn overwhelmingly on the issue of high prices, scarcity of essential commodities, the sugarcane price and the availability of agricultural inputs . . . needed by the *kisans* [peasants] in the previous growing season. . . . Whether or not a voter blamed the government for the economic difficulties and scarcities . . . depended more on the caste status of the respondents than on their economic position. . . . Brahmin voters favorably disposed to the Congress . . . blamed the Janata government. . . . Yadav *kisans*, who were inclined toward the Lok Dal, however, blamed only the Janata government and excused Charan Singh who had been in office only a short time. . . . In other words, the [economic] issues in the campaign were as much the excuses for voting behaviour as reasons for it. The really central issue . . . in Uttar Pradesh at

20 Qualitatively, the problem is the same as that of a strong women's movement finding it difficult to turn itself into a women's party despite the fact that women typically constitute more than half of a given population.

least . . . was whether the voters identified with the middle cultivating castes or with the Congress coalition.[21]

The difficulty presented by multiple selves also explains why the leaders of nonparty movements failed miserably whenever they tried to convert their movements into parties and contested elections. Worse still, such mistakes ended up sapping the strength of their movements in Tamil Nadu and Karnataka, at least temporarily. The conversion of movements into parties cuts away the ground on which these leaders gained strength in the first place – namely, that they were not organizing for the sake of political office but, since all parties were untrustworthy, they were going to build a strong movement that would force whichever party ran the government to pay attention to the farmers' cause.

More critically, consider some direct evidence. Faced with the rising religious sentiment in the country's politics, Sharad Joshi, the most successful peasant mobilizer in the country, laments how difficult it has become for a movement based on economic demands to go beyond where it stands today:

Men do not like to appear to be fighting for bread or even for butter. They like to feel . . . that there is a principle involved. Castes, language, religion and region provide ready-made principles for which men can be made willingly to die and brutally to kill. It is perhaps related to the primary urge to seek security in community. Maybe, the fraternity of an economic class has identity of interests but not the means and structures for securing them.[22]

Finally, consider two more observations. In Punjab, the peasant movement led by the Bhartiya Kisan Union (BKU) acquired strength and popularity in the late 1970s and early 1980s. However, after 1984, when Mrs. Gandhi ordered an invasion of the Golden Temple, the most sacred shrine of the Sikhs, and after her subsequent murder by her Sikh bodyguards in retribution, Hindu–Sikh religious strife rose dramatically. And it completely overwhelmed the peasant movement led by the BKU. Between June 1984, the month in which the Golden Temple was invaded, and 1994, the BKU was unable to lead a single movement in Punjab. The BKU leaders were rendered helpless and immobile. Once the political agenda was redefined, their constituency disappeared.

One may say that the situation in Punjab is exceptionally unfavorable for any democratic political movement. Once an insurgency breaks out, all other movements get sidetracked, not simply peasant movements. A conceptually similar situation, however, emerged in the country's politics after the recent rise of the

---

21 The Congress coalition was normally considered to comprise the upper and lower ends of the social system – the higher castes (except the traders), the minorities, and the ex-untouchables. The quote is from Paul Brass, 1985, "Congress, the Lok Dal and the Middle Peasant Castes: An Analysis of the 1977 and 1980 Parliamentary Election in Uttar Pradesh," in Brass, *Caste, Faction and Party in Indian Politics*, vol. 2, Delhi: Chanakya Publications, p. 198.
22 "The Outlines of the Second Indian Republic," *Bharat Eye-View*, Ambethan, Pune: Shetkari Sanghathan, 1988, p. 67. Also, interview with Sharad Joshi, Delhi, January 12, 1991.

Hindu nationalist BJP. In 1989, three competing idioms of political mobilization were floated in India: urban versus rural by Devi Lal, upper-caste versus lower-caste by V. P. Singh, and Hindu versus Muslim by the BJP. In the end, the election was fought over caste versus religious identities. Devi Lal's rural mobilization was overwhelmed by the caste and religious mobilization. Never a force in the countryside, the BJP penetrated rural India too, getting as much as 17.5 percent of the rural vote. Always a force in the villages, the Janata Dal got a mere 11.3 percent of the rural vote.[23] And as for Devi Lal's peasant-based splinter party (a breakaway from the Janata Dal), it was able to win a mere 4 percent of the vote.

While not defeated for good, rural power may not be able to alter dramatically the fiscal (or investment) priorities of the government unless farmers define their identity primarily as farmers, not as members of a caste, linguistic, or regional community. The challenge before the farmers' movements is to create these necessary conditions – that is, transform the way farmers perceive their interests and identities. It seems, however, that farmers will continue to view themselves both as farmers and as members of communities defined in other ways. This being so, rural power will continue to be a political force without becoming the most significant determinant of economic policy.

Finally, until these conditions can be met, the most effective form of politics for the nonparty movements will continue to be nonparty. It enables them to exercise pressure on *all* parties without the movements turning into parties themselves. Another strategy lying between these two extremes would be to align with the least objectionable party (or a set of parties) and work out a programmatic agreement while using the base of the movement to deliver electoral support and votes to the party concerned. The choices, in other words, are (1) staying nonparty, thereby making do with less in terms of desired policy outcomes but having a substantial political presence; or (2) converting movements into sectorally based parties in an attempt to maximize power, only to run the risk of losing even the existing political strength. In either event, best-case scenarios may not be realizable; but the first strategy, more rational under the current state of peasant consciousness, will ensure that political pressure on the state continues and the second-best scenarios obtain.

7.4 CONCLUSIONS

Four factors have determined the evolution of farm incomes in India: the rising power of the peasantry, the differential rhythms of technical change, the income distribution in the society, and the fiscal burden of farm subsidies on the government. All these factors can work in the same direction if technical change in agriculture does not slow down and the incomes of the poor can be raised. A

23 Based on an exit poll in India, reported in *India Today*, July 15, 1991, p. 35.

positive-sum game for all then becomes possible. If, on the other hand, technical change decelerates, and the poor continue to lack purchasing power, a series of political and economic contradictions emerge. The working of the state comes under increasing strain, as the state is heavily involved in the agricultural economy and its policies have a crucial impact on farm incomes.

Since the rise of food surpluses the behavior of the Indian state toward the countryside has reflected two conflicting imperatives. Giving producer incentives (and disseminating subsidized new technology) has been the first imperative, required by political exigencies now but owing its origin to a policy principle. This principle – price incentives combined with a new technology – has led to the impressive production performance of Indian agriculture after the green revolution. At the same time, however, the food situation since the late seventies has become quite ironical. Even as surpluses mount and the state bears a heavy fiscal burden, the poor remain underfed while considerable amounts of grain routinely rot due to lack of storage.

These surpluses have led to the second state impulse, which conflicts with the first. The fiscal implications of a huge surplus stemming from a lack of purchasing power in the economy impose constraints on the state functioning, given its other goals. If the poor were to have greater purchasing power, consumer prices could be increased more than they have been, which would both reduce the fiscal burden and increase farmers' incomes.

The state has so far showed an unwillingness to meet the farmers' demands fully. Other expenditure goals have competed with farm subsidies. The ultimate reason for the unwillingness of the state to alter fiscal priorities stems from the paradox of farm power. Rising rural power in party and nonparty politics has not been matched by a corresponding increase in rural power within the state institutions. Moreover, given that rural electoral behavior continues to reflect interests and identities that go beyond the economic, it is unlikely that the pressure on the state would significantly increase and the fiscal priorities would drastically shift in favor of the countryside.

One may wish to end on a normative note. If the benefits of food production are to be made positive-sum, it may indeed make sense for the state to spend, on the margin, greater resources on technology than on prices and subsidies. An emphasis on the latter, while the income distribution stays unchanged, puts the poor at a terrible disadvantage while clashes between the state and farm sector increase. The route of technology – greater water and input supplies in areas deficient in them, higher investment in research and extension, and a shift of food crops to less advanced areas while the advanced areas move to a high-value-added crop mix – is likely to make costs lower. Such *cost reductions* will not only benefit the entire economy but also farmers, whose profit margins may decrease but whose overall incomes, as a result of higher productivity, will increase. Moreover, by bringing prices down, the cost reduction will also put food within reach of the poor. Finally, it may also lighten the burden of a conflictual situation between the state and the countryside. How far this positive-sum normative scenario will be realized depends, among other things, on whether rural politicians agree with this logic and push for it politically. In the absence of the latter, the state will continue to perform a balancing act between prices and subsidies, on the one hand, and investments in the technological base of the country, on the other.

8

Democracy and the countryside

I have argued so far that India's rural sector has acquired substantial power since independence. I also contend that serious constraints limit the further evolution of rural power. Of the two claims, the first is more surprising for a developing country. Typically, the early stages of industrial development are characterized by a powerless rural sector. It is only after industrialization has reduced the countryside to a small proportion of the total population that an empowerment of the rural sector takes place, as is true of the developed countries today. Since a powerful countryside in a developing economy is rare, it calls for an explanation.

Rural empowerment in India has two aspects. Rural representation and voice in the *politics above* (parliamentary politics, state institutions) has significantly increased and, simultaneously, the *politics below* (mass political mobilization) is also marked by increasing rural organization. A democratic political system is related to both.

8.1 HOW DEMOCRACY MAKES A DIFFERENCE

8.1.1 The changing configuration of political elites

Universal franchise came to the West long after the industrial revolution. Independent India, on the other hand, was born in poverty with universal franchise. In a poor and largely agrarian country, the first politicians were predominantly urban. A substantial number of them were trained in law, the profession that led the national movement. The nation's democratic leadership, however, made a conscious decision to involve the countryside in mainstream politics. Nehru's economic model was driven by an industrializing zeal, but his political model was animated by a desire to politicize the rural periphery in a nation-building effort. Consequently, the Congress party moved into the villages to enlist popular support. Moreover, the Congress government involved itself in development though various schemes – building roads, schools, better communication systems, irrigation systems, cooperatives, and so on. The Congress party and the government were thus increasingly visible in the rural areas and were also great sources of patronage and power. As a result, the district and state wings of the party ruralized first. Over time, rural politicians built their careers upward to reach the topmost central level. Delhi was the seat of ultimate power. Moreover, as prices and subsidies came increasingly to dominate agriculture and, after 1965, as the central government started making the decisions concerning them, Delhi was the place to be. By now, the face of India's Parliament has been altered.

Political judgments on rural representation in the political system have markedly changed in the last three decades. Recall Myron Weiner's observation about agrarian politics in the late 1950s: "There is a marked change in attitudes . . . as one leaves the offices of ministers and planners in New Delhi and enters the homes of state legislators. . . .[T]he distance of the national leadership from rural political pressures disposes them toward a program which they justify on economic grounds, while state and local leaders are sensitive within their constituencies and are therefore disposed towards policies on political considerations."[1] A decade later, Rajni Kothari noticed a change: "State [and district] leaders. . . . control a good part of the election machinery of the Congress Party. This is partly due to the size of the country which keeps the central leadership remote from the bulk of the population, and partly to the increasing importance of rural patronage and influence in the outcome the election."[2] Two decades thereafter, the *Times of India* was editorializing, somewhat alarmingly, that "a new specter of peasant power is likely to haunt India in coming years."[3] About 20 percent of the *Lok Sabha*, the directly elected lower house in India's parliament, was rural to begin with: over 40 percent of it states agriculture as its family occupation now. If one adds those who only recently took to urban occupations and still have substantial agricultural interests, the proportion of course would be much larger.

Rural pressure on the nonelected state institutions was partially a result of the changing social base of political parties. In 1965, Agriculture Minister C. Subramaniam was shocked to discover that the Agriculture Secretary – the bureaucratic (as opposed to political) head of the Agriculture Ministry – could see agriculture "only in the files."[4] A decade later, the first rural politician to the Commission for Agricultural Costs and Prices (CACP) had been appointed in response to the unending parliamentary uproar that the Commission members were urbanites, having knowledge of agriculture but no direct experience thereof. By 1985, the Commission was split into two halves – one technocratic, the other rural-political. Unfortunately for rural politicians, compared to the major bureaucratic players in economic policy (Finance and Planning), the CACP is much less

1 Myron Weiner, 1962, *The Politics of Scarcity: Public Pressure and Political Response in India*, Chicago: University Of Chicago Press, p. 152.
2 Rajni Kothari, 1970, *Politics in India*, Boston: Little Brown; and Delhi: Orient Longman, p. 120.
3 *The Times of India*, February 3, 1988.
4 As reported in Chapter 3.

powerful. Nonetheless, compared to earlier times and as a consequence of the functioning of a democratic system in a largely rural society, not only has the Indian politician changed; a good deal of bureaucracy has also, though to a lesser degree. Rural politicians may want the upper levels of bureaucracy to follow their wishes more often or to be more like them; but that is a statement of what they would ideally prefer, not a judgment of how the present looks compared to the past.

Nonparty peasant leaders, however, maintain that a party politician having rural origins does not necessarily push for the rural sector. For a member of Parliament, says a leading nonparty farm leader, "many pastures are greener than agriculture."[5] If the political parties have been forced to take pro-rural ideological stands in the last decade, it is due, Joshi argues, to the sustained pressure of rural mobilization organized outside the formal political process. Joshi may be wrong in believing that a pro-rural stand taken by political parties is simply ideological window dressing with no material consequences for policy. He may, however, be right in asserting that rural politicians do not necessarily represent rural *economic* interests: the bright lights of the city may lure them away, or they may construct rural interests in *ethnic*, caste, or regional terms.

By now, of course, no political party is opposed to the main demands of the farmer's movement over prices. Even agricultural loans have been waived for some segments of the peasantry. But it is true that, until the mid-seventies, by which time India's parliament was considerably rural, the ideological platforms of political parties had not included remunerative agricultural prices, higher subsidies, and loan waivers. After Mrs. Gandhi's fall in 1977, the arrival of the peasant-based Lok Dal party as a member of the ruling coalition and the presence of a powerful rural partisan, Charan Singh, in the government started to change party programs. Charan Singh and the Lok Dal (and still later, the Janata Dal) enjoyed only brief spells of power. Just as Mrs. Gandhi returned to power in 1980, price agitations flared up in different parts of the country. With many fewer seats in Parliament than the Congress party, the peasant-based parties have been relatively weak in the 1980s. It is therefore fair to say that, even though it had origins in the elite politics of 1977–80, the non-party agrarian movement has been a critical source of rural pressure on the party system since the early 1980s.

8.1.2 Explaining rural collective action

The difficulties of organizing the countryside are well known.[6] Why some groups in the society are more organized than others is by now typically viewed as a "collective action" problem, the literature on which has grown out of two generic

---

5 Interview with Sharad Joshi, Pune, December 2, 1984.
6 Samuel Popkin, *The Rational Peasant*; Robert Bates, *Markets and States in Tropical Africa*; James Scott, *Weapons of the Weak*; also see Robert Wade, 1988, *Village Republics*.

insights of Mancur Olson.[7] First, if individuals follow their own interests, then they may not follow the interests of the group to which they belong, for it can be shown that, under many conditions, individual interests contradict group interests. Workers may find it more individually rational to compete with other workers in search of higher wages rather than working to strike collective wage bargains. A capitalist may find driving another capitalist out of the market more in his interest than working for the entire capitalist class. Even Marx, it may be added, was aware of this problem: "organizations of the proletarians into a class, and consequently into a political party, is continually being upset by the competition between the workers themselves."[8]

Olson's second insight has to do with group size. The smaller the group, the easier it is to organize; conversely, the larger the group, the harder it is to organize. If a group is small, every individual gets a large share of the benefit, so he has an incentive to engage in collective action. Larger groups, however, increase the temptation to tag along for a "free ride": a single individual's share of the benefits is small, but if he cannot be deprived of the benefits that do accrue from collective action, there is an incentive not to participate. There is, of course, a paradox here. If everyone thought this way, collective action would not take place. That is precisely why the free-rider problem tends to cripple large groups.

On *rural* collective action, as opposed to collective action per se, Bates extended Olson's logic. To (1) the size of the group, he added (2) dispersion and poor communication of rural communities and (3) the strategy of the state (reward compliance and punish recalcitrance). The three factors taken together, argued Bates, would explain the absence of collective action in the African countryside despite the exploitative agricultural policies of African states.

Collective action, nonetheless, does occur in large groups, as we know from history. So how should we explain it? Simply put, collective action is equal to overcoming "the free-rider" problem. How the free-rider problem is overcome has given rise to many theories. One need not investigate this vast literature at length here. To explain rural collective action, four proposals deserve special attention: (1) *coercion* may be exercised formally (by depriving nonparticipants of benefits) or informally ("the agent may feel guilt or shame about abstaining, based on an anticipation of informal social sanctions that can be brought to bear upon him")[9] by organizations or communities over its constituent members; (2) participants may have their eye on some *future gains* accruing from the act of participation itself (building networks that may enhance future mobility); (3) a *tradition of cooperation* (or what would be functionally equivalent, the existence

---

7 *The Logic of Collective Action*, Cambridge, MA: Harvard University Press, 1965.

8 *The Communist Manifesto*, reproduced in the Karl Marx and Friedrich Engels, *Collected Works*, London: Lawrence and Wishart, p. 493.

9 Jon Elster, 1985, *Making Sense of Marx*, Cambridge: Cambridge University Press, p. 362. Elster's discussion of the problems and potentialities of class action is exceptionally clear and thought-provoking. See, in particular, pp. 344–71.

of an ideology) may characterize a given community, group, or class; and (4) reversing the assumption about human nature, human beings may be viewed as agents that do not simply enjoy the benefits of action but also the very *process of seeking*.[10] The first two solutions retain the instrumental view of human nature; the latter two contest that view, assuming that human beings are more value- or norm-oriented, and less consequentialist. Clearly, community traditions or the intrinsic (as opposed to instrumental) pleasures of participation would make atomistic calculations of interests, costs, and benefits less relevant to an explanation.

The specification of the problem above is entirely deductive. Its value, as that of deductive theorizing in general, lies in setting up the problem with simplicity and indicating the possible lines of explanation. But without an empirical investigation, one cannot establish which factor(s) would explain *rural* collective action in *India*.

Strategy versus culture in rural mobilization.   The most common solution of the free-rider problem is cultural. It has been proposed for India too. Invoking Sen and Hirschman's objections to the instrumental view of human nature, Lloyd and Susanne Rudolph have argued that collective action of Indian farmers is a non-problem because, "for many rural Indians, political participation is like pilgrimage and sport. The increased self-consciousness, the sense of community and adventure that collective action can yield, even the exhilaration of 'combat' experiences by cultivators in *padyatras, gheraos*, or *rasta rokos* (marches, sit-ins, and road blockades) can benefit them as much as the realization of policy or electoral objectives."[11]

The culture-based objection to "rational-choice" accounts of mobilization is a serious one, but it has its customary share of serious problems – of explaining variations with respect to space and time. Why has the new agrarian mobilization taken place only in some states and not in others? Is it because in Bihar, Orissa, Andhra Pradesh, and Rajasthan the rural folk are less driven by a sense of community than in Maharashtra, Uttar Pradesh, Gujarat, Punjab, Karnataka, and Tamil Nadu, where price movements arose? Second, even in this latter, new agrarian club of states, how does one explain the ups and downs of movements in Karnataka and Tamil Nadu? Finally, collective action, like a *mela* (fair), may be

---

10 See Amartya Sen, "Rational Fools: A Behavioral Critique of Economic Theory," originally published in *Philosophy and Public Affairs*, reproduced in *Choice, Welfare and Measurement*, Cambridge, MA: MIT Press, 1984; Albert Hirschman's "Against Parsimony: Three Ways of Complicating Economic Discourse," *Economics and Philosophy*, vol. 1, no. 1, 1985; and Pizzorno's "Some Other Kinds of Otherness: A Critique of Rational Choice Theories," in A. Foley, M. McPherson, and Guillermo O'Donnel, eds., *Development, Democracy and the Art of Trespassing: Essays in the Honor of Albert Hirschman*, Notre Dame, IN: University of Notre Dame Press, 1986.
11 "Lakshmi Defended," *The Journal of Comparative and Commonwealth Politics*, November 1988, p. 279.

quite enjoyable irrespective of what one buys in the *mela*; but getting shot at or *lathi-charged* (beaten up) is not enjoyable. Farm-price agitations are known to have incurred such costs.

Now, consider the following remarks on the problem of organizing the countryside by Sharad Joshi, leader of the most vibrant peasant movement of the 1980s:[12]

Our biggest difficulty is that we work in villages. . . . One cannot even enter so many villages for . . . months due to the rains. If you have a district level meeting, it is so hard to reach some villages. . . . Comparatively, it is easier to organize industrial workers. . . . Communication is such a problem in organizing farmers. (P. 93)

(Even otherwise), it is so hard to organize in the villages. If two neighboring villages have had quarrels in the past, one village will come but the other will not. If one family in a village comes, the other will not. If the smaller people come, the *kothiwalas* [the bigger people] may not come. . . . There are so many of these disputes. . . . Villages are far apart. [And] disputes among farmers are many. . . . How we should organize in these circumstances calls for serious thinking. (Pp. 93–4)

Organizing villagers runs into [yet another] peculiar problem. Every village has people belonging to various parties. These parties look at farmers' mobilization with some skepticism. . . . thinking their turf might be overtaken in the village. . . . With respect to parties, our understanding is clear. . . . They are all against remunerative prices. The question of a good or bad party does not arise. But that is not the reason for antagonizing villagers in the various parties. . . . That doesn't help. . . . We should actually use them. . . . If they belong to Mrs. Gandhi's party and believe in the twenty points of her program, . . . tell them we have only one point [remunerative prices]. Give us support on this point only. . . . Fight your elections. We won't contest against you. (Pp. 96–7)

The theory that posits that the task of rural mobilization is easy due to communal bonds and the cultural pleasures of "pilgrimage and sport" does not, thus, resonate well with the account of the leading practitioner of peasant mobilization.

It may be that human motivations cannot be understood in purely instrumental and selfish terms, as economic theory attempts to do. It may also be that traditions of cooperation or community consciousness do exist in the countryside. The point is simply that, despite such traditions, collective action is tough. Community consciousness may exist *within* castes or kinship networks, but not *across* several castes; *within* party clusters, but not *across* parties; *within* a village, but not *across* villages. And even if it does exist across villages in some cases, communication may be a problem. A community orientation does not make rural collective action unproblematic. As an explanation of rural collective action, the cultural argument does not sufficiently distinguish between the "within" and "across" elements and is also unable to account for the ups and downs of a given movement.

Just as need does not create its own fulfillment, as the rational-choice theorists

12 Translated from Hindi. The source is Sharad Joshi, 1983, *Kisan Sanghthan (Vichar aur Karya-Paddhati)*, Varanasi: Sarva-Seva-Sangh Prakashan. The Hindi translation of the title would be *Farmers' Organization (Thought and Strategy)*. All interpolations (in brackets) are mine.

have forcefully argued,[13] so the existence of community traditions does not automatically lead to collective action. For between the culture of cooperation and collective action lies a long shadow: of seizing an issue; convincing farmers that it is a real issue, not yet another political ploy; converting it into a slogan; mobilizing people with an organization of some sort; showing that mobilization can lead to success (so that the collective momentum can be maintained). And for all of this to be achieved across castes, classes, and villages, leaders, organizations, and strategies are required. If they do not exist or emerge, then despite community traditions, there will be no collective action within the community, let alone across villages.

What might an effective strategy be? One can identify two necessary components of a successful strategy for new agrarian mobilization. First, we have the axiomatic truth that higher agricultural prices must be, or must be seen to be, in the interests of agrarian producers. This is not without problems. Buying more and selling less, smaller farmers are typically net buyers of foodgrains; higher food prices hurt them, at least in the short run. Consequently, the crop for which agitations are launched must generally not be food crops (wheat, rice) but commercial crops (cotton, sugarcane), which are produced for the market by all farmers irrespective of farm size. Only in regions where the food crop is heavily marketed can it be turned into an issue of mobilization (Punjab, Uttar Pradesh, and so on), because these happen to be areas where, due to technological diffusion, even smaller farmers can produce a surplus. Alternatively, the credibility of the movement can be built first by starting agitations around commercial crops, and once this has been done, food crops can also be considered, on the theory that, over the medium run, higher foodgrain prices will benefit small farmers by providing more employment or higher wages (small farmers typically work on others' farms to supplement their incomes). Finally, a demand for raising *all* agricultural prices must be made, so that the farming community is not divided. A clever balancing act between the general platform and specific mobilizations must be performed by the leaders and organizations.

Second, these movements must be led by *nonparty* organizations which should resist converting themselves into political *parties*, so that the new leaders cannot be viewed as chips off the old block, as power-hungry party politicians. The organizations that lost sight of this and contested elections – for example, in Tamil Nadu and Karnataka – were set back by many years. Moreover, once contestants in elections, these leaders lose the advantages of an issue-specific rural mobilization and run into the cross-cutting cleavages of their own constituencies. In the act of voting, caste, ethnic, and other considerations may override the interests expressed in price protests. The popularity of price-based protest may thus be electorally deceptive. That these noneconomic identities and inter-

13 Special Issue of *Theory and Society* on "Game Theory, Functionalism and Marxism," Fall 1981, built around Jon Elster's work.

ests can be extremely powerful is dramatically illustrated by the fact that Punjab, India's leading agricultural state, also had a powerful price mobilization in the late 1970s and early 1980s, but the Sikh insurgency in Punjab in the 1980s finally led to the *Sikh protest* becoming hegemonic, completely overwhelming the *price protest* in the process. Much the same may happen in the rest of India if the Hindu nationalist BJP goes further electorally in the countryside.

An excessive emphasis on strategy, however, leaves another issue unresolved. If strategy is the only difference between India and Africa (where the size of the farm group is large, villages are dispersed, and communications poor), then it is clearly worth asking why farm leaders in Africa did not develop these strategies. Rational strategies can surely not be the exclusive preserve of Indian farm leaders.

It is at this point that the role of the political system or, more broadly speaking, the role of the state can be more fully appreciated. India's democracy not only leads to a ruralization of the power structure; it also facilitates rural collective action. The logic of this relationship can be stated as follows. Rural price mobilization is, after all, a protest against state policies. If the state can repress farmers without any electoral or political sanctions, rural mobilization can be easily stilled at its birth. However, a democratic system places serious constraints on the state's repressive capacity vis-à-vis the peasantry, particularly as farmers themselves are well represented in the upper tiers of the polity.

This is not to say that the Indian state has not repressed farm mobilization: peasants lost their lives to state police in the initial stages of the mobilization. But such repression had to cease after the initial stages. Every police firing on the agitating farmers in Maharashtra led to an explosion in Parliament in the first years of price protest.[14] Subsequently, the state developed a strategy of conciliation. Or, if it found farmers' demands excessive, it simple adopted a posture of protracted inaction, hoping to win the battle of attrition: farmers, after all, must return to their farms at critical junctures in the crop cycle. After twenty-seven days of sit-ins in early 1987, farmers led by M. S. Tikait in Meerut returned to their fields. No bullets were fired; Tikait simply withdrew the agitation after he had captured enough national attention without having all his demands met.

Repression, I should further clarify, was not really the planned strategy of the Indian state, even to begin with. Rather, the sight of rural dwellers blocking roads was enough of a frustrating novelty for *district-level administration* to treat the crowd as dispersible with a show of might. Once such mobilization acquired legitimacy, thoughts of dispersing agitators through police firings withered away.

---

14 Parliamentary Debates in 1980 and 1981 reverberate with rancorous debates over the police repression of Joshi-led agitation. The state legislature in Maharashtra, too, exploded with charges and countercharges between the treasury and opposition benches. Police firing on agitating farmers ceased after that.

Thus, the legitimacy of these movements has made a difference to the behavior of the coercive institutions vis-à-vis agitating farmers.

Rural collective action, even in a democracy, has costs. Being away from the farm can lead to losses. Time and energy must be spent on organization. Weather is not always kind to those blocking roads or participating in sit-ins. And the possibility of police repression, despite its improbability, always remains.[15] What is critical is that in democratic systems, the costs of collective action are significantly lower because *repression cannot normally be exercised with impunity*. Opposition parties have a vested interest in embarrassing the government, as they do in India. A free press puts constraints on the government, as it does in India. And support groups form easily, as they do in India. Mechanisms countervailing repression are built into the system.[16] Controlling for all the customary obstacles to rural collective action in the third world (size, dispersion, poor communication), the nature of the political system thus makes a difference. With respect to rural collective action, a democratic polity may well account for the observed differences between India and most of Africa.

To sum up, rural collective action concerning prices and subsidies is a result of three factors:

1. The various segments of the peasantry have an interest in higher agricultural prices and subsidies. However, this is truer of commercial crops than food crops, as the smaller peasantry, which buys more food than it sells in the market, may or may not benefit from higher food prices (depending on the assumptions one makes about the indirect effects of food prices on employment, wages, and so on). Political reasons for supporting movements for higher food prices may nonetheless exist. Organization helps the small peasantry negotiate with the bureaucracy that dominates the supply of inputs. A small peasant, on this level, needs the organization more than the richer peasant does. The distinction between food and cash crops is not necessary, however, in high-productivity areas. Functionally, food crops in such areas become commercial crops, its surpluses being marketed even by smaller peasants.
2. Given the basis in interests, cultural explanations of group solidarity may be invoked to explain why some castes participate; but given that mobilization cuts across castes, party clusters, and villages, one needs to go beyond cultural assumptions of solidarity to focus on the organizational strategies of the leaders. Two aspects stand out. Nonparty movements and mobilization have generally been for commercial crops, or, if for food crops, such mobilization has remained mostly confined to the green revolution areas.

---

15 Moreover, political opponents can always plant criminals in such rallies, provoking the police and the administration, normally through the destruction of public property. Such political games are not unknown in movement politics.
16 The repression-resisting capacity of a democracy, as Robert Dahl explained with great clarity, will not apply to some groups – groups whose numbers are so meager that they are electorally unimportant, or the case where a dominant ideology in the system makes discrimination toward certain groups more acceptable than toward others. Dahl explained the position of American blacks before the mid-1960s in that way; the argument can be extended to quite a few groups in India, but not to farmers. See Robert Dahl, 1971, *Polyarchy*, New Haven, CT: Yale University Press, 1971, esp. chaps. 2 and 3.

Organizations and leaders that, moreover, developed electoral ambitions as a result of the increasing popularity of the movement were defeated, their movements set back by many years. Cross-cutting cleavages of rural identities and the original nonparty justification of the movement constituted the source of these declines. In some states these mistakes were not made and the movement is still vibrant.

3. The democratic nature of the political system constitutes an autonomous factor. The interests of farmers and suitable organizational strategies in themselves would not have turned into movements if an authoritarian system, instead of a democratic one, had significantly raised the costs of organizing as a result of its repressive capacities. The limited repressive capacities of a multiparty democracy lower the costs of collective action. Moreover, the increasing ruralization of the top tiers of the polity put additional constraints on state repression of farmers.

Democracy thus accounts for the rural empowerment in two related ways: it explains the expanding rural presence at the upper levels of the polity and it facilitates rural collective action, the latter continuing to exist pressure on the former as well as being rendered easier by it.

8.2 HOW FAR CAN RURAL POWER GO?

Chapter 7 identified two constraints on the power of India's countryside. First, the rural sector has a large presence in the elected tier of the polity (the legislature), but not within the state institutions (the executive). Second, rural power is also self-limiting due to the cross-cutting cleavages – caste, ethnicity, religion – that make it difficult for a rural party to emerge with a Parliamentary majority.

An underlying economic factor may now be added to this explanation. The tendencies unleashed by a democratic polity are, at this point, increasingly at odds with some of the institutional properties of a poor economy.

As we know, powerful rural sectors exist in first world democracies, where the development process has already reduced the size of the agricultural sector to less than 10 percent of the economy. Rational-choice analyses of group power may well be right in claiming that the small size of agricultural populations in the developed countries facilitates the organization of the rural sector. Two simple economic facts, however, also stand out. In a developed economy, the small size of the agricultural sector, and the meager proportion of the average household income spent on food, reduce the political and economic strains of subsidizing that sector. Western governments, of course, point to the drain on their public exchequers caused by agricultural subsidies. But, if a low-income country were to follow in the footsteps of the rich countries, imagine the drain caused by subsidizing a sector that holds 60–70 percent of the population and produces 35–40 percent of the national income. In rich countries, the politics and the economics of the farm sector run in the same direction. In a poor country with a *democratic* political system, the two tendencies diverge. Democracy in India exists in a low-income country.

There is a sense in which, after a point, agriculture cannot prosper if the rest of the country is poor. India's food economy already shows several symptoms of the food economies of the first world. Food surpluses have been substantial and so have budgetary subsidies to agriculture. On the other hand, the economy is also inevitably burdened by typical third world features. The most important is the lack of purchasing power: the country's poor simply do not have the incomes to buy food at the prices at which it is offered. In a hypothetical, politically uninfluenced world, if government intervention in the food economy were to cease and market forces were allowed to operate, food prices would sharply decline.

How would the clash between the two institutional tendencies – one political, the other economic – develop in the future? Two scenarios can be envisaged. The first is a stagnation (or decline) in rural pressure as a result of religious or caste identities overwhelming economic ones. If caste, kinship, and ethnicity – that is, noneconomic identities – had existed simply as bases for social, not political, groupings, one would have expected a monumental rise in farm power in India's democracy. If politicians can win votes on ethnic or religious slogans, economic issues may recede into the background.

At the other extreme lies the second scenario – that of increases in rural power and pressure in the polity. For the reasons outlined above, it is an unlikely one. However, as politics are open-ended in a democracy, and as even the unlikely can happen in real life, the implications of this scenario are worth considering.

Given the lack of purchasing power in the economy, rural power may become counterproductive for the rural sector. If producer prices are increased by higher margins due to increasing political pressures, agricultural subsidies will undoubtedly increase, and/or consumer prices of food will increase at a rate higher than they have so far. An endless increase in consumer food prices while food surpluses also continue to mount is potentially explosive. So far, the ideological legacy of a historically exploited peasantry has not created serious urban political resistance. But an urban backlash in the future cannot be ruled out.

If this scenario should appear farfetched, consider the following analogy. In the 1950s, no one resisted the policy of affirmative action (quotas for the depressed castes in public-sector jobs and institutions of higher education); nor was the possibility of a backlash seriously entertained. But, as the lists of castes for job reservation increased under the political pressure of a democratic polity, some of the most violent clashes erupted in urban India in the 1970s and 1980s. The nature of conflict has often changed in Indian politics, and it can do so on the issue of food prices. Food riots are known to have taken place in many countries. The resistance may come from the urban poor, or it may emerge from the urban working class and lower-middle classes.[17] At some point in the future, an urban

---

17 One may argue that the former is less likely than the latter, for (*a*) mostly concentrated in the informal sector, the urban poor have a smaller capacity to organize, and (*b*) the migrants into the informal sector typically maintain strong roots in the countryside. The organized working class is

backlash against increases in food prices, while surpluses in the country mount, is one of the possible outcomes. This would be unfortunate, as the rural sector still needs to be supported.

The real issue is how to support it. *Cutting costs* rather than *increasing prices* is the best possible route. Producer price incentives for crops other than food can still exist. It is food that creates the biggest town–country tensions in the early stages of development. A policy of price incentives for food producers was well conceived in the circumstances of the mid-1960s when increases in supplies were badly needed. The urgency of the need legitimated *both* producer price incentives *and* technological investments. That policy has served its purpose by increasing food supplies as well as making the agricultural sector better off.

Now, decoupling producer price incentives from technological investments is a necessity for food crops. On the margin, public resources *invested* in technological improvements instead of being *spent* on producer price increases would benefit all sectors of the society, including the farmers. With technologically induced cost reductions, even a lower increase in producer prices can increase farm incomes. Meanwhile, due to a halt in food prices (or to lower increases), the urban sector will be less hard-pressed, and the public exchequer will also have a greater degree of freedom. Most of all, this will be the kindest solution for the millions of Indian poor.

Technology thus seems to be a rational way to end the embarrassment of food surpluses coexisting with widespread hunger. Yet another factor is worth considering. Incomes in the countryside, dependent on prices, subsidies, and technology, are not the only measure of rural welfare. Clean drinking water, education, roads, electricity, and hospitals also have to be made available. Private investments rarely go into these so-called infrastructural activities, for they are public goods, typically supported by public investment. Moreover, both the landed and the landless need them. A visit to the town hospital when the patient is about to die is often self-defeating. The more state resources go into prices and subsidies, the less money is available for infrastructure.

That India's villages can, and *should*, be further improved is beyond doubt. At this point, there are two roads to that objective: higher prices, larger subsidies, and loan waivers, on the one hand; technological and infrastructural improvements, on the other. Which road will be taken is hard to predict.

---

less constrained by these factors, but it is also partially protected from increases in the cost of living. One has less need for it but greater capacity, and the other vice versa. Since wages are only partially indexed, the bigger thrust will, in all probability, come from the organized sector, in which, however, the unorganized sector will also participate.

Appendix: Liberal trade regimes, border prices, and Indian agriculture

In keeping with the overall trends in economic theory, an important argument has, of late, emerged about the negative impact of relatively closed trade regimes on agriculture. Anne Krueger and her associates have called attention to two sets of policies that have a bearing on agricultural incentives: direct agricultural policies (pricing, taxation, investment), on which scholars have mostly focused; and indirect policies, especially those concerning trade and exchange rates, which have traditionally been neglected in the scholarly discussions of agriculture.[1] Though directly aimed at protecting industry in developing countries, these latter policies, by making "import-competing" industrial goods bought by the agricultural sector dearer and discouraging exports, typically impose a tax on the countryside.

In her study, Krueger came to three conclusions. First, the indirect policies were more significant than direct policies in their impact on agriculture. Second, however, discrimination was primarily against export agriculture, not against the entire agriculture sector. A relatively closed trade regime protected import-competing sectors in general, both industry *as well as* agriculture. Third, such discrimination was lower (or countered) where agricultural interests were part of the governing coalition or where rural support was seen to be critical by the ruling party, as in Sri Lanka, Malaysia, Turkey, and South Korea after 1971.

India was not one of the cases studied by the Krueger team. Moreover, two other theoretical reasons seemed to indicate that in Krueger's own terms, India would escape the charge of a "strong discrimination against agriculture." The bulk of Indian agriculture (wheat, rice) has been primarily "import-competing," not "exportable" in the Krueger sense (tea being a major exception); and India's democracy has made the rural sector powerful in the polity.

However, following the Krueger framework, a widely noted argument claim-

---

1 Anne Krueger, 1992, *The Political Economy of Agricultural Pricing Policy*, Vol. 5, Baltimore and London: The Johns Hopkins University Press for the World Bank. Krueger's main associates in the five-volume series were Maurice Schiff and Alberto Valdes.

ing a "marked and continuing anti-agriculture bias" in India has recently been made.[2] Pursell and Gulati admit that internal trade in agriculture has "for the most part" not been restricted over the last 15–20 years. Moreover, they also note that agricultural subsidies are substantial; and agricultural incomes are not taxed in India. Yet – that is, even after allowing for subsidies and exclusion of agricultural incomes from direct taxation – the anti-agricultural bias, according to them, is "marked." A systematic gap between the international ("border") and domestic agricultural prices since 1973 is the primary basis for their claim.

In the absence of alternative estimates, it is not analytically proper to question the statistical calculations of Pursell and Gulati. Serious conceptual difficulties, however, remain. Consider two of the more significant issues. Even if international prices were higher than domestic prices in Indian agriculture, does that mean farmers were discriminated against? And should a country like India be governed by international prices in agriculture (as opposed to industry)?

Typically, when border price arguments are made about the developing world, the aim is to illustrate how low farm incentives lead to low production. And the implication is that to encourage production, farm prices need to be brought up to the level of international prices. An argument based on border prices runs into difficulties in India because *unlike the 1960s, India's key agricultural problem today is not one of production, but of distribution.* India's experience since the mid-1960s is quite unlike Africa's, where a long-term decline in production took place in response to lower relative domestic prices. Indian farmers have continued to produce surpluses since the late 1970s – to the extent that India does not even have adequate storage capacity for its public stocks. If the bias was so "marked" against agriculture, how did production climb so steadily? Either the gap between domestic and international prices was not significant, or it did not matter.

Let us consider first why the gap, if it did exist, did not prevent India's farmers from producing surpluses. Unit costs of production, as a consequence of technical change, have in all probability declined since the green revolution. Even if international prices were higher than the domestic prices, the latter gave substantial returns to farmers due to increasing yields.

Indian farmers, thus, were not exploited as far as their costs of production were concerned. One can, of course, say that they might have made (and produced) more had they been given international prices. But the latter would almost certainly have led to higher food surpluses. International prices, by making food dearer, would have put more of it beyond the reach of the poor, or, alternatively, would have made the budgetary burden of a fiscally strapped state higher. Neither situation can be a preferred alternative.

An important counterfactual question is also worth asking. Would international

2 Gary Pursell and Ashok Gulati, 1993, *Liberalizing Indian Agriculture: An Agenda for Reform,* Policy Research Working Papers: Trade Policy, Washington D.C: the World Bank.

prices have been higher than domestic prices if India had entered the world market as a seller of its surpluses? This counterfactual question is not important for smaller countries, for they are unable to affect international prices singly. Given the size of their agricultural economies, however, big countries like China and India can depress prices when they enter the market as sellers, and push them up when they buy. This is especially true of rice, a commodity in which the size of the international market is only about 8–10 million tons. The border price of rice would go down significantly if India sold 1–2 million tons of rice in the international market. Wheat markets are larger in size, but so is the wheat surplus of India. India's overall impact on the international prices of wheat would not be as dramatic as on rice prices, but wheat prices would also come down if India sold its wheat surpluses.

In short, if India had become a seller, border prices would have been lower, and the so-called anti-agriculture bias, using border prices as a benchmark, would have been significantly reduced. The *size* of the agricultural economy and surpluses thus matters. The African story about border prices does not naturally extend to India or China.

Ultimately, however, questions about the relevance of the border price paradigm for Indian agriculture boil down to something more fundamental than an empirical or methodological dispute. *Should* analysts be so concerned with international agricultural (as opposed to industrial) prices, while analyzing Indian agriculture?

Both the level and instability of border prices call for a critical reflection. International prices are typically higher than domestic prices, though I have already argued that the gap between the two in India's case is not perhaps as large as Gulati and Pursell think. In a country like India, which has surpluses as well as substantial hunger, to raise farm prices in line with border prices is to mount the wrong horse. It is more important to find a fiscally effective or innovative way of distributing the surpluses that already exist, so that hunger can be alleviated. Pursell and Gulati estimate that India's agricultural prices would go up by 15–20 percent if border prices ruled, with food prices rising higher. The implications of such price increases for hunger are self-evident. Moreover, a food price inflation of over 20 percent is also a serious political matter. Such increases in the price of food have taken place twice since 1947 – in the mid-1960s and between 1972–4. Both times the ruling party experienced a serious erosion of support. Whatever one's judgment of the economic worth of border prices, the attendant political economy is seriously flawed. No political party in India in the foreseeable future can raise food prices by 20 percent, and yet feel electorally secure.

Finally, due to the weather dependence of agricultural production, the world market is also highly volatile. That is why so many developing countries have concentrated on food price stability as a policy objective. Even East and Southeast Asia, though generally following a more market-oriented economic policy than India, have been quite preoccupied with food price stabilization, registering significant deviations from the border price levels.[3] At the same time, they have viewed international prices as a more defensible standard for the industrial economy.

Why did they do so? The reasons are not hard to discover. Fluctuations in industrial prices do not have the same welfare implications as food prices, which can be a matter of life and death for the poor.[4] That efficiency should be an important concern both in industry and agriculture cannot be denied. However, the existence of hunger amidst unstable grain prices in international markets means that countries must look for what has come to be called food security. A buffer stock of grain permits price stabilization, and "buys" food security, especially for the bigger developing countries. In developing agriculture, objectives other than efficiency can be normatively important as well as politically pressing.

To sum up, while long-run deviations from border prices will obviously hurt an economy, food, because of its association with hunger, calls for an approach that views efficiency as one of several important policy objectives. The border price paradigm is "monistically preoccupied" with efficiency.[5] India's villages do need to be helped. Producer prices are, however, no longer the way to do it. Investments in health and education, and making food cheaper while protecting farm incentives would be a better path to follow.

3 C. Peter Timmer, 1993, "Rural Bias in the East and Southeast Asian Rice Economies: Indonesia in Comparative Perspective," *Journal of Development Studies*, vol. 29, no. 4, July. Also in Ashutosh Varshney, ed., 1993, *Beyond Urban Bias*, London: Frank Cass.

4 This, of course, is a major argument in Amartya Sen, 1981, *Poverty and Famines*, Oxford: Clarendon Press.

5 I have borrowed the phrase from the late Raj Krishna, 1982, "Some Aspects of Agricultural Growth, Price Policy and Equity in Developing Countries," *Food Research Institute Studies*, vol. 12, no. 3, p. 244.

Index